W0082488

PROFANING
PAUL

CLASS 200 NEW STUDIES IN RELIGION

EDITED BY Kathryn Lofton AND John Lardas Modern

PROFANING PAUL

CAVAN W. CONCANNON

The University of Chicago Press
Chicago and London

The University of Chicago Press, Chicago 60637

The University of Chicago Press, Ltd., London

© 2021 by The University of Chicago

All rights reserved. No part of this book may be used or reproduced in any manner whatsoever without written permission, except in the case of brief quotations in critical articles and reviews. For more information, contact the University of Chicago Press, 1427 E. 60th St., Chicago, IL 60637.

Published 2021

Printed in the United States of America

30 29 28 27 26 25 24 23 22 21   1 2 3 4 5

ISBN-13: 978-0-226-81563-3 (cloth)

ISBN-13: 978-0-226-81565-7 (paper)

ISBN-13: 978-0-226-81564-0 (e-book)

DOI: https://doi.org/10.7208/chicago/9780226815640.001.0001

Library of Congress Cataloging-in-Publication Data

Names: Concannon, Cavan W., 1979– author.

Title: Profaning Paul / Cavan W. Concannon.

Other titles: Class 200, new studies in religion.

Description: Chicago ; London : The University of Chicago Press, 2021. | Series: Class 200: new studies in religion | Includes bibliographical references and index.

Identifiers: LCCN 2021013926 | ISBN 9780226815633 (cloth) | ISBN 9780226815657 (paperback) | ISBN 9780226815640 (ebook)

Subjects: LCSH: Paul, the Apostle, Saint. | Paul, the Apostle, Saint—Influence. | Bible. Epistles of Paul—Criticism, interpretation, etc. | Bible. Epistles of Paul—Criticism, interpretation, etc.—History.

Classification: LCC BS2651 .C66 2021 | DDC 227/.06—dc23

LC record available at https://lccn.loc.gov/2021013926

♾ This paper meets the requirements of ANSI/NISO Z39.48-1992 (Permanence of Paper).

For Éowyn and Scout
with all my love

———————

To deny a people the man whom it praises as the greatest of its sons is not a deed to be undertaken light-heartedly especially by one belonging to that people.

SIGMUND FREUD, *Moses and Monotheism*

CONTENTS

SEARCHING FOR PAUL
IN THE BATHROOM

We have become like the slag of the world, the dirty dishwater of all things, and we still are.

1 Cor. 4:13

I think they're shit.

Phil. 3:8

I HAVE LONG TAKEN PLEASURE in having my picture taken while sitting on ancient Roman toilets. As a biblical scholar who works with ancient material culture, I often joke that the best place to "walk in the footsteps of Paul" is to sit on a public toilet from the first century CE. That's your closest chance of being where Paul once was, if you are into that sort of thing.

And lots of people are into that sort of thing. For centuries Christians have made pilgrimages to Pauline places, whether reliquaries, churches, or archaeological sites. Paul's is a presence, like that of many Christian saints, often sought in physical spaces as a means of filling the gap between his writing and his whereabouts. Yet it is not just Paul's saintly life that has caused him to be an object of holy fascination but also his words. Paul's words, jotted down by his secretary (amanuensis) and (usually) worked out collectively with his colleagues, were meant to stand in for his presence, to put the apostle of the absent Jesus in the midst of his audience, separated often by great distances. For those who venerate those words, physical places associated with Paul extend that promise of presence from antiquity to the present.

My penchant for directing devotees of the apostle to his shit stems from a desire to trouble the veneration that Christians have long directed at Paul. This is not because I have some animus toward Christianity but because I harbor a deep concern about the impact of Paul's letters—not just within the fuzzy boundaries of Christianity but also within the larger history of the West. I am not alone in this. While there have been many, many Christians who have found guidance, comfort, and insight from Paul's writings, it is no secret that those same writings have long been found to be useful tools of the powerful against the weak. If we cannot count the souls in heaven who have benefited from Paul's theological musings, we also cannot count the bodies that have been left behind.

Take, for example, the issue of Christian support for slavery in the antebellum American South. In Paul's letters (and 1 Peter) we find exhortations for slaves to be obedient, remain as slaves, and otherwise just go along with being enslaved. The most common texts used in the ideological support of slavery were 1 Corinthians 7:20–21; Ephesians 6:5–9; Colossians 3:22 and 4:1; 1 Timothy 6:20–21; Philemon; and 1 Peter 2:18–25. Many of these texts have been identified by academic biblical scholars as pseudepigraphic, meaning that they were written not by the historical Paul but by a later fan writing in Paul's name. Yet even if we pare this list down and read Paul with as much sensitivity to the cultural and historical distance between our time and his as we can muster, we still do not find a Paul who stood clearly and forcefully against the enslavement of millions of humans.

For many this is a hard truth to hear, and it is a truth often repressed in the service of keeping Paul on the "right side of history." It is easy to assume that the Bible, within which we find Paul's archive of letters, is fundamentally a (or *the*) "Good Book." How could it not be? Is it not god's Word to a fallen humanity? Does it not tell a simple story of god's love for the world? Does it not offer a morality and an ethics that have shaped the best of Western culture? This assumption that the Bible is fundamentally good has a long history and a circuitous path from antiquity to (post)modernity.[1] It is a hard habit to kick. The same impulse attaches itself to Paul, although his archive of writings unquestionably bears responsibility for supporting the ideology of slavery, both ancient and modern. His complicity cannot be erased just because his writings are in the Bible.

This phenomenon doesn't stop with slavery. Paul's letters, his concepts, and his turns of phrase have supported anti-Semitism, the oppression of women, the pogroms of dictators, and the expansion of neoliberal capitalism, to name just a few atrocities. How many oppressive governments have been propped up ideologically by Paul's claim that god has instituted all governments (Rom. 13:1–5)? There are ways to parse this passage that allow Christians to critique immoral governmental authorities, but how much suffering could have been avoided if Paul had said, "Respect good governments and resist evil ones and always strive for a better society"? How many women have found themselves trapped in suffocating patriarchal families or fenced off from institutional power because Paul argued that man is the "head" of woman (1 Cor. 11:3) and that women should be silent in church and listen in full submission (1 Cor. 14:34–35)? Someone might point to Paul's claim that "in Christ there is neither Jew nor Greek, slave nor free, male and female" (Gal. 3:28), but that pesky "in Christ" has given interpreters so much wiggle room that could have been easily avoided by Paul's saying, "Women and men are equal. Full stop."

As a historian, I can step back and historicize the problem. It would be foolish to expect Paul, who was born, raised, and socialized in the patriarchy, misogyny, hierarchies, slaving, and violence of the first-century Mediterranean, to share the values of modern liberal Westerners. Slavery seemed natural to him, and he probably feared slave revolts in the same way that Roman elites feared them.[2] But here is precisely the problem: Why should anyone looking for resources to challenge neoliberal capitalism or the rising current of racist fascism trust the insight of someone who couldn't see that the forced bondage of human beings was an unconscionable wrong? Why does someone like that remain scripturally or culturally relevant?

Since the Enlightenment, Christians, theologians, historians, and even some radical philosophers have tried to redeem Paul from his own words, unwilling to eject him from his place in the (Western) canon in the face of changing cultural values. As a result, Pauls have proliferated. Luther's Paul waged war against the "legalism" of the Roman Catholic Church. F. C. Baur's Paul represented the universalizing Hegelian progression of the Spirit in history. Karl Barth's Paul addressed his eschatological vision to the crisis of existence. In the postwar West, Paul was transformed again into a multiculturalist, a liberal, and, more recently, a radical, anti-imperial leftist.

Paul continues to play his old role as the ideological support for racism, state power, and reactionary politics. Resurgent anti-Semitism spews its bile laced with Pauline echoes of Jewish legalism. Romans, chapter 13, is quoted from the lecterns at the White House to support concentration camps at the US-Mexico border. Paul is still gonna be Paul, after all. But the apostle of the ancien régime has also become a darling among radical Marxist philosophers over the past few decades. Often traced back to Jacob

Taubes's final seminar on Paul and political theology at Heidelberg in 1987 and to Stanislas Breton's *Saint Paul*,[3] radical readings of the apostle have become something of a cottage industry among the most influential names in European philosophical circles.[4] For these philosophers, Paul has become a resource for renewed fidelity to rethinking what Alain Badiou has called the "communist hypothesis,"[5] by which he means not a return to twentieth-century communism but a renewed commitment to resistance to capitalism, neoliberalism, fascism, and the otherwise oppressive political economy of (post)modernity.[6]

Developing in tandem with this philosophical turn to Paul has been an uptick in an interest in empire in the academic study of Paul. Occasionally drawing inspiration from postcolonial writers, liberation theologians, and the new Paulinist philosophers, academic biblical scholars have created their own niche market of Paul as somehow resistant to the imperialism/colonialism of the Roman Empire.[7] For these biblical scholars, there has been a conspiracy afoot for the past two millennia, in which the radical historical Paul was captured by the conservative forces of church and state.

I am suspicious of these rehabilitation projects. They remind me, uncomfortably, of G. K. Chesterton's *The Man Who Was Thursday*, in which the main character is recruited by the state to infiltrate an anarchist cell, only to discover that the entire leadership of the cell are likewise state spies. I suspect that Paul's redemption and co-optation into radical politics or liberal Protestantism will do more harm than good. Like Ananias in the Acts of the Apostles, we should wonder of a Paul who wants to join in the struggle for justice: "Lord, I have heard from many about this man, how much evil he has done to your saints" (Acts 9:13, NRSV).

Feminist, womanist, and queer biblical scholars have long been among those at the forefront of urging caution about inviting Paul to join in the movement for justice, though their warnings have seldom been heeded.[8] For example, Clarice Martin has shown how Christian ministers have found ways to critique or circumvent the pro-slavery passages in the so-called Household Codes, passages related to ancient household management found in the canonical letters of Colossians, Ephesians, 1 Timothy, and 1 Peter; however, as she shows, they have not brought similar critical attention to bear on what those passages say about the subordination and submission of wives, women, and children to male authority.[9] Bernadette Brooten has shown that Paul's views on sexuality depend on a set of assumptions about the subordination of women to men according to nature (*kata physis*).[10] To take Paul's advice on celibacy or same-sex desire means, according to Brooten, that the reader is implicitly drawn into a broader set of assumptions with which she may not agree. This is my first suspicion with projects that attempt to rehabilitate Paul: whatever snippets of liberative thought we might draw out of Paul will always be undermined by the totality of his archive and the assumptions embedded within it. What his archive gives with one hand it takes away with the other.

My suspicion against rehabilitating Paul also rests on unexamined assumptions about Paul's authority and importance in both the Christian and, more broadly, the Western tradition. The veneration of Paul as a touchstone for Christian theology, as a saint whose words carry the force of the divine, ensures that his letters will always have the potential to be grafted onto the apparatus of oppressive systems. Because his archive is found within the Christian Bible, modern readers, academics, theologians, and laypeople alike tend to start with a series of assumptions, among them the assumption of white Christian hegemony over Western culture. Because the Bible is a sacred text, it is presumed to be good and relevant. Paul benefits from this assumption by association: readers assume that he is good, that he is relevant, and that he can illuminate and answer our problems with his solutions. This is what I would call, riffing on Michel Foucault, the "canonical function," the discourse that surrounds Paul as a canonical author and shapes how he is read before his letters are even picked up.[11] Historians and biblical scholars are not immune to this tendency, though they would argue that Paul is good and relevant when read within his historical context. Even Marxist philosophical readings of Paul make the same assumptions about his quality and relevance, though they do not share Christian presuppositions about his sacrality. Interrogating Paul's assumed place as a canonical author is therefore a necessary starting point to any conversation about his rehabilitation or reuse.

Paul presents us with questions that sit at the heart of what counts as canon, whether that be what's in the Bible, what's in the Literature 101 syllabus, or what Star Wars stories are *really* Star Wars. What are the pleasures that cause some to set a text apart as special—the joy of insight, the thrill of verbal intimacy? What pleasures come from wielding such a text to enlighten or to force obedience? What are the ethical limits that a text can push? At what point must we stop our faithful interpretive betrayals, our near-infinite capacity to resignify canonical texts? Are there pleasures too in rejection, in profanation? Few literary archives have straddled the lines of these disparate pleasures more adroitly than Paul's, able to incite the blisses of exegetical ecstasy, masochistic self-destruction, and sadistic oppression.

I want to press on these tensions between the evils that have been wrought in and through Paul's letters and the sacralizing effects of his place in the Christian canon, his canonical function. I want to wrestle with the pleasures of reading and rejecting Paul, with the ethics of proximity or distance, desire or hate, that come from reading Paul as canon. I take as my jumping-off place the redemption of Paul within radical European philosophical circles, a turn ably assessed and critiqued by Elizabeth Castelli.[12] I read these philosophical appropriations of Paul alongside professional biblical scholars who have sought to co-opt him into their own liberal political projects. To read Paul alongside these philosophers and biblical scholars is to read a Paul who has been redeemed for radical and liberal politics through strikingly similar strategies and tactics of interpretation. But is this necessary or wise or even possible? Can Paul be redeemed? Can an archive of texts that supported slavery, demonized Jews, propped up dictators, naturalized the submission of women, and endorsed a whole host of other atrocities be welcomed into the struggle against racism, capitalism, fascism, and other ills? I argue no. I do so by engaging feminist, womanist, enslaved, and queer biblical readers and scholars who have developed ways of reading Paul's archive without reinscribing the effects of his canonization as the saint of Western theology and philosophy. They do so by a countererotics of reading, bringing to Paul's archive not a desire for the absent apostle and his pleasurable insight but an ethics of communal love, survival, and fidelity. Paul can't be redeemed; however, paying attention both to why he can't and to what happens when interpreters try opens up space to hear new perspectives and forge new alliances that are necessary in the face of human futures that look increasingly polluted, authoritarian, and unequal.

Since I will make the claim that Paul can't be redeemed, the place to start might be to think about that most unredeemable substance: shit. We begin here on a first-century toilet, sitting—shitting—with the specter of the apostle. Shit has a messy history. Contemporary theorizing about excrement, waste, and garbage offers a way of seeing both the messy processes that keep Paul in his place as the canonical theologian of the West and the marginalized reading strategies that might offer new ways of using and subverting the Pauline archive. Listening to readers whose lives have been most harmed by the apostle and his archive challenges the radical political projects envisioned by his modern philosophical readers.

Brian Thill has observed that everything becomes waste, given enough time.[13] In a similar way, shit is surprisingly ubiquitous. Shit and the discourses that surround it swirl around the borders of civilization and barbarity, purity and impurity, sin and redemption. As a result, shit and sanitation go hand in hand. Since its inception, academic biblical scholarship has played the role of the Bible's sanitation department, quietly removing scriptural waste from the sight of the Bible's cultured readers. The primary mode by which this waste removal occurred (and still occurs) is through the historicization of the Bible. Paul becomes a hero for modernity precisely by a complex process of historicization that sifts the waste from the recycling.[14] However, as Timothy Morton has noted, there is no Away to which we can banish our waste, scriptural or otherwise.[15] It always gets dumped on someone else and always, always finds a way back.

This reality applies to other modes of redeeming Paul by biblical scholars and atheist philosophers alike, each of which finds in him a kernel of radicalism, a touchstone of the political. These constructions of a radical Paul are built on a pile of waste that must be transmitted elsewhere. Thill notes that waste, at least for now, is not a problem for the (relatively) affluent and powerful. We can clean our houses, ship our trash out to landfills, and flush our waste down the drain, all the while clinging to the fantasy that we have gotten rid of our filth. But that isn't the whole story: "The more precarious your life is, of course, the less sustainable that fantasy of expulsion and removal. Every breath of toxic air you breathe, every drink of carcinogenic water, every handful of polluted soil, reminds us that our trash always comes back to us—just not always to *us*, specifically."[16] That waste has its most pernicious effects on those whose lives are most precarious should prompt us to wonder where the detritus of our biblical interpretations falls. Further, it should prompt us to ask: What shit are we dumping on the marginalized and oppressed in order to make Paul their advocate? Who pays the price for us to feel good about Paul's politics? We should be suspicious of political and theological projects that ground themselves in Paul's archive while claiming the mantle of the radical, inclusive, egalitarian, and universal.

It is for this reason that the later chapters of this book look to theorists who have wrestled with the pain wrought by the Pauline archive, including some who have felt Paul's boot on their necks. These readers push back against the archive's inscription through the deployment of discourses and systems of oppression: racialized slavery, patriarchy, and heteronormativity. If there is a way to think with, around, or without Paul's archive, I suspect that we had best look there for guidance. Following their lead, I turn to passages where Paul explicitly invokes imagery of waste, filth, and excrement. He deploys this imagery to construct his authority and to advance his own interests among the communities to which he writes. By contrast, feminist, womanist, and queer biblical scholars read against Paul's rhetoric, seeing in his excremental invocations paths not taken toward dwelling with and among what Zygmunt Bauman has chronicled as the "wasted lives" of global capitalism.[17]

The task of thinking about trash and the lives that it has and will waste is vital. The accumulation of trash, on land, in the sea, and in the air, jeopardizes any linear, teleological, optimistic vision of human futures, especially for those whose present is already characterized by poverty, pollution, or systemic violence. We need new visions of shit futures and recycled progress, a living with the wastes we can't wish away. Rethinking what a future with our shit might look like requires additive and coalitional organizing, enacting new configurations of thought that scramble existing boundaries.

This book intentionally disrespects boundaries between biblical studies and Continental philosophy and political theory. It also refuses the respectable detachment of biblical studies, following instead the intimate, impassioned, and resistant voices of minoritized and marginalized scholars. The scholars I engage offer readings that disrupt Paul's claims to authority while also gesturing toward new figures of thought and action.[18] I put the work of these readers of Paul alongside predominantly white, securely tenured, leftist political theorists and philosophers. I endeavor to stage for the reader a conversation that might go otherwise than when these same political theorists and philosophers have sat with a Pauline archive ensconced securely within the white, Western (cultural) canon. I invite those who might look to Paul for guidance in the struggles ahead to join me in listening to the voices of those who have challenged Paul(inism) and, in so doing, imagine different configurations of thought, action, and alliance. To do this, we must start by throwing Paul out with the garbage.

———————————————————————

What do I mean when I say that Paul needs to be thrown out with the garbage? First, we must get our Pauls straight. The Paul who lived and wrote letters in the first century CE is not who I have in mind for the garbage heap. While such a person undoubtedly existed, we have no access to this Paul that isn't always already mediated by the archive of letters that bear his name. This Pauline archive is a collection of thirteen letters that were preserved, edited, rewritten, and collected through processes that remain opaque to modern historians.[19] This archive, continually edited in antiquity and reconstructed by modern editors from a myriad of textual remains, is coded by modern readers in two interconnected movements for producing Pauls: canonization and secularization. Each of these movements operates within what Kwok Pui-lan has identified as a white, Protestant logocentrism, the belief that writing is derivative of speech, meaning that it depends on the existence of a speaker/author for its meaning.[20]

In the canonizing movement, Paul's letters are named as part of the Christian biblical canon, where sacrality is marked by divine inspiration.[21] God's words become, via a saintly human author, the written Word. Saint Paul is invented in this process as the author who writes the words given to him by god. Saint Paul and god come to form a braided author, imparting authorial intent to the Pauline archive that becomes the intertwining of divine speech and human writing. This process creates both a sacred archive and a saintly author. To read Saint Paul's archive is to hear the words of god. To question Saint Paul is to question god.

Secularization works in a parallel way for historians and nonconfessional readers of the Pauline archive. Paul's archive is treated as a written record of a historical author, located in a particular time and place. This Paul is reconstructed through the traces of the ideas, style, moods, and tempos of the Pauline archive. The archive is assumed to be a window on this Paul's psychology, beliefs, identity, or genius. Historians treat it as a collection of historical sources for a Historical Paul, sifting authentic from spurious writings there to arrive at Paul the historical person behind the archive.[22] Once constructed through parts of the archive, the Historical Paul becomes the author who governs the interpretation of the whole. A theoretical reconstruction is converted into a flesh and blood author whose "intentions" determine good or bad readings of the text. Failed readings are deemed insufficiently historical for not connecting the Historical Paul to the meaning of the text correctly.

Others secularize the archive as the literature of an approachable author, much as they would a novel by Dostoevsky or a philosophical argument by Nietzsche. Though they may refuse to affirm Saint Paul's metaphysical preoccupations, these readers pick up the Pauline archive precisely because its sacrality has ensured a perpetual presumed relevance for engaging such a cultural icon. Rather than a saint inspired by god, Paul becomes a genius, a touchstone, a theorist, a central voice in the Western cultural canon. He becomes a saint by another name for a differently confessional community. In either case, secularization leads to a Paul rendered human. This rendering is achieved by assuming that the archive bridges the gap between writing and speech, between text and author.

Both movements, canonization and secularization, construct what I have called Paul's canonical function. In both movements, an author is constructed as a (useful) fiction to ground interpretations of the Pauline archive. Whether inflected as theological, historical, or literary readings, good interpretations are said to reflect Paul's intentions, while bad ones fail to capture them. "Paul" is an invention to authorize certain ways of reading over others. This canonical function is thus a way to mask power: the power to set the terms as to which interpretations count and which don't.[23]

Canonical function identifies an interpretive metastructure similar to what Vincent Wimbush has called "scripturalization." In *White Men's Magic*, Wimbush describes scripturalization as "the ideology and power dynamics and social and cultural practices built around texts."[24] In other words, "there are no scriptures per se; there are only scripturalectics—social-political relations and psychosocial dynamics, and the human beings who invent and manage these dynamics or are managed by them."[25] With scripturalization, Wimbush shows how assumptions about a text make it interpretable and shape the interpretations that can be produced. This shaping is tied to the power relations that course through society. The ability to shape meaning resides not in the text itself but in the power relations surrounding it.

Wimbush's work shows that scripturalization is a linguistic prison policed and maintained by the dominant and built to house and constrain minoritized bodies, "the system of slavery that would control seeing and reading itself."[26] Those who claim to be just interpreting what the texts "say" (as if texts had the magical capacity for speech) mask what makes their interpretations possible in the first place: "What is real is the politics and uses of language, the work of the metadiscursive regimes that enslave, that control language use and the effects of such."[27] The trap of scripturalization means that biblical interpretation functions much like Nietzsche's notion of the eternal return, which is ultimately the return of the same: the status quo never changes. The task, then, is learning how to break out.

Feminist biblical criticism offers one potential pathway out of the prison of scripturalization. As Kwok has argued, if the scriptural is taken to be not sacred but "one form of human construction to talk about God," then interpretive possibilities open up that are not constrained by the logic of scripturalization, allowing for experimentation and new combinations with noncanonical texts.[28] Elisabeth Schüssler Fiorenza has similarly called for recasting the Bible as a "structuring prototype of women-church," in which biblical texts are sorted and tested for the extent to which they have supported patriarchal structures in the past and present.[29] For both authors, the locus of evaluating interpretation and setting canonical limits (or not) is a community seeking liberation. As Schüssler Fiorenza puts it, revelation is located "not in biblical texts but in the experience of women struggling for liberation from patriarchy."[30] Such interventions in the processes of scripturalization orient the ethics of interpretation around ideals of equality or liberation and around a communal pragmatics.[31]

Wimbush has shown how some Black readers of the Bible in early modernity turned the trap of scripturalization, "white men's magic," toward the possibility of liberation. Focusing particularly on the autobiographical writings of the eighteenth-century ex-slave Olaudah Equiano, Wimbush shows how Equiano came to recognize a scriptural regime at the heart of the British Empire's colonial apparatus, analyze it, and turn it to his own ends in a quest for agency, survival, and the emancipation of his fellow Africans. Wimbush's reading of Equiano shows an "ex-centric" subject who "did not so much exegete and perform the texts called scriptures as he excavated and analyzed the regime that is scripturalization."[32] Wimbush's descriptions recall Gilles Deleuze's reimagining of Nietzsche's eternal return: rather than a cycle where nothing ever changes, there is an ex-centricity that returns the same but with a difference.[33] That difference might be another way out. The "mimetic excess" identified by Wimbush in Black readers like Equiano points to the possibility that the improvisational readings produced by and through those oppressed by regimes of scripturalization might break open the regime itself. This begins when scripturalization has been "fathomed, critiqued, resisted."[34] This, I will argue in what follows, is the work of profanation.

Resistance does not promise liberation, but resistance must be the starting point: "Identifying that which enslaves does not guarantee but it facilitates salvation."[35] The space between the necessity of critique and resistance and Wimbush's hesitancy about salvation is where the argument of this book takes place. Or, rather, forestalls the closing of that space. While a robust critique of Paul's canonical function might seem to create an opportunity for liberation, I hesitate at attempts to turn Paul from a persecutor into a liberator. They remind me of the shallow calls for racial reconciliation often made by white evangelicals to move past the history of slavery and present-day racism.[36] My hesitation hovers over passages in the Pauline archive that have been complicit in regimes of violence, patriarchy, and racism. How far can critique take us if those passages remain, merely waiting for the right social and interpretive conditions to come to life again?

I don't think there is an easy path to making Paul safe. In fact, it is probably an impossible task. What we can do, I think, is sit in the place of hesitancy and resist, for now, the inexorable scripturalizing drive to redeem Paul, to create yet another (useful) Pauline fiction to obscure who gets to control the Bible. To return to the metaphor that drives this book: Paul is shit. Don't make him into fertilizer just yet. Rather than recycle Paul, let's pause, hesitantly, between what Eve Sedgwick has called paranoid and reparative readings.[37] For Sedgwick, paranoid readings emerge from the drive to critique systemic oppressions, to such an extent that the reader is left always in a state of constant anxiety. You can never be too paranoid. Sedgwick sees paranoid reading as the default option for academic critique. She challenges the dominance of this critique by noting its naïve trust in a politics of exposure to solve systemic problems.[38] Sedgwick urges that reparative readings be given their place in the academy as well: "This is the position from which it is possible in turn to use one's own resources to assemble or 'repair' the murderous part-objects into something like a whole—though, I would emphasize, *not necessarily like any preexisting whole*."[39] She is right to note that critique alone is not sufficient. Following Jennifer Knust's work on the history of Noah's curse of Canaan (Gen. 9:18–29), I question the extent to which reparative work requires that we begin the work of repairing Paul's archive after, or instead of, critiquing it.[40] By pausing the transition from paranoid to reparative readings, I invite the reader to join me in sitting in the shit, refusing recycling or redemption (for now). At the end of the day, I, as a privileged, tenured, cis-male academic, am not the one who can pronounce Paul redeemed. I hope that repair is possible for those who are and have been harmed by Paul's archive. I remain unconvinced that repairing Paul is either possible or a more urgent task than repairing the lives of his readers. By dwelling in the space between profanation and redemption, trashing before recycling, sitting in the shit, we leave open the possibility of being surprised by the fact that redeeming Paul won't save us from the shit that's all around us. That's up to us.

STAYING WITH THE SHIT

SO WHAT ARE WE DOING HERE in this ancient bathroom? Imagining Paul shitting on a public toilet near the marketplace of Corinth is a way to humanize Paul the Saint, to pull him back from the heights of theological speculation and back to the messiness of human life. But merely humanizing Paul does not address the apostle's allure despite the myriad evils associated with his name. Why would someone follow Paul into an ancient public bathroom? We know what happens in here. Come to think of it, what am I doing sitting here? In this chapter I will try to explain why it is worth sitting with shit. Along the way we'll meet garbologists, philosophers, and historians who have excavated the subterranean connections between shit, capitalism, Christianity, and, finally, Paul. I beg the reader's indulgence as we think about what it is we are doing, here where Paul did the same thing two thousand years ago.

Defecation, shit, feces, piss, cesspools, foul language. Human excrement and the processes by which it is produced, transported, treated, and disposed of represent fecund sites for thinking about how distinctions are made with regard to what counts as human and what does not. As Giorgio Agamben notes, "Separation is . . . exercised in the sphere of the body, as the repression and separation of certain physiological functions. One of these is defecation, which, in our society, is isolated and hidden by means of a series of devices and prohibitions that concern both behavior and language."[1] Following Agamben, I want to wade through the shit and what it "means," not to naturalize it or comically enjoy it, but as "a matter of archaeologically arriving at defecation as a field of polar tensions between nature and culture, private and public, singular and common."[2] I want to press past the secularizing injunction to sit on the toilet with Paul to find a way to profane him thoroughly, to imagine a return to Paul's archive that is emptied of its sacrality and authority.

A HISTORY OF SHIT

A good place to start is Dominique Laporte's *History of Shit*.[3] Laporte's history troubles the clean lines that shit demarcates between bourgeois and proletarian, city and country, health and sickness, beauty and ugliness, and civilization and barbarity. He shows how shit divides and is itself divided discursively at the site of tensions inherent in Western history. His work provides the space for us to think productively about how to profane Paul's shit, his language of the outside, the Other, and the unthinkable.

Laporte's story begins in 1539 in France with the publication of two edicts of François I: one that made French the official language of civil administration in the kingdom and another that defined how the citizens of Paris would henceforth be required to handle their own shit. No more emptying chamber pots out the window, people![4] These edicts juxtapose what for Laporte, following Freud, are three interconnected drives: "Cleansed language corresponds to the three requirements of civilization declared by Freud: *cleanliness*, *order*, and *beauty*, a definition, we might add, that has absolutely nothing to say on the subject of use. To cleanse, to order, to beautify: the fact that this discursive triad manifests itself so openly in the policing of both city and speech should give us pause. Perhaps it's not filth per se that troubles history's gaze, but the compulsion toward cleanliness that can locate its pragmatic function after the fact."[5] For Laporte, the cleansing of language and excrement is part of an obsession to separate the civilized from the barbarous. Scrubbing language of its foulness and draining excrement out of the streets thus represent parallel endeavors and ought to be read together. Civilization is what happens when you bleach out all the stains, rinse out the effluent, and scrub the floors.

In his work on waste, Brian Thill has made a similar argument about garbage as a discursive and physical marker of the lines between barbarity and civility. Rereading Italo Calvino's famous essay on taking out his trash each morning, Thill argues that our relationship with trash is functionally similar to that with shit: "As Calvino tells us, he takes out his trash every day not just out of a natural concern for hygiene or as an opportunity to rhapsodize about sanitation workers, but so that on waking up the following morning, he may begin his day fresh and new. Waste for him is a disgusting remnant of things we processed, and now want or need to expel, to separate from ourselves by policing what we believe to be the proper boundaries of our selves."[6] Waste for Calvino demands a ritual of purification that renews and purifies the self, that marks a deferral of our materiality and animality, the distinction between what is disposable and what is permanent.[7] Thill also notes that waste shapes our imagination of human and alien futures. From postapocalyptic thrillers to the clean hyperspace of science fiction, trash marks the line between utopia and dystopia.[8]

The civilized drive toward waste removal represents the public discourse of shit as that which must be removed to make us properly civilized and therefore human. But Laporte notes a parallel return of shit that goes unarticulated by the public discourse: "Shit comes back and takes the place of that which is engendered by its return, but in a transfigured, incorruptible form."[9] What Laporte means is that shit acts as a cipher for the cycle of waste and (re)production that sits at the heart of capitalism.

By way of explicating this counterintuitive claim, Laporte turns to a famous vignette from Suetonius's life of the emperor Vespasian (ruled 69–79 CE).

> But [Vespasian] particularly resorted to witticisms about his unseemly means of gain, seeking to diminish their odium by some jocose saying and to turn them into a jest. . . . When Titus [his son] found fault with him for contriving a tax on urinals, he held a piece of money from the first payment to his son's nose, asking whether its odor was offensive to him. When Titus said "No," he replied, "Yet it comes from urine." . . . He did not cease his jokes even then in apprehension of death and in extreme danger; . . . as death drew near, he said: "Woe's me. Methinks I'm turning into a god."[10]

Vespasian's famous quip is the source for the famous Latin saying "pecunia non olet" (money does not smell). For Laporte this saying "patently states a truth that all political economies ceaselessly deny"—namely, that commerce functions by denying and scrubbing its smell and converting it into capital.[11]

At the café where I am writing these words, I am presented with a beautiful façade of machinery, baked goods, and branding materials. The delicious coffee that I order is served to me in tactilely pleasing mugs. I offer the barista my credit card. With a few beeps a signal is sent, telling my bank to add a few digits to the café's bank account. What I don't see, and what is hidden from me, is the process by which this coffee made its way from the soil to me and where the ground coffee will go once it has been stripped of its aroma and flavor and deposited in hidden garbage bins next to the espresso machine. From the manure that fertilized the coffee trees to the refuse that will be quietly removed and shipped to a garbage dump after the shop closes (or maybe a compost pile somewhere, if the proprietors are really "eco-conscious"), the entire process from production to exchange is designed to give the appearance of "*cleanliness, order,* and *beauty*" while hiding the shit. What this performance produces, finally, is a clean exchange of capital and a hidden and disavowed excrement. Calvino's ritual of purification is not a personal rite but rather tied to a capitalist culture of "clean" consumption that functions only by masking its waste. "Money does not smell" is at the center of a capitalist discourse that disavows its remainder, a remainder, it should be noted, that is rapidly asserting itself in the form of ecological and climatic crises.

Calvino's trash and my coffee grounds might seem like quaint examples of what seems to be a manageable problem, but things are quite a bit more dire than we are accustomed to think. Most waste produced by human society is industrial and corporate rather than personal, a fact often hidden from public-policy discussions that focus on the "personal virtues" of recycling, carbon footprints, and simpler living.[12] The charade that we, as individuals, are responsible for fixing the coming ecological catastrophe through our individual actions is another iteration of the disavowal at the heart of our economic system. Capitalism functions because of an ability to shit without consequence.

This deferral of responsibility for shit from the collective to the personal has a long history. One effect of the turn in early modern Europe toward a civic landscape of cleanliness, order, and beauty was the production of both the household and the individual as autonomous from the state and society.

> We witness the *domestication* of waste, as a result of which the subject sees the object assigned to its "true" place; that is to say, to his home, *in domus.* . . . Mind your own business, and I will mind mine, says the individual to his neighbor. What happens in my home, in my family, my dirty laundry, and all the rest is no affair of yours. This little heap in front of my door is my business; it is mine to tend. Mine to see to; mine to mind. Thus it was that the politics of waste branded the subject to his body, and prefigured, not so insignificantly perhaps, the Cartesian ideology of the *I*.[13]

When Parisians in the sixteenth century were forced to handle their own shit, to collect, transport, and dispose of it on their own, they began to see themselves and their homes as private spheres distinct from the public sphere: "I am the one who cleans up my shit." "We take care of our business in this family." This relegation of excrement to the private sphere is one among many processes by which the individual becomes abstracted from her community, foreclosing further on the possibility of collective action and resistance.[14] It is this same "I" that is now enjoined to be eco-conscious through the personal virtues of reduce, recycle, reuse, forestalling the need for systemic changes to how capitalism writ large produces waste without consequence.

The contradiction at the heart of this formation of the "I" who handles her own shit is that it relies on a fiction that there lies, out there, an Away in which her excrement will be eradicated.[15] For Laporte's Parisians, the Away was outside the city in the French countryside. For industrializing economies, it was the dump. For a globalized economy, it has become the garbage cities in developing nations and the floating garbage islands in the Pacific. These attempts to push garbage further and further away have, paradoxically, brought us to the point where it has no place left to go. As Thill notes, "If our era is beginning to teach us anything, it is that here on earth, whatever objects we've dumped somewhere beyond us always come back to us, over and over again, and often with a vengeance."[16] Because there is no exit from our ecosystem, there is no place for our waste to go. Therefore it will always find its way back to us. The individual selves that emerged to handle our own shit are thus built on a fiction of clean divisions separating the private, the public, and the Away. This fiction is the self that can engage in consumption and keep itself clean, that need not concern itself with where its shit ends up, so long as it isn't in its own backyard.

FROM SHIT TO GOLD

This is where the story of shit carries with it yet more twists. As Laporte notes, "Civilization does not distance itself unequivocally from waste but betrays its fundamental ambivalence in act after act."[17] Just as Vespasian's tax turns urine into odorless cash for the imperial family, so, too, does shit return in surprising ways to the cycle of production and consumption. Though nominally excluded from civilized society—we recall Donald Trump's infamous claim that undocumented immigrants to the United States come from "shithole" countries—shit is transformed, through a variety of mechanisms, to render it a commodity. Though dirty as sin, shit can be redeemed.

This redemption comes first in the use of excrement as fertilizer, once it has been removed from the city: "In waste's initial phase of transmutation, the earth is nourished and enriched and thus bears the fruit so beneficial to the city. The city, in turn, is enriched by this metamorphosed fruit that no longer smells of earth or shit" (31). Under François I's edict, the city removes its shit, but in its passage to the country shit is transformed into fertilizer that returns wealth to the city, much as Vespasian's urinal tax turned pee into gold. Kate O'Neill has documented the contemporary communities and global economies that have emerged around the transformation of garbage into capital at the massive dump sites where the first world has deposited its wastes.[18] Shit has never stopped being recycled into gold. Here we can pause briefly to reflect on Vespasian's other morbid witticism: as he faced death, the emperor joked that he was becoming a god. The state and the economy have the power to transform shit into gold, "channeling and purifying it" (Laporte, *History of Shit*, 46). Why can't it also transform a man into a god?

The key to the transformation of shit into gold lies in the management of odor. Money, after all, doesn't smell. Neither does the beautiful (85). We have become used to a sensorium in which "bad smell—whether of shit or of a corpse, from the cesspool or the cemetery—is perceived as intrinsically noxious" (82). We assume a clear line between health and odor, that the beautiful and the good does not smell. However, Laporte meticulously shows how blurry the line is between shit and gold, stench and aroma. Corpses become relics (60). Cesspools are disinfected by "bergamot, orange and lemon essence, distilled lavender, orange blossom essence, clove, and countless other essences and oils" (80). Urine becomes a salve, a balm, and a curative (98–100). Animal dung is converted into remedies for constipation (101). Shit is distilled and deodorized into perfume and makeup (102–6). This commerce between pollution and purification is blurred by the olfactory: "Taste and disgust ('dis-taste') cannot be organized along the schism of civilization and barbarity" (103).

RUINS

It is in this hazy space between taste and disgust that we can locate the complicated rituals and narratives of memory that emerge around ruins, the wasted remains of the past.[19] About a century after François I's edicts, Europeans began to travel to the Mediterranean on tours of the remains of its ruined empires. The Grand Tour, as the route that moved from England to France, Geneva, Italy, and back through Austria and Germany was called, inspired young European intellectuals who viewed the remains of the Roman Empire with a sense of Romanticism and imperial ambition.[20] Gibbon was inspired by his tour to write his great opus on the decline and fall of the Roman Empire.[21] For others, the Tour was considered integral to a cultured education.[22] The proper discernment of ruins was seen as key to the dispositions of the elite. It was also in this period that archaeology emerged, the discipline that made it possible for me to sit on all those first-century toilets alongside the absent apostle. Archaeologists even found fragments of Paul's archive and other biblical texts in ancient garbage dumps.[23] Digging up more ruins of the Roman and Greek past, first as an elite hobby and then as a disciplined exercise, fed different forms of nationalist and pan-European identities as the power of these new nation-states began to extend beyond the borders of Europe.[24]

If early modern ruin hunters were motivated by cultural, nationalist, and imperialist drives, the role of ruins in the cultured imagination has shifted in postmodernity. In his study of plant closures in Detroit, Paul Clemens rails against the effete hipsters who would make their way to deindustrialized sites "armed with telephoto lenses, French theory, and poetic notions."[25] Brian Thill writes of the variegated nature of the fetishistic journeys, variously called ghetto tours, toxic and disaster tourism, Detroitism, and ruin porn. Though the locales and stated goals of these tours differ, Thill sees them as two sides of the same coin: "We are either meant to see the gritty and authentic underbelly of the American metropolis as we breeze through its seedier parts on safari, or we are meant to contemplate the horrible spectacle of smokestacks, bilge ponds next to playgrounds, and waste dumps to goad us into action. In either case, we are still comfortably ensconced in some role as outsider to them; otherwise the tour part makes no sense. And it is the shared reliance on voyeurism, spectacle, and perceived difference that joins these otherwise distinct phenomena."[26] Thill ultimately settles on *ruin porn* as his preferred term for these rituals, since they rely, like pornography, on detached voyeurism, a distance from the thing itself.

That space between thing and voyeur allows for the experience of *jouissance*, the perverse pleasure at seeing the horror of a despoiled and toxic landscape. The telephoto lenses of Clemens's Francophile tourists serve as shields as much as frames for seeing something beautiful in capitalism's nightmares. As Thill rightly points out, "No one actually living through the decimation and end of all things, no one dying from pollution or surviving in a community choked with filth, would look upon the decay of the world and find beauty in it; but a sufficiently comfortable subject-citizen, on tour among the necropolises of old, indulging in a day trip into the remnants of the past, can allow himself to find something majestic and noble in the demise of peoples and communities and civilizations that are not his."[27] Thill may be understating the capacity for those living amid blight to find beauty in decay, but his point remains apt: it is easier to romanticize desolation when you can see it from a comfortable distance. Ruin porn is the fetishization that finds beauty in that which capitalism works to hide. Our global economic system relies on the constant churning of consumption into waste. At some point, the reality of what this cycle of consumption has wrought, what Morpheus in *The Matrix* famously dubbed the "desert of the real," will grind to a halt the wheels of the capitalist machine.

Don't shit where you live. The old adage is a good one. François I was right that his capital city would flourish if people were forced to handle their own shit and keep it out of the streets. But it is also true that we live here, in one fragile, global ecosystem. There is no other where we can live. We have nowhere else to shit, and it's already starting to find its way back.

REDEEMING SHIT

It might be easy to think of shit in Mary Douglas's terms as fertilizer out of place. Douglas famously argued that dirt is merely soil in the wrong place, an example that, for her, unlocked a way of thinking about the difference between purity and pollution, between that which is sacred and that which profanes.[28] Dominique Laporte's genealogy of shit complicates Douglas's (and Durkheim's) clean lines between the sacred and the profane, a distinction to which we will return in a later chapter. Shit is framed in binary terms: it is private, polluting waste that must be separated from society. Yet at the same time it returns, not as matter in the right place, but via economic systems that transform it. Shit is not fertilizer out of place but matter in need of redemption by economic transformation. Shit must be redeemed to return as gold.

Laporte's account of the circulation of shit shows the interwoven economic and theological logics of redemption. Purity and pollution are not merely religious categories but economic ones. Paris must be purified of its shit, then enriched by its redemption. This braiding of the theological and the economic, the redemption of shit at the heart of capitalist circulation, should make us look differently at Christian theological discourses of redemption, how human souls are saved from sin. Wide swaths of Christian theology posit all humans as stained by original sin, so dirty in the eyes of god that divine sanctity cannot abide our stench. Thus interpellated as filth, humans are in need of redemption by Christ, to be washed clean. Paradoxically, it is blood that somehow cleans us, provided we "do not cease purging" ourselves of our abjection.[29] John's vision of the end of time, the heavenly city of Jerusalem made of gold and jewels descending from heaven, allows no pollution or filth or death: "Nothing unclean will enter it" (Rev. 21:27).

As Julia Kristeva notes, Christian consciousness is forged through interiorizing our abjection: "Man is a spiritual, intelligent, knowing, in short, speaking being only to the extent that he is recognizant of his abjection—from repulsion to murder—and interiorizes it as such, that is, symbolizes it."[30] Jesus and Paul, on Kristeva's reading, rearrange biblical laws regarding purity, such that impurity/abjection is no longer an external concern but a permanent threat from within (113–15). This sense of permanent internal defilement eventually gives way to guilt for sin (116). The purging of this guilt is ongoing but never finished, a debt that is never paid in this life but continues to accrue both principal and interest. It is continually deferred to the future, feeding a spiritual hunger that is never quenched (120). This debt system parallels economic imperatives under neoliberalism. We are enjoined: consume! constantly—a telos infinitely deferred because there can be no end to consumption's demands. When have we bought enough to be done? And we are always followed by guilt: guilt for not consuming the right way, not buying organic, not using our own bags at the grocery store, not taking on debts. The history of shit shows how this cycle by which humans are made into shit so that they can be redeemed parallels the redemption of shit and its inscription into a capitalist logic of production and consumption. The history of shit shows that a Christian theology of human redemption is tied at its core to a capitalist logic. Is there any way to break out?

The cycle of Christo-capitalist shit is one of redemption with a remainder. In the cycle of capitalist consumption, some excrement gets reclaimed as fertilizer or any of the myriad products described by Laporte. Like other recycled refuse, it is transformed into two braided things: consumer products and capital. But not all shit can be redeemed. There is matter that cannot be expunged as waste and returned as value. This matter collects as a remainder, in the form of landfills, waste, pollution.[31] Shit that can be redeemed feeds the system that produced it in the first place, while the remainder that cannot be redeemed becomes a threat to the system of consumption and reuse. From the carbon in our atmosphere to the toxic chemicals in our groundwater to the acidification of the oceans, the remainder of human consumption has gathered a force that threatens not just capitalism but human existence.

THE "MANURE AND SILT OF HISTORY"

The paradigmatic example of the machinery of shit operating at the intersections of capitalism and theology is the plantation and its inscription of Black flesh as both the fodder and the waste of capitalist consumption. As Achille Mbembe has written, the slave trade, the plantation, and the colonial regime itself have not been left behind: "In these baptismal fonts of modernity, the principle of race and the subject of the same name were put to work under the sign of capital."[32] In writing wisdom to his son, Ta-Nehisi Coates refuses to sugarcoat the cost of capitalism's birth on the plantation: "The soul was the body that fed the tobacco, and the spirit was the blood that watered the cotton, and these created the first fruits of the American garden. And the fruits were secured through the bashing of children with stovewood, through hot iron peeling skin away like husk from corn."[33] The neoliberal system that now sends out poor Black and Brown bodies as "essential workers" to die for the sake of keeping capitalist consumption going while paying them less than a living wage was christened in the baptismal font of the plantation. "In America," Coates reminds his son, "it is traditional to destroy the black body—*it is heritage*."[34] Capitalism makes all flesh into fodder and waste, though it is Black and Brown bodies that have always been seen as the easiest flesh to churn through the system.

The abject in the Christian theological imagination has always been the flesh, the unredeemable remnant that must be sloughed off so as to enjoy a glorious heavenly body. The Platonic binary between the spirit and the flesh runs right through Paul's archive, where it is intensified as the glorious body promised to believers.[35] The flesh, the body that works, breathes, eats, smells, sins, prays, excretes, and decomposes, is a fecund organizer of the intersections between the capitalist and the theological discourse of shit.

The dominant philosophical tradition that analyzes the inscription of the body into political economy has been that of biopolitics, associated primarily with Michel Foucault and Giorgio Agamben.[36] Biopolitics has been a frame for studying how the state has become interested in the control and management of life. Working in the Black feminist tradition of Hortense Spillers and Sylvia Winter, Alexander Weheliye has argued that the biopolitical analysis of thinkers like Agamben has been insufficiently attentive to race as central to the work of the state in the management of life.[37] For Agamben, the symbol of biopolitics is the *homo sacer*, an obscure figure from Roman law who could be killed at will. Agamben sees the *homo sacer* as representative of bare life, a life that precedes racial or social particularity but which can be rendered outside the law by the (ultimately arbitrary) decision made by the sovereign (whether a king, an oligarchy, or the people). Weheliye argues that we need not look to the murky history of ancient Roman law to find a potent symbol of biopolitics: it can be found on the plantation in the flesh of the enslaved Africans of the antebellum South.

Enslaved Africans were the engine that drove the machinery of early modern capitalism. As Kathryn Yusoff rightly notes, race was enfolded into slavery as a "material technology of extraction" that "weaponised the redistribution of energy around the globe through the flesh of black bodies."[38] It was as flesh that enslaved Africans became the "manure and silt of history," to use Mbembe's phrase.[39] Rendered as objects, machinery, animals, subhuman, enslaved Africans were the energy that drove capitalism, fodder for the expansion of extractive processes.[40] They were fuel for the fires of modernity but also the slag and ash thrown away when value had been extracted.

The interpellation of African flesh as fertilizer and garbage extended beyond the dehumanizing practices so carefully laid out by Orlando Patterson, who famously argued that slavery is a kind of social death.[41] As Mbembe shows, slavery was violent theft—the loss of autonomy, of one's body, but also of kinship, family, and community—as well as a form of racialized biopolitical containment.[42] Theological discourses, most important for our purpose the writings in the Pauline archive, were attached to this machinery, supporting and smoothing over its contradictions.[43] In a letter sent to the colonies in 1740, the famous evangelist George Whitefield sought to advance the cause of slavery on Christian grounds, refuting the view that "Christianity would make [slaves] proud, and consequently unwilling to submit to Slavery."[44] As Katharine Gerbner has shown, Christian missionaries helped forge a discourse of Protestant white supremacy that adapted with the slave system in the Americas.[45] Christian theology and the slave economy were intertwined from the start. The plantation is thus the site where we can see most plainly how the discourse of shit braids capitalism and theology through the flesh of Black bodies. Coates eloquently states this connection: "You cannot forget how much they took from us and how they transfigured our very bodies into sugar, tobacco, cotton, and gold."[46]

Mbembe's intervention in the discursive and material structures that render Black flesh as shit finds a fertile potentiality in this flesh.

> As a slave, the Black Man represents one of the troubling figures of our modernity, and in fact constitutes its realm of shadow, of mystery, of scandal. As a human whose name is disdained, whose face is disfigured, and whose work is stolen, he bears witness to a mutilated humanity, one deeply scarred by iron and alienation. But precisely through the damnation to which he is condemned, and because of the possibilities for radical insurgency that he nevertheless contains, and that are never fully annihilated by the mechanisms of servitude, he represents a kind of silt of the earth, a silt deposited at the confluence of half-worlds produced by the dual violence of race and capital. The enslaved, fertilizers of history and subjects beyond subjection, authored a world that reflects this dark contradiction. Operating in the bottoms of slave ships, they were the first coal shovelers of our modernity.[47]

The enslavement of African flesh is the ultimate expression of how shit sits at the center of our economy as both driver and by-product. It is also the confluence of the forces of racism, theology, and alienation that drove the subsequent conquest of the colonial period and the extractive logics of financialized global capitalism. Mbembe suggests that at the core of this machinery is a possibility for revolt, a fecundity that cannot be annihilated by servitude. That possibility may only be available to those willing to become shit themselves.

BECOMING SHIT

In her work on how war and violence are "framed," Judith Butler shows how a frame "does not simply exhibit reality, but actively participates in a strategy of containment, selectively producing and enforcing what will count as reality."[48] These frames shape who counts as human, whose life is grievable, whose death can be relegated to a statistic, and who must be mourned. Butler shows how we can be completely unfazed by news reports of drone attacks that kill scores of humans in Yemen, while the death of a white teenager by an undocumented immigrant in Missouri can call forth breathless news reports, public outrage, and rapid political action. Both are tragedies, but only one is grievable. Only one counts as a *human* tragedy.

Butler's frames are the strategies of containment that divide the world into human and nonhuman. They separate out the shit and toss it out. While I have emphasized the all-too-real fact that the unredeemable remainder of our collective shit is wreaking havoc with our world, it is also important not to forget that that which is tossed out and discarded can be a resource. As Butler notes, "The frame is always throwing something away, always keeping something out, always de-realizing and de-legitimating alternate versions of reality, discarded negatives of the official version. And so . . . [the frame] is busily making a rubbish heap whose animated debris provides the potential resources for resistance."[49] What sort of resources for resistance might be found on the rubbish heap?

Karen Bray calls attention to the potential resistance that might be named "becoming feces."[50] Shit, as Bray notes, sticks to those whom society has deemed disposable, those who are not otherwise counted as countable and therefore fully human—grievable, to use Butler's term. But it is equally true that "feces are incredibly generative. Without organic waste, nothing new can grow. The gap between the linguistic animacy and the actual animacy of feces is precisely the abyss from which a new theological and ontological construction might be found."[51] Feces call our attention to that which has been excluded or thought to be unproductive. It thus creates space for new ways of thinking, feeling, living, and acting: "Feces can be rethought as a site from which we find new ways of thinking our very beings and our energetic responsibilities to become along with all other actants in our assemblages. We might rethink the importance of the theological insights, the mattering of those bodies too often made inanimate and considered degenerative. . . . In order to practice a fuller recognition of one another we will need both to understand alternate forms of generativity *and* to be willing to risk finding solidarity in the feces."[52] Paying attention to shit is not just about attending to the ecotheological catastrophe of global capitalism. It is also a site around which to organize resistance.

A model for this way into the cesspool is the matsutake mushroom, chronicled so brilliantly by Anna Lowenhaupt Tsing. These mushrooms grow and thrive in places despoiled by human civilization. They are even said to have been the first thing to grow after the atomic bomb was dropped on Hiroshima.[53] Tsing describes them alongside other scavengers of human waste: "Like rats, raccoons, and cockroaches, they are willing to put up with some of the environmental messes humans have made. Yet they are not pests; they are valuable gourmet treats. . . . Through their ability to nurture trees, matsutake help forests grow in daunting places. To follow matsutake guides us to possibilities of coexistence within environmental disturbance. This is not an excuse for further damage. Still, matsutake show one kind of collaborative survival."[54] Following matsutake into the wastes created by humans offers a model for seeking life amid ruin, not as voyeuristic porn but in the struggle with others in our asymmetrically shared precarity. We might find a way to live and think differently by looking to "what manages to live despite capitalism."[55]

MEANWHILE, BACK IN THE BATHROOM . . .

So what does all this have to do with Paul? I convened us all here in this ancient restroom because I wanted cheekily to transgress the pietistic desire to connect with Paul. With my liberal colleagues in Pauline studies, I thought that I might bring him down to earth a bit, render him a little less sacred by proximity to human excrement, maybe even disrupt his allure by the foul stench.

In this chapter I have shown that shit is not just what gets flushed away in places like this. Shit is everywhere. I have waded into the history of shit to call our attention to four things. First, excrement and waste name a discourse that separates the civil from the barbarous, the clean from the unclean, the righteous from the unwashed masses. Excremental language, which we also find in Paul's archive, names both the waste that we produce and the people, populations, and places that we choose to mark as less deserving of full humanity and attention. Shit frames them as Other and Away.

Second, shit is tied to complex ancient and modern economies of production, consumption, and reuse that make it central to thinking about the modalities and realities of contemporary neoliberal capitalism. In fact, shit is central to capitalist modes of production precisely because it is that which must be concealed and disavowed for the system to function. Even the memory of its plantation origins must be forgotten. For those who come to Paul's archive looking for resources to fight neoliberal capitalism and its global empire, attending to this weak point in the system might be worth their time.

Third, the cycle of consumption and reuse that marks capitalist modes of production names not just an economic but a theological logic: the language of redemption marks both the reclamation of the believer's immortal soul by god and the five cents I get from recycling a Coke bottle. While redemption is the public face of corporate responsibility and individualized ecological ethics, redemption always leaves a remainder that cannot be reused and recycled. This takes the form of toxic dumps, nuclear waste disposal sites, carbon dioxide, and acidifying oceans, all massive ecological disasters at various tempos of becoming.

Finally, shit is fecund, productive, and life-giving . . . sometimes. While shit can be recycled in the flows of global capitalism, it can also stand for something that has been tossed out, thrown away, left uncounted that, under the right conditions of felicity, becomes a surprising resource. Achille Mbembe points to the insurgency that can never be annihilated by oppression. There is always a site of resistance, so long as it can be found. However, the only way to find out whether a cesspool or a garbage dump contains something of worth is to get down into the muck itself.

In what follows, I want to press on the process of redemption and its remainder as it relates to the Pauline archive. How do biblical scholars and philosophers alike redeem Paul for their political projects? What is left as a remainder when that work has been done? Who pays the price? I will argue that biblical studies is itself a machine that has always been in the business of (re)producing and sanitizing new Pauls (and new Bibles), without attending to the waste left over in the process. What would it look like to shut down the factory? In later chapters I return to the discourse of shit and waste in Paul's archive itself. I argue that Paul's invocations of excrement and other foul-smelling substances testify to a desire for escape from the struggle rather than strategic interventions against the politics of capitalism and empire, as his biblical and philosophical fellow travelers have argued. However, by reading against the grain of Paul's archive, by profaning Paul as shit, marginalized biblical scholars have traced lines of thought that are better resources for the struggle against global capitalism than Paul's—but only for those who risk becoming shit themselves.

When I was a child in the late eighties, I thought my father was larger than life. He owned a high-end car dealership and so might show up one evening with a new Porsche someone had traded in. That usually meant an invitation to drag race around the neighborhood. Everything for him and with him was an adventure. His work running the dealership kept him there for long hours, but when he was home he was very present with my younger brother and me. We played video games together. He coached our Little League teams. I looked up to him in that way boys do to their fathers.

When I was in the fourth grade, my family moved, quickly and inexplicably. We rented a new house a few blocks away from the familiar one. It was bigger and darker, the interior design noticeably a stale leftover from the early seventies. My father was around a lot more now.

I didn't ask why he was suddenly home so much. At least I don't remember doing so. I demurred when he tried to get me interested in building a model engine with him. I relished his letting me sneak downstairs at night to watch TV shows my mother didn't think were appropriate. Things were different now. I felt the tension but couldn't name it.

Then I happened upon something my parents had been endeavoring to conceal. I had discovered hiding places around the new house: lofted storage spaces, a secret crawl space connecting the pantry to the den, walk-in closets. One summer day I was hiding from my younger brother in my parents' room. Under the bed I found a recent edition of the local paper. On the front page was a large photograph of my father in handcuffs. His face was turned down toward the ground. The bars of the county jail were clearly visible in the background.

My father had been arrested and charged with numerous felony offenses. His business had apparently been floundering, and he had cut too many corners to get by. Bankruptcy is what had led to our move to the new house.

By the end of the summer, my father was gone. I didn't see him again until his prison term was up. My brother and I were never allowed to visit him. My mother didn't want us to see him there. Every so often I accepted a collect call from him. He worked jobs at the prison, for mere cents per hour, to pay for magazine subscriptions for my brother and me.

Money was tight. My mother and brother and I moved again, to a smaller house on the other side of town, our nice furniture I had grown up with crammed awkwardly into the new normal. I had to change schools. My mother went to work full-time. She wore herself out making it work and trying to shield us kids from how hard it all was, but I could see the strain. Even when her door was closed, I could hear the sobs if I listened quietly.

When I pulled that newspaper out from under my parents' bed, I don't think I quite knew what it all meant. I remember sitting with it for a while, piecing together what had happened. The details of that moment are seared into my memory, not because I was traumatized by the photograph, but because of how my father's arrest would ripple through my life in the months and years ahead.

The town we lived in was wealthy and tight-knit. Everyone knew everyone. It became clear to me over time that my father's legal troubles were common knowledge among my friends and classmates. Kids brought it up on the playground at school. My friend's father awkwardly did his best to say nice things about my dad in the car one day: "He was such a great Little League coach." I could hear the silences gathering around my father as parents would stop midsentence when I came within earshot. Sometimes people brought hand-me-downs or dropped off other things at the house. I remember the discomfort of the older kids whose parents had sent them on these humanitarian missions. We had become charity cases. I started to detect subtle condescension and sympathy in the tone of voices addressing me at social events.

This was the second trauma that came from my father's absence: the assumption that our shame was known and the simultaneous uncertainty about how that shaped my friends', neighbors', and classmates' perceptions of me. The story was out there for anyone to hear . . . but who knew? That uncertainty morphed into a simmering paranoia that extended well past the time of my father's imprisonment. What did they say about me when I left the room? Did they read some sign of my proximity to criminality in a mannerism or a phrase? Was I wearing the wrong clothes? Was I gauche, a joke, a charity case? They knew I didn't fit in. Of course they did. I couldn't get the stink off me.

Shit isn't just a discourse or a system. It isn't just a repertoire of metaphors. We also *feel* shitty sometimes. It felt shitty to lose my home and my school and my father. It felt shitty to watch what it all did to my mother, strong as she was and is. But I also felt like shit. I was shit. And everyone knew it.

I'm drawn to shit, from ancient toilets to modern dumps, not just because it is a fecund analytic window on social and textual processes. I find myself drawn to shit because I feel I know something about what it means to feel like shit. It's easy to name a rhetorical device that pits us against them, that renders someone or something Other. There's an analytic distance that theorizing creates. It's quite another thing to know what it feels like to be Othered, to be interpellated as shit.

Shit is material. It is what we throw away and perhaps redeem. It is discursive. It polices the boundaries of self and other, civilized and barbaric, human and nonhuman. But it is also, in Donovan Schaefer's words, a "sedimentation of how we feel."[1] Shit is a feeling that emerges from a body affected by forces often beyond our conscious control or understanding. It is, for far too many people, a way of being in the world. It can't just be flushed away. It is something that we carry, not to deposit at the county dump, but to hold in our bodies. And it stinks.

My shit was felt in two ways: as loss and shame. I missed my father, but I felt shame in front of others who saw our loss from the outside. I heard their pity and judgment, and that sense of shame settled in my body, affecting how I saw myself, how I thought others saw me. It percolated through me as anxiety, doubt, and depression that has stuck with me decades later. As Silvan Tomkins notes, "At that moment when the self feels ashamed, it is felt as a sickness within the self. Shame is the most reflexive of affects in that the phenomenological distinction between the subject and object of shame is lost. Shame . . . generates the torment of self-consciousness."[2]

Elspeth Probyn shows how shame is not just a thing or a personal feeling but an emotion arising through "the specific explosion of mind, body, place, and history."[3] Shame is not a psychological, personal affliction but an affect both felt and systemic, personal and distributed. "Shame is an affect that crosses many different orders of bodies."[4]

I live in a country that imprisons more people per capita than any other. Millions of people have been affected by the prison system like my family was, and millions more are subject to the cruelties and indignities of the criminal justice system every day. These millions are disproportionately Black and Brown bodies. Like me they have been made to feel shitty, but they carry shit that has piled up at intersections of race, gender, sexual orientation, class, and nationality that I have not had to carry. And that shit is deadly. Writing to his son, Ta-Nehisi Coates warns, "And you know now, if you did not before, that the police departments of your country have been endowed with the authority to destroy your body. . . . All of this is common to black people. And all of this is old for black people. No one is held responsible."[5]

The shame that comes from intersectional injustice is compounding and is a way of describing what Frantz Fanon called the "aberrations of affect"[6] that trap the colonized into social, political, and psychological (ultimately intersectional) prisons of inferiority. Fanon called this affective state "a massive psychoexistential complex" that is simultaneously personal and structural.[7] Shame crosses many different bodies, each of which feels shame, feels shitty, caused by explosions at the intersections of forces, biographies, and histories.

Shame is simultaneously particular and universal, meaning that we can only understand it, feel it, by hearing one another's particular shit. Discussing Primo Levi's writing about his experience at Auschwitz, Probyn shows how the narration of our particular shit requires a hyperattention to its specificity, a resistance to abstraction, in order for others to approach it with any degree of proximity.[8] I do not share my own story of feeling shitty to authorize me to speak for others. I share my story because it's what led me to approach those who have felt like shit as they read Paul or felt dehumanized as his words were preached at them. I share because I think that there is some way in which feeling like shit together in our specificity makes a different kind of existence possible from that offered by calls to the future, to progress, to nation, or to religion. With Alexander Weheliye, I wonder whether listening to our "distinctive understandings of suffering [might] serve as the speculative blueprint for new forms of humanity."[9] *Distinctive* is perhaps the most important word in Weheliye's gesture toward the future. Eve Sedgwick has argued that shame is not a toxic part of our individual or group identity that must be expelled to be healed. Rather, shame is integral to the formation of identity and thus available for transformation and resistance.[10] It is also contagious. Feeling shitty is a starting point. Getting down in the shit and listening comprise a process, a form of grieving-with, opening ourselves up to hearing one another's shame in its distinctiveness. It is a place not to get stuck but to create new speculative forms of humanity.

My father came up the side path to the front door. I could hear his footsteps on the concrete walkway. I was so excited as we waited for him to arrive. Our house had a white Dutch door. It was a warm day, and the top had been opened to let a breeze blow through the living room. I sat on our blue velvet loveseat, which had once been stylish but now felt and looked threadbare.

He had a beard and had lost a lot of weight. He wore an ill-fitting polo shirt and a dark mesh baseball cap. I ran to the door with my brother and hugged him. He felt smaller. I had grown, of course, since I had last seen him. But that hug felt different. It would always be different.

He moved into a motel a few blocks away for a few weeks, then into a studio apartment at the back of a small apartment building in a different neighborhood. He built a new life and tried to build it with my brother and me. He wanted so much to be forgiven. He wanted me to look at him the way I had before all this happened. Until the day he died, I could see it in his eyes every time he looked at me. I heard it whenever he tried to explain to me why he did what he did. He felt like shit too.

But I kept him at arm's length. I was embarrassed by him. I was paranoid about what people said about me. I worried even more at every social inter-action where he mingled with my friends and their families. I was trying so hard to get the smell off myself. I wanted so badly to have a clean slate. I was throwing back what had been thrown at me.

I loved my father then, and I love him still. He died when he was fifty-five. He died never knowing how shitty he had made me feel. I never felt I could trust him with that. Or maybe I didn't want to let go of it. By handling my own shit, I could hold on to my anger and my hurt. That's the thing about feeling shitty. Sometimes you just want to keep your shit to yourself. I wish that I hadn't. I wish I had taken the risk. I chose to stay with my shit, which meant that neither of us could ever climb out of the cesspool.

THE BIBLE DOESN'T SMELL

IN A LETTER TO THE CORINTHIANS, Paul criticizes his audience in first-century Corinth for the manner in which they engage in their communal meal. There seem to be divisions regarding who eats with whom and when. Some eat and drink before the rest arrive, leaving some members drunk and others hungry. Some biblical scholars have argued that these divisions cut along lines of class and status. Others have suggested competing theologies among the Corinthian factions. Putting those debates to the side, I want to dwell briefly on what gastrointestinal results come from improper digestion of the Lord's Supper. In other words, what are the assumptions about what happens when the Lord's Supper is consumed the wrong way?

> Whoever, therefore, eats the bread or drinks the cup of the Lord in an unworthy manner will be answerable for the body and blood of the Lord. Examine yourselves, and only then eat of the bread and drink of the cup. For all who eat and drink without discerning the body, eat and drink judgement against themselves. For this reason many of you are weak and ill, and some have died. But if we judged ourselves, we would not be judged. But when we are judged by the Lord, we are disciplined so that we may not be condemned along with the world. So then, my brothers and sisters, when you come together to eat, wait for one another. If you are hungry, eat at home, so that when you come together, it will not be for your condemnation. About the other things I will give instructions when I come. (1 Cor. 11:27–34, NRSV)

Centuries of Christian liturgical practice and thinking around what would become the Eucharist have obscured a logic here worth interrogating. Paul suggests that the conditions under which the Lord's Supper is consumed can make people sick and even kill them (11:30). This ritual meal, for Paul, acts as a *pharmakon*, an ingestible substance that can be either a cure or a poison.[1] During the meal, the bread and wine are transformed into Christ's body and blood. This gives the food a pharmacological potency that has different effects on the body, of both the community and the individual. Proper consumption is not just about the food but the social and ritual context in which it is ingested. If this social context is characterized by unity, then the meal is curative; if not, then eating the Lord's Supper can lead to sickness and death.

The text's logic of liturgical eating and digestion rests on assumptions about food that are, when read carefully, probably strange to most modern readers. Strange, too, might be the belief that god punishes people in tangible, bodily ways through how they consume sacred food. While this is not the shittiest thing that Paul ever wrote, I dwell on it here because the logics involved in this critique of the Corinthians involve strangely banal assumptions about the relationship between food, digestion, and divine violence. Biblical scholars have spilled a great deal of ink historicizing Paul's argument, rendering it properly foreign for today's readers; but historicizing this passage does not address the morality of believing in a god who sickens and kills people for not eating the right way.

This points, in instructive ways, to the limits of historical critical examination of Paul's archive. In this chapter I lay out very briefly the history of how (mostly white male) academic biblical scholars largely gave up on offering moral critique of the sacred texts they study. Biblical studies was birthed out of European colonialism and conquest. The historical turn that marks contemporary academic biblical studies emerged as a response to increasing criticism of the Bible's morality in early modernity, even as that same modernity was founded on systemic violence and enslavement. Academic biblical scholarship came to serve as the Bible's sanitation department, taking out the shit so that its texts could be kept fresh and clean. The Bible had to be clean if it was to be used to regulate white citizens and convert and discipline nonwhite bodies. The philosophical turn to Paul follows a similar path into and out of the Pauline archive, seeing in his rhetoric potential for radical political theorizing while ignoring potential moral critiques of his intellectual project. In both cases, "historicizing" Paul offers a way of ignoring some of the terrible shit he says.

A (BRIEF) HISTORY OF BIBLICAL STUDIES

When biblical scholars narrate the history of the biblical studies discipline, they often start with the Enlightenment (with an occasional nod to the Protestant Reformation) and the challenge that confronted Christians with the rise of new epistemologies, sciences, and political orders.[2] These factors are important to the history of the field, but often overlooked in the discussions is the role that colonialism played in shaping biblical studies. As European colonizers invaded what for them were vast new territories, they brought missionaries and Bibles with them.[3] These played the double role of justifying colonialism and explaining the peoples, practices, and cultures that the Europeans "discovered."[4] Indeed, an emerging consensus among scholars of religion is that the very category of religion itself was forged in the fires of colonial violence.[5] Before the Europeans' conquests, the spread of the Latin Bible throughout their continent created the conditions for consolidating Christian identity around the Bible, a phenomenon intensified by the vernacular translations that circulated after the invention of the printing press.[6] As Christian theologians confronted the new diversity of their colonial conquests, they reworked earlier epistemological and hermeneutical frameworks to invent "biblical" histories for non-European peoples; undercut, demonize, and eradicate local textual and ritual traditions; and justify Europe's national and religious superiority and its concomitant right to rule over new "barbarous" Others.[7] These moves were necessary, as Katie Cannon argued, to dehumanize Africans to the point that their very enslavement would go unremarked by Christians.[8] Paul was at the center of these new uses of the Bible, both as the idealized Christian missionary who attacked native religious traditions wherever he went and as the ideological supporter of the slave trade and the plantation system.[9] In addition, the academic study of the Bible emerged when Europe's colonial empires reached their greatest extent toward the end of the nineteenth century, which has meant that colonialist and racist ideologies have been written into the field since its inception.[10]

Running parallel to and in dialogue with European colonialism were shifting political and epistemological debates that are often referred to as the Enlightenment. These debates played a key role in shaping the history of biblical studies.[11] Up until the sixteenth century, biblical interpretation was determined by the "rule of faith," a ceaselessly debated set of assumptions about the Bible, theology, and the limits of meaning-making within

Christianity. A key epistemic shift occurred in early modernity around the seventeenth century, in which the nature of the Bible as theological, moral, and political guide was increasingly subject to interrogation.

Modern readers might be familiar with polemics that began to circulate in this period around the Bible's historicity: Was the world created some six thousand years ago? Did the Israelites part the Red Sea? Was there a King David? But critical questions about the reliability of the Bible as a historical narrative were subsets of a larger, mostly forgotten conversation about the morality of the Bible. Taking particular aim at the violence that is justified throughout the biblical narrative, early modern European authors suggested that the Bible might not be the ideal guide for forming modern moral citizens.[12] What kind of role model is a god who endorses genocide and conquest like that found in the book of Joshua? What kind of god demands that Abraham sacrifice his son Isaac? For cultured Europeans of a certain disposition, there was no answer to these moral critiques of the Bible. But even in the Age of Enlightenment, it was hard to imagine calling god and the Bible immoral.[13]

By way of dodging this uncomfortable conundrum, the Bible was recast as a cultural and literary touchstone for the West that could be subject to historical rather than moral critique. To preserve the Bible's cultural role in the West, one solution was to trim, recast, and excavate down to a deeper moral core behind the "human" accretions to the text. The core that remained after the work of this dissection would form what Jonathan Sheehan has called the "Enlightenment Bible,"[14] which is the Bible construed not as purveyor of theological truths but as the source of Western culture. Anyone who has heard valorizations of the Bible's "impact" or "influence" on cultural traditions or civilization has met the Enlightenment Bible. But, as Sheehan shows, this assumption that the Bible's importance lies in its role as cultural touchstone was forged in the heat of the criticism of the Bible in early modernity.[15] The Enlightenment Bible is, at its core, bound up with the Christo-capitalist discourse of shit and redemption. When the Bible began to give off a foul, immoral odor, it was subject to a process of redemption: some parts were hidden, unable to be cleansed of their human stain, while others were bleached, polished, disinfected, and sold back to us.

Biblia non olet.

A classic example of this process at work is the Jefferson Bible.[16] Famously skeptical of religious practice and belief in his own time, Thomas Jefferson nevertheless believed that one might be able to access a transcendent moral philosophy through a critical sifting of the Gospel narratives about Jesus.

Working at night with a razor, Jefferson trimmed the canonical Gospels down to create a Jesus who was like the moral philosophers admired by our third president. Jefferson's justification for this sanitizing work was that there was something at the core of biblical religion that could be excavated for his own personal edification from the human accretions that had built up around Jesus. Jefferson could save Jesus through a critical scrubbing of the all-too-human filth that had accumulated around him. In a letter to John Adams, he described the core of the Christianity he had produced as "diamonds in a dunghill."[17]

Another avenue away from the critique of biblical immorality was a turn toward historicism. Biblical theologians, drawing from new methodologies of historical analysis, were more comfortable debating the historicity of the biblical narrative than its morality.[18] Historicism rendered the unpalatable aspects of the Bible "historical," by which was meant culturally and historically specific human accretions, while leaving a pure, universal core that could be retained by right-thinking moderns. Historicism was thus deployed to foreclose a line of inquiry into biblical morality. The historical study of the Bible covered over and hid the base assumption that the Bible's morality, properly contextualized, could not be questioned. To let the Bible's morality be subject to criticism would jeopardize its role as the foundation for ethics and morality in the West.[19] One of the guardrails for historical scholars of the Bible was a certain deference to the text of the Bible itself. Someone might question whether Jesus walked on water but not his morality. Biblical scholars could be critical but only in the service of understanding the Bible on its own terms: "For the overwhelming majority of New Testament scholars . . . it has sufficed to gloss, paraphrase, amplify, annotate, or otherwise elaborate on the theology, Christology, pneumatology, ecclesiology, and eschatology of the New Testament authors."[20]

This process of reworking the Bible and biblical authority marks academic biblical studies as a thoroughly modern enterprise. Zygmunt Bauman has argued that the most apt image of modernity is mining.[21] Mining, as opposed to farming, involves destruction and waste in the production of the new.

> The new cannot be born unless something is discarded, thrown away or destroyed. The new is created in the course of meticulous and merciless dissociation between the target product and everything else that stands in the way of its arrival. Whether precious or base, pure metals can be obtained only by removing slag and cinders from the ore. And one can

get down to the ore only by removing and disposing of layer after layer of
the soil that bars access to the ledge—having first cut down or burnt out
the forest that barred access to the soil. Mining denies that death carries
in its womb a new birth. Instead, mining proceeds on the assumption that
the birth of the new requires the death of the old. And if so, then each
new creation is bound to share sooner or later in the lot of that which has
been left behind to rot and decompose to pave the way for a yet newer
creation.[22]

Biblical studies has constructed itself as a mining exercise, in which the
Bible's historical slag is discarded so as to preserve a moral or culturally
relevant (c)ore.

In her intervention in the discipline of geology, Kathryn Yusoff has
reminded us that it is not enough to point out that extractive processes like
mining leave behind waste and destruction. Mining, as a figure for the modern, is one of many extractive processes that relied on Black and enslaved
bodies as fuel for the acquisition of the products central to capitalist accumulation and consumption.[23] It is telling that the quest for an "enlightened"
Bible by European intellectuals took place in the context of the conquest and
enslavement of Brown and Black bodies. The enlightened Bible as symbol of
universal, civilized values hid its whiteness. The European project of enlightened, liberal civility was built on the backs of the unacknowledged humans
whose bodies were fodder for European culture. The production of whiteness not only shaped the study of the Bible but was suffused throughout all
the disciplinary structures of knowledge production that emerged from the
Enlightenment.[24]

Within the field of academic biblical studies, it has been feminist, womanist, and postcolonial biblical scholars that have challenged this mining
project, pointing out how the biblical sanitation department has consistently worked to produce a white male Bible. Kwok Pui-lan has shown that
biblical studies was shaped by European-specific quests for and anxieties
about "cultural origin, national identity, and racial genealogy."[25] Fernando
Segovia argues that by enforcing neutrality and impartiality on the interpreter and demanding an interpretation that universalizes the biblical text,
biblical studies ultimately calls for a "dehumanized" interpreter, one who
brings nothing of herself to the interpretive process.[26] Renita Weems has
shown how the assumption of the interpreter as Platonic form, stripped of
all particularity, ultimately ignores the androcentric nature of biblical texts
and how women who read them are forced to read from a male perspec-

tive.[27] The operations Segovia and Weems identify allow whiteness to remain unmarked, rendering it the normative frame for identifying "proper" interpretations as opposed to those marked as raced or gendered.[28] At its core, biblical studies attempted to forestall moral critique of the Bible by placing the white male biblical scholar in the position of speaking for the text. They were the men who owned the mines from which the historical Bible has been extracted.[29]

Bauman lifts up Michelangelo's famous saying about sculpture as an example of the ideology behind the modern fantasy of mining the new: all we have to do is remove the superfluous bits to reveal the beauty within a block of marble.[30] Hidden beneath the formless slab of marble is a beautiful sculpture waiting to be revealed. As Segovia and Weems, among others, have pointed out, white male biblical scholars have chipped away at the biblical text to reveal a white male Bible.

PAULUS NON OLET

We can extend this broader argument to Pauline studies. While the Historical Paul has been subject to a dizzying array of historical reconstructions, what is rarely questioned is the assumption that whatever Paul is historically reconstructed via these operations will serve as a foundational figure for ethics, morality, politics, and theology. Cut away some pseudepigrapha here, contextualize an embarrassing statement over there, build a few analogical links between his context and ours, and we will get a Paul that can ground our ethics. Of course, not everyone in the field is invested in Paul's continuing relevance, but I think most Pauline scholars are interested in him because, at some level, they are convinced that a properly historicized Paul has something to say to their corner of (post)modernity.

A good example of how this process works is Eric C. Smith's recent monograph *Paul the Progressive?*[31] Smith, a historian of early Christianity, writes for a progressive Christian audience while drawing from the rhetorical techniques of historicism to transform Paul into a modern progressive ally: "After years of studying Paul within the academic field of biblical studies, I have come to see [Paul] as one of the most misunderstood figures of the Bible and the Christian tradition. . . . The Paul that is revealed in careful study of his letters is nothing like the person so many progressive Christians hate, and, in fact, he shares many progressive Christian values" (ix–x).

Speaking from the position of an academic biblical scholar, Smith lays out a framework within which Paul ought to be read so as to bring out his true, progressive side. In what he calls the ground rules for reading Paul, Smith instructs his readers to

1. Remember that Paul didn't write all the letters that bear his name;
2. Trust Paul's own words;
3. Trust his actions over his words, when necessary; and
4. Recognize that we all bring our own lenses to reading Paul (3–4).

Smith's process is like that of most biblical historians. He endeavors to isolate Paul from not-Paul, recognizing that ancient Christians often wrote in Paul's name long after he had passed from the scene. Smith's second rule is also a challenge to the historicity of the canonical Acts of the Apostles, written by the same author who edited the Gospel according to Luke. Most historians recognize that Acts is not a reliable account of Paul's life and work but rather a legendary account of Christian origins. Finally, Smith encourages his readers to stick to the text, paying attention to where we can see Paul's actions through his words, and to be careful not to read Paul anachronistically. These are the standard tools of biblical historians; however, Smith uses additional rhetorical tools outside his formal list of rules to render Paul "progressive."

Take, for example, Smith's chapter on Paul and slavery (89–104). He is at pains to absolve Paul of criticism for the historical support that the apostle's archive has given to slavery, ancient and modern. His approach takes several steps, some of which follow his scholarly "ground rules." First, he subtracts from Paul any references to slavery that come from deutero-Pauline literature (notably Ephesians, Colossians, and the pastoral Epistles). This gets rid of the most baldly pro-slavery passages in the Pauline archive. Turning to the uncontested letters of Paul, Smith argues that Paul's advice to slaves in 1 Corinthians 7 to remain in their state is much more ambiguous than most modern translations suggest and that Paul might be encouraging slaves to take the opportunity to gain their freedom if the possibility presents itself. But even this reading of Paul's advice hardly counts as "progressive." Manumission was a regular part of ancient slavery, something many slaves could count on and expect. Manumission was also used by ancient slavers as an inducement to good behavior that ultimately served as a means of maintaining the system itself, a point made forcefully by Jennifer Glancy.[32] Paul's advice to slaves, charitably read, was to work within the system as it was set up.

Smith then turns to Paul's letter to Philemon, which was a major biblical support for the Fugitive Slave Act before the American Civil War. Smith does not argue that Philemon is evidence for Paul's critique of slavery; rather, he rightly recognizes that the text is ambiguous and, at best, shows Paul speaking affectionately about an enslaved Christian (Onesimus). In both 1 Corinthians and Philemon, Smith shows, the most charitable readings show Paul assuming that slavery was normal.

We might think that accepting the institution of slavery would disqualify Paul as a progressive, but this is where Smith's rhetorical moves subtly shift the goalposts. First, he compares his pared-down Paul with the worst excesses of the American slave system, which gives the impression that Paul was not *that* bad. Pointing to the explicitly pro-slavery statements in the deutero-Paulines, Smith concludes that "it was not Paul's writings that were to blame, or Paul himself, but it was the misuse of Paul, both deliberate and accidental," that put him on the side of slavery as an institution (*Paul the Progressive?*, 102). Smith assumes that the Christian texts written after Paul in his name represent a *betrayal* of Paul's theological vision. He does not entertain the possibility that these later devotees of the apostle saw him as an ally in their support for the ancient status quo and not as a problematic progressive needing to be contained.

Second, Smith recontextualizes Paul so as to take away the blame somewhat for his acceptance of slavery. He does this by claiming Paul believed that the world would soon end, thus making him less likely to try to overturn accepted social institutions. Paul's world was one in which slavery was normal, and he should not be blamed for accepting slavery as a given. Finally, Smith can conclude that Paul was not a "slavery apologist," which is the question that frames the entire chapter. What is so rhetorically clever here is that the entire chapter sets the goalposts in the most convenient location for Smith: Paul is absolved of being a full-throated supporter of slavery. What Smith has shown is that Paul accepted slavery as normal; he even felt comfortable enough playing with the terminology of human enslavement in his own self-descriptions (103). This hardly strikes me as an argument that Paul ought to be reclaimed as a progressive.

Even Smith seems somewhat abashed at making such an argument: "With the help of modern biblical scholarship we can recover a Paul who is far from a slavery apologist, and who might even be an ally in the struggle for emancipation" (91). Smith's tepid endorsement of a Paul who "might even be an ally" should force us to ask the question, At what cost have we paid for Paul's own emancipation from his entanglement with slavery?

Smith has pared Paul down, recontextualized him, lowered the bar, and still can't produce a Paul who can say that slavery is wrong, full stop. What are we saying to readers who have lived with the historical weight of the Pauline archive's support of slavery when we ask them to welcome someone who only "might" be an ally in their struggle? This strategy is what Joseph Marchal has recently called "pinkwashing Paul," in which a progressive figuration of the apostle is offered, "while ignoring or downplaying his letters' ambivalences, complicities, and recapitulations of imperializing and sexual naturalizing trajectories."[33] More to the point: Why is Paul's purity so important? Why does he have to be the hero of our historical work? *Must* we value (or revere?) the corpora we study? Why can't Paul smell bad? This is, after all, someone who thought that god made people sick and let some die because they were not properly celebrating the Lord's Supper.

We begin to suspect that Smith and many other biblical scholars with him are trying to have their cake and eat it too. Recognizing that his coreligionists have been either turned on or turned off by Paul's reactionary views, Smith has mobilized historicized and rhetorically useful arguments that can (1) trouble Paul's inscription in the conservative politics that Smith and his audience of progressive Christians reject; (2) keep Paul relevant enough so that Smith can continue to read the parts of the archive that are convenient for his political and theological sensibilities; and (3) maintain Paul's central position in a progressive canon, leaving Smith and the guild of liberal biblical scholars as the key interpreters that keep the Bible from falling into the hands of conservatives. By claiming that the Historical Paul was, without scholarly intervention, "progressive" in his time just like we are in ours, biblical scholars do just what theological readers have always done: recast Paul in their own image.

PAUL AFTER THEORY

The guild of biblical scholars turned, with the rest of the humanities and social sciences, to theory in the waning years of the twentieth century. While historicism has remained the dominant mode of respectable analysis in the field, in recent decades biblical scholars have taken up a wide variety of new methods, theories, and perspectives with which to approach and analyze biblical texts. This turn to theory was premised on the idea that new modes of analysis would radically transform the biblical studies field; however, as

Blossom Stefaniw has noted, these theoretical resources have only been integrated in part of the field, such that "methodological customs and theoretical allegiances correlate with diverging levels of collusion with patriarchy and commitment to the intellectual habits and academic customs entailed by it."[34] The new tools look fancy, but they are still being used to shovel shit for the Enlightenment Bible.

The theoretical turn has done little to dislodge the presumptions of the historical-critical method, authorial intent, and textual deference that characterize biblical scholarship more broadly.[35] Partly this is because some practitioners have remained committed to the same biblicism that forestalls ethical critique of the Bible, as R. S. Sugirtharajah has pointed out.[36] Even with their theoretical frameworks, the Bible is still presumed to be inherently good, when interpreted rightly. Theory, then, has allowed biblical scholars to say the same old things with new words.[37] In this sense, theory was really just the introduction of a new politics of respectability for (largely white) biblical scholars.[38] It allowed them to sound like modern, critical members of the university, countering the suspicion that biblical scholars were simply preachers without a pulpit.[39]

In resisting the early modern deferral of biblical morality, feminist biblical critics challenged the Bible's ethics as well as the strategies of identification with the Bible deployed by (mostly male) biblical scholars.[40] This has led to a far more complex ethical evaluation of biblical texts by feminists and other marginalized scholars; however, these minoritized readings have remained sidelined by the mainstream of the field. Many scholars writing from the margins have taken what Moore and Sherwood call a "reading as" approach, which means reading the Bible from particular identity-based positions. What this means in a practical sense is that such readings "can easily be accommodated to the democratic ethos of the discipline ('You read your way and I'll read my way'; 'Let many flowers bloom') and accorded a place in it—but precisely on its margins, where they can be both visible from the mainstream of the discipline and extraneous to it."[41] As Stefaniw has shown, this acceptance at the margins has been used as evidence of progress, a rhetorical posture paralleling white dismissals of the endurance of "real" racism after the Civil Rights movement.[42] This limited acceptance applies as well to naïve approaches to inclusion: having more women and people of color in the discipline than before doesn't solve the problem.[43] By letting the margins have the margins, traditional historical approaches to biblical studies can maintain their dominance of the center.

This problem is compounded by institutional structures that intersect with and shape the field, inhibiting changes from making their way to the center. Only in recent decades have scholars of color been admitted into the prestigious graduate programs that allow entry into the guild of biblical scholarship.[44] Limited citation and access to avenues for publication have been other structural impediments.[45] Finally, the study of early Christianity remains tied to theological or confessional schools, whose faculty are required to hold theological views that do not recognize women and/or LGBTQ+ persons as fully human. Consequently, many of the avenues for employment in biblical studies are open only to those who will resist transforming the field.[46] Moreover, these scholars find ready avenues to publication through confessional or parachurch publishing houses. Such structural forces allow the center to hold in the face of critique from the margins.

In their study of the field, Moore and Sherwood suggest that the ideological tension between universalist and particularist frames at the heart of biblical "reading as" is also a factor in maintaining the status quo. On the one hand, "reading as" requires a rejection of universal, homogenizing categories and presumptions of objectivity. But, on the other hand, most of these projects ground their ethics in alternative universal values, such as rights or justice.[47] Ultimately, for Moore and Sherwood, "reading as" fractures marginalized voices into different camps based on ever-narrower slices of identities, precluding transformation of the discipline itself by preventing the formation of a critical mass to contest the white male historicism at the center.

Moore and Sherwood's point is thought-provoking and in a later chapter will return as a concern in the work of Alain Badiou and Ward Blanton; however, it relies on a politics of difference that need not be accepted. For Moore and Sherwood, the dominance of identity-based approaches, and the moral and ethical imperatives that attend them, needs to be paired with a return to "the Big, Flabby, Old-Fashioned Words" in order for biblical studies to change (123). What they mean by this is that the Bible should come "to be seen as a key site where foundational, but unsustainable, 'modern' separations were made" (128). Such work would interrogate the history of biblical studies itself to understand more fully "the process whereby the critical discourse on the Bible became a means for the consolidation of certain antitheses foundational to modernity" (128).[48]

Moore and Sherwood suggest that a salutary direction has been charted by the philosophical turn to religion, the Bible, and Paul: "The Bible, like religion, is now being used as a resource for philosophers to think beyond the limits of empiricism, ontology, and metaphysics. . . . The Bible has become a resource for unsettling settled identities and shaking up the way we think about established concepts" (*Biblical Scholar*, 129). Biblical scholars can revive the field by engaging with and extending the work of these philosophical approaches to the Bible, "while resisting the temptation simply to repeat the protective mantra that they are not reading Paul, say, as they should (read: as we would)" (130).[49] I agree with Moore and Sherwood that an interesting conversation could be had with philosophers who have become enamored of Paul, particularly when biblical scholars cease critiquing these projects as insufficiently historical or theological. But I am not so convinced that the use of Paul (and the Bible more generally) as a "resource" for philosophical work offers a clear way out from the moral and ethical problems of biblical interpretation. It is, rather, more of the same, with a different name.

By turning Paul into a resource for thought, most philosophical readers of Paul bring with them many of the worst tendencies that have clustered around Pauline interpretation while they celebrate the Pauline archive. Paul gets "pinkwashed" in the transition from saint of conservatism to prophet of revolution. The preoccupations of white male scholars remain unmarked. Take, for example, the opening salvo of Simon Critchley's philosophical reading of Paul:

> Saint Paul is trouble. It is simply a fact about the history of Christian dogma that a return to Paul is usually very bad news for the established church. . . . So, the spirit of Paul is the movement of reformation. It is the attempt to clear away the corruption, secularism, and intellectual sophistry of the established church and to return to the religious core of Christianity. . . . Paul is the proper name of a ferment in the history of Christianity. Indeed, it is a ferment that places even the specificity of Christianity in question. . . . If Paul's essence consists in anything, then it is surely activism. This spells trouble for any and every church that sees itself as founded, funded, and well-defended.[50]

Critchley's praise of a Paul who takes on the establishment has a long tradition in Christian anti-Judaism and Protestant anti-Catholicism, whose effusive praise of Paul lifts him up as a hero of activism, reform, and revolution. Such valorizations of Paul cut across the various philosophical rereadings of his archive, and they suggest the importance of evaluating these readings critically before seeing them as resources for revitalizing biblical studies. In what follows, I will argue that Paul needs to be profaned, stripped thoroughly of his canonical function. Recycling Paul doesn't get us to a radically new place. He needs to be trashed so that we can write new counternarratives.[51] We must return to and extend the incomplete ethical critique of Paul's archive before we can ask whether it is useful for radical universalisms.

The centrality of evaluating the ethics of biblical texts and their interpretations has been a main feature of feminist biblical criticism for decades.[52] Shaped by the experience of patriarchal oppression, feminist biblical scholars, many writing in dialogue with the work of Elisabeth Schüssler Fiorenza, developed a hermeneutic of suspicion that, among other things, sifted and sorted, filled in and looked around, challenged and reimagined the shitty things that Paul said—not just about women but about wo/men, an intersectional term designating those subject to gendered, raced, classed, or colonized systems of domination.[53] Over time the centrality of ethical analysis has been picked up by postcolonial, queer, and womanist readers,[54] many of whom have pushed on feminist biblical criticism's blind spots to address intersectional issues of race and colonialism.[55] The ethical critique of Paul's archive, these scholars have shown, must also include the decolonizing of the field itself and its reliance on presumptions that whiteness and masculinity = proper scholarly analysis. Most biblical scholars have ignored these interventions as insufficiently "historical" and continued looking to Paul as moral exemplar (notice how the invocation of *historical* still functions to halt ethical critique!).

In fact, scholars regularly try to "rescue" Paul from the grip of his conservative interpreters as though he was the one who needed rescuing. Paul's long dead, after all. We'd be better off paying attention to how readers rescue themselves or others *from* Paul and from the oppressive assemblages within which his archive fits so comfortably. What might the texture of such stories look like? What might it mean to kill the presumption of Paul's authority over moral and ethical matters and reject our collective moratorium on ethical criticism of the Pauline archive? What would happen if we let Paul's shitty statements, assumptions, beliefs, and arguments be shitty? In other words, what would happen if readers of Paul stopped being sanitation workers, carting off his shit and hoping we don't see it stashed behind the apostle's sparkling theological statements, and embraced a different role as public health workers? As Schüssler Fiorenza has suggested, Paul needs a warning sign: "Caution, could be dangerous to your health and survival!"[56]

Owning My Shit

A few months ago, I found some old notebooks and journals from when I was in college. Reading the thoughts of my younger self feels both embarrassing and enlightening. I have forgotten more than I can remember, and these textual artifacts open up space for memory. It's not that I trust these documents. Other than dates and basic descriptions of events, what I wrote to and for myself back then was just as much a story about me as is this one. The me that wrote in these journals knew himself about as well as the me who is now reading them, which is to say not very well at all. Through these semilegible scrawlings (at least my handwriting hasn't changed) I can reimagine the past, my past, so as to rewrite my present. In one of the notebooks, I found an outline of an argument, sketched sometime toward the end of my junior year, about why the Bible doesn't condemn homosexuality.

Judging by the dates on surrounding entries, I wrote out this argument sometime in the spring of 2000, my junior year at UCLA. It was there that I was introduced to the historical-critical method of biblical scholarship. Though I had been raised a nominal Catholic, at the time I was a recovering evangelical fundamentalist, with one foot in the door of a softer form of evangelicalism and one foot out. I was, in other words, someone whose biography mirrored the historical conditions from which biblical scholarship emerged. The origin story for biblical scholarship replicates itself in many individual students/scholars that find their way into the guild. This replication is not merely ideological but affective. Historical criticism was exhilarating for me. It offered me strategies for sorting the biblical text into that which could be historicized, and thus offloaded to a dump of orientalized, patriarchal, primitive, or otherwise human accretions, and that which could be recycled as timeless, or timely, truth. The text of the Bible, particularly the Pauline archive, felt vibrant again, as it had when I entered a fundamentalist Christian world convinced that the Bible held secret codes implanted in it by god to reveal prophecies and prove the Bible's divine origins. Passages that felt dull were illuminated by what Adolf Deissmann long ago called the "light from the ancient East."[1]

Paul soon emerged for me as a new hero, first as an organizer who resisted forms of patriarchy, slavery, and state violence and then as a touchstone for rethinking divisions between race, gender, and class. He had to be trimmed down, of course, to fit into these various new suits. The deutero-Paulines had to go, as did the story of Paul in Acts. New frames helped me see new meanings in Paul's words and phrases, as when I began to learn that the New Perspective trajectory of Pauline scholarship had radically recentered his theology away from justification by faith. It was not just that this was intellectually interesting for a bookish young man. It also *felt* exciting.

As a fundamentalist evangelical, cognitive command of the Bible and its meaning allowed me to feel like I was doing something countercultural. I was listening in on secrets and guidance that the rest of the world had missed. Because of my own baggage, I had felt like an outsider most of my life. For a while, it felt thrilling to be able to choose to be an outsider to "the world." Historical criticism, as we saw earlier, ran along the fissure that developed between the Bible and early modernity. For me, historical criticism intensified the fissure I felt between myself and evangelical Christianity. I was now an outsider on the inside.

The historicizing frameworks I imbibed in the classroom spilled out in Bible studies and church gatherings. In a Bible study I co-led on Job and Ecclesiastes, my co-leader grew frustrated at how I pressed against theologically comfortable readings of these texts. My college youth pastor sat me down at lunch one day on campus to ask whether I had made the theologically heretical comments some fellow students had heard me make. Maybe I shouldn't be in leadership in the group if I believed what I had said. The Campus Crusade for Christ liaison became increasingly concerned as I suggested that Paul didn't really think that all humanity needed to be saved through the substitutionary atonement of Christ.

At the time, I felt I was standing on conviction, fighting for historical truth against theological naïveté. It was a softer form of the fundamentalist drive for purity that I thought I had walked away from, though now directed against fellow Christians and not worldly outsiders. Christians, so I thought, needed to read the Bible historically, or else they wouldn't understand their own scriptures and, implicitly, were missing out on what *god really wanted* them to do.

Rediscovering my journal entry from the spring of 2000 helped me see how this ideologically driven narrative of my conversion to academic biblical studies misses what it felt like to become a biblical scholar. The entry itself is nothing particularly noteworthy. It is mostly a distillation and curation of arguments that circulated in the mid- to late nineties in the wake of John Bosworth, challenging the idea that the Bible, particularly the book of

Leviticus and the letters of Paul, condemned homosexuality.[2] The arguments are the undergraduate versions of those still made to let Paul and the Bible off the hook for the long history of Christian homophobia.[3]

Read at the level of analytic content, the entry is an exercise that sits at the very heart of historical-critical work: deploying historical arguments to show that the Bible doesn't really say what we think it does on an issue. In this case, most Christians and non-Christians in the late nineties would have probably said that Paul condemned homosexuality, that it was considered by the apostle, and hence by Christianity, to be a sin. As a budding historian, I was arguing that this consensus was all wrong, that it wasn't sufficiently attentive to the historical differences between then and now. These are good things for historians to note, of course. Careful attention to the difference between then and now is a crucial aspect of what it means to study the past. But I was deploying these tools for something more than just intellectual curiosity.

What I remembered when I found my journal entry was that I had put all this together while sitting in my car waiting to meet someone for coffee. This was not just any someone. I had first met Sara when we were both first years in college. We attended the same church. We spent a good deal of time together, and I wanted it to be something more, something romantic. Coffee was a chance to figure out, awkwardly, how to get there. Our church at the time was what one might call theologically left of center. It seemed progressive that our church's denomination (the Presbyterian Church, U.S.A.) ordained women. But what the church ought to "think about" homosexuality was a hot topic. I wanted to impress Sara by convincing her. I wanted her to feel an attraction to what felt to me like a rebellious way of reading the Bible. I wanted that feeling also to translate into attraction to me too. I was playing the part of the exegetical rebel. Wouldn't a woman who also loved the Bible find that sexy? Seduction by biblical exegesis. Only a biblical scholar in the making could be so foolish.

This twenty-year-old journal entry reminded my older self of what it was like to be young and stupid, and it provoked a realization about how I came to love not the Bible itself any longer but the historical study of it. What I had wanted to say, but couldn't, was that I wanted Christianity, as I had known it, to be something else, to shift as I had shifted. I hadn't directed these swerves of perspective from some central cognitive "I," but they had swerved nonetheless. Lacking that level of self-reflection, I acted the part of the rebel. It felt good to be seen as pushing buttons, saying the things that weren't supposed to be said. It felt thrilling, as only juvenile acting out can.

I'd like to think that I have moved beyond the impulse to shock people to get attention. Given the amount of foul language used in this book, I'm not so sure. I am embarrassed that I acted as if being a theological rebel would fix what I was missing, replace what had already slipped away from me, even get me the girl. In effect, what I was doing was pinkwashing myself through Paul, using a kind of interpretive tolerance to grant me something like Foucault's "speaker's benefit" and to achieve my own heteronormative fantasies.[4]

As I looked at this faded paper, I wondered whether the attraction of academic biblical studies for many of my colleagues was precisely what it had been for me: the thrill of being able to say no to what could no longer be believed. I have always told myself that I became a biblical scholar because I found the work intellectually engaging. In my younger days, I even told myself that I wanted to bridge the gap between the church and the academy. But I suspect it was because I felt a thrill from using my intellect and the tools I was handed in the classroom to act out. That thrill, I am loathe to admit, made me a biblical scholar before I had decided on it.

Or did it? I suspect now that the idea that there was a natural fit between my biography and a career in biblical studies misses something about both.

Before my world came undone and my family came apart, I had been a bookish kid. I read constantly. After my father went to prison, I remember reading more and more, devouring the books in my new school's library. A few years later, the panic attacks started happening. I had questions about death and what comes after. Through a family friend I found myself at a Calvary Chapel outreach service, and sensing that the thing for me to do was go down front to the altar at the minister's invitation, I gave my life to Jesus Christ. Then I was given a Bible, warned not to go back to a Catholic church, and told I had been saved.

It took a while for me to start going to church. Frankly, the thought hadn't occurred to me. But I started to devour books and tapes, mostly on apologetics, theology, and end times prophecy. That road took me to talk radio, Rush Limbaugh, and Republicans. Even today I find QAnon conspiracies discomfortingly understandable (if no longer appealing).

I could now redescribe my formative fundamentalist period as a failed attempt at learning the tools of scripturalization. I heard in sermons and read in books that the Bible was the answer to everything, that it told the future . . . that it would be a way to build a new family. If I gave myself over to this book, if I learned it inside and out, if I devoted myself to studying it, I would have what I wanted. I'd get married; I'd have kids, a house, a purpose. No more shame. Oh, and I'd be saved from the coming apocalypse.

It's clear from my journals that I never really learned how the Bible was scripturalized in evangelical communities. I never really learned the white men's magic of using the Bible to get what I wanted, to forge a stable identity, and to build a community. My attempts to study the Bible seemed to confuse people around me. I couldn't seem to dance to the right beat.

To say that this inability to dance to the worship music around me made me into a biblical scholar before I even knew it is to hide a fact that I came to understand too late: it wasn't that I was made to be a biblical scholar, but that biblical scholarship was made for me, a cis hetero male who presents as white. At the time that I encountered academic biblical scholarship, I was feeling that the fabric of evangelical theology was coming apart, but I was desperate for something to keep it all together. Biblical scholarship offered me a place where others have had to struggle to get in.

I picked up the rhythms of biblical scholarship quickly. I learned the languages. I read books by white male liberal scholars that helped me differentiate myself from my evangelical tribe, while still thinking I was an insider. I wrote and wrote and wrote. I learned to name check the right way, to suggest persuasively that I had read more than I had. I played that role with more depth in grad school. I networked. Sought out patrons. I adapted to new beats and rhythms, new methods, theories, perspectives. I danced well.

Part of why I could do this was because I had been, without consciously knowing it, invited to the dance, while many of my fellow classmates had to fight their way in. From the other side of the curtain, I can see it in the statistics of who gets published, who gets read, who is marked as "classic." I can hear the subtle inflection added to a critique of someone's work for being . . . too theoretical . . . too sloppy . . . too feminist-y. I can see how I participated in the fraternity party, knowing that so long as the club's rules and membership didn't change too much, I'd have a place. Learning this truth came from listening to those who had to fight so much harder than I did to be heard and recognized, and who still must fight that fight.

I'm a product of a discipline that, while not alone in academia for being so, rewarded me for performing masculinity and whiteness. That is shit I must own. It's all well and good for me to listen and then name how I have benefited from privilege and patriarchy. Even Paul can look on his past life and call it shit (Phil. 3:8). Whether I am just full of it or not will depend on whether I keep sitting here staring at old notebooks or get to work on dismantling the structures that made me feel welcome in the first place.

REDEEMING PAUL

IN HER FANTASTIC ETHNOGRAPHIC ACCOUNT of the *catadores* (sifters, collectors) who gather recyclables at Jardim Gramacho, one of Rio de Janeiro's garbage dumps, Kathleen Millar asks, "Why do the *catadores* return to the dump?"[1] The work of scouring a dump site for such materials is not a job many humans would choose for themselves. Images of catadores sifting through mounds of garbage conjure postapocalyptic futures, though theirs is a future present. Millar's work on the catadores of Jardim Gramacho challenges the desperation we attach to such work, even the category of work itself. The catadores don't return to the dump because they have no other job opportunities. They don't come out of a sense of desperation. Rather, they return to the dump because the informality and plasticity of their labor and the community that has formed around the dump's economy offer them a "form of living," a livelihood and a way of life.[2] Anna Tsing has documented similar communities that have formed around the work of gathering matsutake mushrooms in despoiled landscapes.[3] These workers return to damaged and dangerous landscapes because they have found ways to make lives at the margins of the "formal" economy. I will return later to this juxtaposition between death and life and the forms of living that emerge when allied with the vital matter of refuse. Here I want to dwell on my variant of Millar's question: Why do biblical scholars and philosophers keep going back to Paul?

I have suggested that biblical studies is a sanitation department that renders the Bible clean by processing its waste. As with any complex institution, there are different functions and different workers. In the next two chapters I look at readers of Paul—a sociologist, a philosopher, a radical filmmaker, and two biblical scholars—who return to Paul's archive much like the catadores in Millar's study return to the dump. In their own ways, all these readers know that this archive is a dump site. However, they also are compelled to return to it, because they sense that something valuable might be found there. Each has cultivated a way of seeing value in this Pauline garbage heap. Some are recyclers. Some sift and sort. Some are looking for treasure, perhaps mistakenly thrown away. Each figures differently what ought to be redeemed and recycled and what can be left to rot with the banana skins, empty to-go cups, and chemical waste.

The Paul invoked here is fecund fertilizer. The logic of these readers mirrors the redemption of shit. Food becomes excrement. Excrement becomes fertilizer or makeup or health remedies. Shit is transformed into gold. But that transformation always leaves an unredeemable remainder.

Readers of Paul, ancient and modern alike, have been presented with a slew of binary options for reading Paul (sinner or saint, hero or heretic, radical or conservative) that ultimately can be summarized in the question, Shit or gold? Is Paul valuable as scripture, as theological authority, as religious visionary, as militant model, or is he an unrepentant reactionary better left to the dustbin of history? To read Paul within the excremental discourse of the West allows us to recognize that the boundaries between shit and gold are blurry, that they often feed one on the other.

But we should also keep in mind Millar's salient observation about the catadores: they return to the dump because they find a life and a livelihood there. For some of the readers in the next two chapters, there is joy in finding a diamond in the rough, a pearl among the swine. Others return to Paul because that is where their community is, so they go back to be with their people, even if that means sifting through the garbage with them.

What these chapters attend to is not just the redemption of Paul but its remainder. What sort of redemptive processes has Paul been wrung through? What remains when he is redeemed? In this chapter I focus on three modern redemptive projects of the apostle by Jacques Ellul, Alain Badiou, and Ward Blanton, while the next chapter focuses on projects by Pier Paolo Pasolini and Brian Blount that split Paul in two, perhaps in order to save him. I have chosen these five projects, not because they represent the diversity of Pauline studies or because they cover all the ways in which Paul has been redeemed or split by modern scholars; rather, I have chosen them because their juxtaposition allows me to explore typical modes of redeeming Paul while also pointing toward a potential path beyond Paul, to his profanation.

I have also chosen them because they are redemptive projects from scholars that share similar political goals to my own and from whom I have learned a great deal. These scholars turn to Paul for resources to grapple with racism, to imagine alternatives to global capitalism, and to theorize radical political change. While I might quibble over the details, these are projects with which I sympathize and identify. My readings of their work, then, strike close to home. In each case I suggest that Paul's reuse in the fight against injustice comes with a remainder.

PAUL THE ANARCHIST

The turn to Paul as a resource for radical political thought seems to have emerged late in the Reagan and Thatcher administrations as the Cold War came to an end and neoliberal democratic governance was poised to become the dominant politico-economic governing system for the globe. Jacob Taubes's seminar at Heidelberg in 1987 has often been regarded as the starting point for this turn to Paul.[4] Taubes's lectures situated Paul's thought within the history of Western messianic and eschatological thought, paying particular attention to the political theology of Carl Schmitt and Walter Benjamin.[5] His Paul influenced ancient historians like Dieter Georgi, Daniel Boyarin, and L. L. Welborn along with the philosophical reflections on Paul by Giorgio Agamben.[6] In a later chapter I will return to the "messianic" trajectory in the philosophical readings of Paul, particularly as it is articulated by Agamben, but here I want to dwell on an understudied attempt at this same time to read Paul in the direction of radical politics.

In 1988 Jacques Ellul, an anarchist and professor of sociology at the University of Bordeaux, published *Anarchie et Christianisme*, one of many books that circled his interests in theology, political theory, and the critique of modern state systems.[7] Ellul's short book sought to create what Bruno Latour might call the "conditions of felicity" whereby Christian theology and the anarchist tradition of political philosophy might see each other as allies. To do this, Ellul attempts to fold Paul into his anarchist critique of the state. He paints Paul as not only a critic of the state but one who rejects all forms of mastery and domination.

Anarchism is a (famously) riotous tradition, so Ellul rightly begins his project by locating his definition of anarchism. He settles on two major axes. The first is the absolute rejection of violence (11). This means that Ellul rejects both the violence inherent in state power and the use of violence to achieve political ends. In fact, participation in politics itself is already too much of a capitulation to state power and must be avoided in favor of conscientious objection (14–15). Ellul's nonviolent anarchism resists participation in neoliberal democracy and "acts by means of persuasion, by the creation of small groups and networks, denouncing falsehoods and oppression, aiming at a true overturning of authorities of all kinds as people at the bottom speak and organize themselves" (13–14). Ellul's second principle of anarchism (*an-arche*) is "no authority, no domination" (45). His anarchism rejects state power and the history of Christianity's alliance with the state (30). This principle creates challenges for the traditional Christian conception of a sovereign god. If there can be no masters, there can be no god (32). Hence Ellul's Christian god is reframed as a self-limited ruler who grants freedom to humans and saves through liberation, which Ellul defines as "love" (33–44). Christianity and anarchism must join, then, in challenging the great disaster that is the assumption, common to the Left and the Right, "that the nation state is the norm" (104).

From this theologized definition of anarchism, Ellul seeks to show that a "general current which points towards anarchy" runs throughout the Bible, Paul included (46). He recognizes, however, that Paul is a problem for his anarchist critique of the state. As such, he turns to Paul last, having included subsections on the Hebrew Bible, Jesus, and Revelation before arriving at Paul out of canonical order. Ellul does not distinguish between Paul and the deutero-Paulines, which means he must explain Pauline support for the state in Romans 13:1–7, 1 Timothy 2:1–2, and Titus 3:1. He chooses to focus on Romans 13, which he admits is "a very embarrassing passage" for his position (86).

Ellul begins by arguing that most interpreters have fixated on Paul's claim that "all power comes from god" (13:1) as a means of justifying a divine sanction for the state (monarchical or democratic) (79). By reading Romans 13 in context, Ellul thinks he can nuance that sanction. Emphasizing Paul's call to a renewed mind that is not conformed to the world (Rom. 12:2), he argues that Romans 13 can be seen not as a support for the state but as an emphasis on god's nonstate sovereignty. On his reading, Paul does four things: he reminds his readers that "the authorities are also people"; as people, authorities deserve to be prayed for; taxes are owed to authorities; and the authorities' powers (*exousiai*) are earthly manifestations of heavenly powers that have rebelled against god (81–83). Ellul builds on this final takeaway by reading Romans 13 in light of Colossians 2:13–15, in which the claim is made that Christ has already stripped the state and the authorities of their power through the cross: "Politically this means that the *exousia* which exists alongside or outside political power is also vanquished. . . . Power is indeed from God, but all power is overcome in Christ!" (84–85) Ellul's Paul supports neither the divine right of kings nor the sovereignty of the people but humanizes government and sees it as always already disempowered through the mythos of the cross.

Ellul's Paul sees the state through something like a realized eschatology: the state may be here, right in front of you, but in the cosmic perspective it is already overcome.[8] While I can see how this might be a position that could embolden Christians against the presumed omnipresence and permanence of the state apparatus, Ellul's goal of a Christianity without masters and without violence is undermined by an individualist, cognitive model of freedom. His eschatology of the state is paralleled by his individualist notion of freedom and liberation, as offered by his anarchist vision of Christianity.

> The biblical God is above all the one who liberates us from all bondage, from the anguish of living and the anguish of dying. Each time that he intervenes it is to give us again the air of freedom. . . . But why freedom? If we accept that God is love, and that it is human beings who are to respond to this love, the explanation is simple. Love cannot be forced, ordered, or made obligatory. It is necessarily free. If God liberates, it is because he expects and hopes that we will come to know him and love him. (*Anarchy and Christianity*, 39)

Ellul's god liberates but only from the bondage of existential dread. Existential freedom is the gift of his god that is exchanged for love. The analogy here to Ellul's view of the state is clear: an anarchist Christianity does not see the state or someone's social/legal/economic standing as real. Each must be overcome through an existential liberation of each individual's thought. Though Ellul doesn't make this connection, this resembles Paul's eschatological relativism in 1 Corinthians 7. For Paul, the impending end of the world creates an eschatological context in which all persons ought to live in their current situation "as if not" (*hos mē* [1 Cor. 7:29–31]).[9] Ellul's realized eschatology lacks the relativizing urgency of Paul's imminent one, but it functions similarly: society and government cannot be changed except by an act of god, so the best we can do is shift perspective.[10]

This leads to a key problem in Ellul's reading of Paul. He is so desperate to claim Paul for an anarchist Christianity that he must avoid critical reflection on how Paul's broader archive breaks with his anarchist critique of violence and subordination. Even if we find Ellul's reading of Romans 13 persuasive, the Paul who encourages women and slaves to be obedient to their husbands and masters must certainly fail Ellul's criteria for participation in anarchist a-politics. This is all the more an issue since Ellul does not distinguish between a Historical Paul (Rom. 13) and a deutero-Paul (Col. 2). The latter is the first text in the Pauline archive to introduce the so-called Household Codes, which regulate subordination within the patriarchal household "as is fitting in the lord" (Col. 3:18). What good is a Paul who relativizes the state but who doesn't call out the masters in his own house?

Clarice Martin long ago called out this selective reading strategy in relation to the Household Codes, showing how modern exegetes work hard to absolve the Pauline archive of responsibility for supporting slavery while at the same time ignoring how these texts enjoin the subordination of women and children to patriarchal authority.[11] Martin's critique of readings like Ellul's is not that they need to be rendered consistent, but that readers—and here Martin is speaking to African American readers specifically—need to "create and implement responsible ethical guidelines for the dismantling of the gender hierarchy of African American men and women."[12] We do not need a consistently liberatory or anarchist Paul. What we need are strategies of reading Paul that foster the kinds of politics or communities necessary for survival or resistance, whether that means using something useful in Paul's conceptual repertoire or actively resisting it. A truly anarchist reading of Paul would call him out for his oppressive views, critically engage what might be salvageable for anarchist politics, and refuse to submit to following Paul without question. Ellul's convoluted interpretation of Romans 13 yields little in the way of a clearly discernible politics that could dismantle the state itself. Such an interpretation seems necessary only if we start with the presumption that a Christian view of the state must cohere with Paul's, no matter what the cost. If anarchism means no masters, then throw all the masters onto the garbage heap, Paul included.

THEORIZING THE UNIVERSAL

Perhaps the most famous attempt to redeem Paul as a figure for radical politics is Alain Badiou's *Saint Paul*,[13] standing alongside similar reclamations by Stanislas Breton and Slavoj Žižek, among others.[14] Like many radical thinkers, Badiou has been in search of tools for breaking the deadlock of global capitalism and identitarian politics, which for him are two sides of the same coin. Over the course of a large body of work, he has theorized pathways that interrupt such politico-discursive deadlocks through a theory of the event. In Paul, Badiou claims to have found the origin of his own intellectual project, a "poetic thinker of the event" and the "foundation of universalism."[15] Paul is for him the first militant, and his (re)turn to Paul is born out of the need for a new militant figure to face the menace of global capitalism. For Badiou, Paul is a surprising and valuable discovery as he scours the garbage heaps of the Western tradition, looking for a replacement for Lenin.[16]

In the sole extant fragment of his epistle to Agathapous, the early Christian theologian Valentinus mused that Jesus "digested divinity; he ate and drank in a special way, without excreting his solids. He had such a great capacity for continence that the nourishment within him was not corrupted, for he did not experience corruption."[17] In other words, Jesus was so otherworldly that he didn't shit. Badiou's Paul is cut from a similar cloth: in order to speak for the universalism that Badiou sees as the ground for radical politics, Paul and his thought must be rendered generic, beyond particularity. While this erasure is problematic in itself as a reading of Paul, it becomes even more so when we look to what (and whom) Badiou must throw out to create his Pauline Platonic form.

To understand how Paul becomes useful for Badiou, it will help to lay out briefly, and without the nuance that characterizes this work, how Badiou conceptualizes his theory of the event, of which Paul is the first theorist.[18] For Badiou, the history of philosophy has been a struggle between the one versus the multitude: "What *presents* itself is essentially multiple; *what* presents itself is essentially one" (25). Badiou solves this problem by arguing that being itself, stripped of all particularity, is pure multiplicity ("the one *is not*"), but that what presents itself to us is a situation, a limited multiplicity of elements counted as one according to a particular structure (26). Because reality is multiplicity, the situation and its count are never stable or complete; however, the mechanism by which the situation is counted and rendered seemingly stable is the state (99). The state is that which staves off anarchy by determining what elements are included in the situation.

Because a situation is only counted-as-one, it is inherently unstable. Every situation contains elements that are not counted by the state of the situation. These uncounted yet present elements form an evental site ("a multiple such that none of its elements are presented in the situation" [183]). Situated on the void of pure multiplicity that threatens to throw the situation into anarchy, an evental site is a potential locus for radical transformation of the situation: "Every radical transformational action originates *in a point*, which, inside a situation, is an evental site" (185). An event names the torsion that occurs around an evental site, because the evental site is outside the situation (not subject to a count). As Ian James puts it,

> An event, should it occur, is not anything that can be identified or verified from within the existing structure or a situation. Since it exceeds anything the situation can count or present, the event *as such* cannot possibly be known or verified in advance or even in the moment of its surging or emerging. . . . An event, if it has occurred, will be that which will have completely transformed the state and structure of the situation and will have done so solely on the basis that the elements of the evental site were not presented in the situation prior to the occurrence of the event itself.[19]

Because of its undecidability, the truth of the event is only knowable through fidelity, which is the "set of procedures which discern, within a situation, those multiples" that depend on the emergence of an event (Badiou, *Being and Event*, 245). That which is thus discerned must take the form of the "generic," which means that the truth of the event must not be located in elements that are recognizable or counted within the situation that has been transformed (345–46). This means that fidelity to an event always comes after the fact and is a risk, in that it names something that cannot contain any specificity or act as a new structure for a situation. The one who risks such fidelity is a subject (413). The subject is, ultimately, that which decides by taking a risk that an event has occurred, names its occurrence, and remains faithful to it, such that it cannot be reinscribed within the situation.

Badiou's theory of the event carries with it an important revolutionary potential, though I will push back on various assumptions that are baked into it. There is something intuitively correct about a model of change that looks to that which remains unaccounted for, what could not be expected, and I think there are ways in which such a project could align itself with the "deep solidarity" called for by Joerg Rieger and Kwok Pui-lan.[20] But the potential of Badiou's theory is, I would argue, actually blunted by anchoring it to the Pauline archive.

In a situation characterized by Jewish particularism and Roman global imperialism, Badiou's Paul announces the event of the Resurrection of Jesus, a foolishness and scandal unaccounted for by the state or the structure of the situation, and becomes a subject through his fidelity to the proclamation of this Good News. In what follows, I press on how Badiou redeems Paul from his role as oppressive Christian saint and repurposes him as a secular, militant theorist of the universal. But this secular gaze merely transfers Paul's

canonical function from one place to another, resurfacing in Badiou's theory
of discourses as the figure of the Master. Like Jacques Ellul, Badiou looks to
throw off the yoke of the Master but does so by submitting to Paul, properly
reconfigured. Finally, because Badiou is unwilling to question Paul's position as an idealized militant theorist, he struggles to reconcile his Paul with
what Paul says in his letters, particularly about Jews, women, and slaves.
Paul's reuse, from saint to militant, leaves an unredeemable remainder.

Badiou opens his book *Saint Paul* with a claim to objectivity, not unlike
mainstream biblical scholars. He sees Paul with no preconditions, no interest in his place as the touchstone of Western religious history.

> For me, truth be told, Paul is not an apostle or a saint. I care nothing
> for the Good News he declares, or the cult dedicated to him. But he is a
> subjective figure of primary importance. I have always read the epistles
> the way one returns to those classic texts with which one is particularly
> familiar; their paths well worked, their details abolished, their power pre-
> served. No transcendence, nothing sacred, perfect equality of this work
> with every other, the moment it touches me personally. A man emphati-
> cally inscribed these phrases, these vehement and tender addresses, and
> we may draw upon them freely, without devotion or repulsion. All the
> more so in my case, since, irreligious by heredity, and even encouraged
> in the desire to crush the clerical infamy by my four grandparents, all of
> whom were teachers, I encountered the epistles late, the way one encoun-
> ters curious texts whose poetry astonishes. Basically, I have never really
> connected Paul with religion.[21]

Badiou positions himself as thoroughly disinterested, unwilling, despite his
anticlerical upbringing, to bring anything to his reading of Paul. As Elizabeth Castelli notes, this is how he establishes his authority as a reader of
Paul.[22] As a dehumanized reader, Badiou constructs his reading of Paul as
objective, as coming from no place but Paul himself. This stacks the deck
from the start: by positioning himself as a disinterested reader, Badiou's Paul
speaks only in universals, because it is only the universal that can address
a reader stripped of all particularity. This is what Badiou refers to as the
generic: a subject and a message without historical particularity. Paul doesn't
defecate, doesn't come down to a particular plot of the earth, and neither
does his ideal reader.

Badiou's Paul can become a theorist of the universal only through this
process of stripping out the particular: "There is in this prose [of Paul's let-

ters], under the imperative of the event, something solid and timeless, something that . . . is intelligible to us without having to resort to cumbersome historical mediations."[23] Badiou thus "secularizes" Paul: rather than returning to Paul "the saint" to ground a new religio-ecclesial configuration, the apostle is recycled to produce Paul "the militant" to ground a new political formation. If a "Christian" framing of Paul would mark him as among the first apostles, canonical, and a saint, Badiou secularizes Paul as the first militant, a classic, and a poet-thinker. The structure of authority remains.

The procedure for extracting the militant Paul from the saintly Paul revolves around the extraction of a universal procedure from the "fable" that Paul tells. Badiou distills Paul's definition of Christianity to a single "generic" statement: "Jesus is resurrected" (4). This statement is the key enunciation by Paul because it "fails to touch on any Real" (4–5). We should remember, according to Badiou, "the event that [Paul] takes to identify the real *is not real* (because the Resurrection is a fable)" (58). The proclamation of Jesus's resurrection is central to Badiou precisely because it is unbelievable in a literal sense and thus becomes a subject-forming gesture that founds the "generic conditions of universality" (6). By reducing the Christian narrative to its "element of fabulation [*point de fable*]," Badiou strips away all the historically situated elements of that narrative to a core procedure that can be universally replicable.[24] In Badiou's terms: the Resurrection of Jesus is the event that Paul proclaims, and its very absurdity means it was not captured or anticipated by Paul's situation. Properly denuded of the encrustations of a religious imaginary or historical particularity, this Pauline declaration reconfigures "truth" by separating the production of truth from any particularity, rationality, historicity, or cultural conditions. It's as if we are watching philosophical reading in the Platonic realm of the forms.

Because he is committed to reading Paul "generically," Badiou is forced to wrestle with Paul's Jewishness. When speaking of Jewish ethnic particularity, he is quick to point out that we can still say that Paul is Jewish, but in so doing we must also remember that "although the event depends on its site in its being, it must be independent of it in its truth effects. Thus it is not that communitarian marking . . . is indefensible or erroneous. It is that the postevental imperative of truth renders the latter indifferent (which is worse). It has no signification, whether positive or negative" (Badiou, *Saint Paul*, 23). Paul's Jewishness and its markings are indifferent and without signification as regards the truth effects of the event. Badiou appears comfortable with designifying ethnic particularity while relying on Paul's historical biography, in some of its particularity, to ground Paul's ability to speak as an authentic antiphilosopher/militant, to offer a satisfactory response to the question, Who speaks?[25]

The effects of Badiou's indifference to Jewish particularity can be seen in his exploration of the four "discourses" in Paul's thought (1 Cor. 1:18–25): Greek, Jewish, Christian, and mystical. His analysis of these discourses reinscribes his Paul within tropes of Christian theological anti-Judaism. For Badiou, the Greek and Jewish discourses stand in for the two central problematics of our present world: the homogenizing system of globalized capitalism (Greek) and the enervating politics of identity (Jewish) (*Saint Paul*, 6–13). The Greek discourse, figured as the wise man and modeled on Greek philosophy, seeks wisdom that "consists in appropriating the fixed order of the world, in the matching of the logos to being" (41). By understanding the cosmic order, the wise man adjusts himself to it so as to find his place within it. Conversely, the Jewish discourse is that of the sign and the exception, and it is figured as the prophet who speaks for and of a transcendent god. As an exception, "the prophetic sign, the miracle, election, designate transcendence as that which lies beyond the natural totality" (41). For Badiou, each discourse mirrors the other as a discourse of the Father, and both envision salvation only as that which is already given within the cosmic totality,

> whether it be through direct mastery of the totality (Greek wisdom), or through mastery of a literal tradition and the deciphering of signs (Jewish ritualism and prophetism). For Paul, whether the cosmic totality be envisaged as such or whether it be deciphered on the basis of the sign's exception, institutes in every case a theory of salvation tied to mastery (to a law), along with the grave additional inconvenience that the mastery of the wise man and that of the prophet . . . divide humanity in two (the Jew *and* the Greek), thereby blocking the universality of the Announcement. (42)[26]

Each of the two discourses fails, because it is tied to law and unable to bear the universality of the event announced by Paul. As such, both are discourses of mastery.

Badiou contrasts these two discourses with what he sees as Paul's Christian discourse, though the term *Christian* is never used in Paul's letters. It is this discourse which can bear universality, because it does not have any recourse to law for its justification. Not a synthesis of the Jewish or Greek discourses, it is "absolutely *new*," an "intervention within History," a "rupture" (43). Badiou sees in Paul's Christian discourse, as a discourse of the

Son, a decline of the figure of the Master, now replaced by the "apostle." The figure of the apostle does not belong to the discourse of the Master because he testifies to an event as neither witness nor guardian of memory: "The apostle, who declares an unheard-of possibility, one dependent on an evental grace, properly speaking knows nothing" (45). That the apostle, like Socrates, "knows nothing" is a function of how Badiou characterizes the event to which the figure of the apostle bears witness.[27] He constructs this Christian discourse of the Son as one lacking a Master because it neither has rational content nor is declared by a subject that knows its truth, in a traditional epistemological sense. The event that Paul's discourse names (the Resurrection) is not real but a fable, thus inscribing within itself no content whatsoever (58).[28]

It is worth pausing here to note what Badiou has done by cycling his theory of the event through Paul. Paul's Jewishness, and all identities as such, is not just erased but figured as one of the discourses of the Master. In its place, Badiou offers the Christian discourse of the Son, but this replacement lacks any content. In his response to Badiou's Paul, Daniel Boyarin wonders what, if anything, this Paul can stand for, or if he is just an empty sophist, seducing with his words.[29] Badiou ultimately is seduced, as so many Pauline hermeneutes are, by Paul's rhetoric and self-presentation. Alain Badiou's Paul becomes a man without content, except for his fidelity to declaring the Resurrection, such that he can stand in the position of abstract universality.[30] Paul doesn't shit, but it seems like that is because he hasn't eaten anything.

Aligning Paul with a philosophical project need not reinscribe the worst tendencies of his archive. In her groundbreaking work on Paul, Elizabeth Castelli put him into conversation with Michel Foucault. In reading him with Foucault, Castelli laid out the subtle mechanisms by which Paul, particularly in 1 Corinthians, seeks to control speech and knowledge, who can speak and who properly knows.[31] By cycling his theory of the event through Paul's rhetoric, Badiou not only renders Paul a man-without-content; he also reinscribes Paul's authority, secularizing him as the apostle-militant of the event.

Badiou's desire for a subject unmarked by particularity precedes his reading of Paul. It arises from a broader antipathy to the discourse of multiculturalism and relativism, which he sees as the inverse of the totalizing effects of global capitalism.

> There is nothing more captive, so far as commercial investment is concerned, nothing more *amenable* to the invention of new figures of

monetary homogeneity, than a community and its territory or territories. . . . What inexhaustible potential for mercantile investments in this
upsurge—taking the form of communities demanding recognition and
so-called cultural singularities—of women, homosexuals, the disabled,
Arabs! And these infinite combinations of predicative traits, what a god-
send! Black homosexuals, disabled Serbs, Catholic pedophiles, moderate
Muslims, married priests, ecologist yuppies, the submissive unemployed,
prematurely aged youth! Each time, a social image authorizes new products, specialized magazines, improved shopping malls, "free" radio sta-
tions, targeted advertising networks, and, finally, heady "public debates"
at peak viewing times. . . . Capital demands a permanent creation of subjective and territorial identities in order for its principle of movement to
homogenize its space of action; identities, moreover, that never demand
anything but the right to be exposed in the same way as others to the
prerogatives of the market. (*Saint Paul*, 10–11).

We can grant Badiou's point that the forces of modern capitalism have
become quite efficient at turning identities into sites for directing the flow
of capital; but the invective on display here suggests that for him there is
perhaps more at stake in a deracinated subject as the bearer of universality.

Throughout his study of Paul, Badiou remains adamant that the universal is indifferent to custom, tradition, and difference itself (29, 57, 74).
What he most fixates on is the question of ethnic or cultural difference. An
oscillating movement occurs in Badiou's prose between his figuration of Jew
and Greek in Paul's writings as discourses or identities. As we saw above,
Jew and Gentile mark the two discourses that the Christian discourse must
be set against as categorically "new." This emphasis on the new, paired with
the figuration of the Jewish discourse as the antecedent to modern identity
politics, trades on the frameworks of supersessionism and anti-Judaism that
have long shadowed Paul's archive.[32]

While Badiou generally tries to treat *Jew* and *Greek* as markers of abstract
discourses, he also uses them as stand-ins for ethnic identity proper, which
are always signifiers that must be cast aside in fidelity to Paul's event: "For
him who considers that the real is pure event, Jewish and Greek discourses
no longer present . . . the paradigm of a major difference for thought. This
is the driving force behind Paul's universalist conviction: that 'ethnic' or
cultural difference, of which the opposition between Greek and Jew is in his
time, and in the empire as a whole, the prototype, is no longer significant
with regard to the real, or to the new object that sets out a new discourse"

(Badiou, *Saint Paul*, 57). Notice the slippage here around *Greek* and *Jew*(ish), from discourses relating to thought to ethnic/cultural signifiers. The "new" discourse, which Badiou identifies with the properly Christian, cannot be tied to ethnicity.

Badiou anticipates that his polemicizing against ethnic and cultural identities, and multiculturalism more broadly, will be read as a problem for his project. Thus he includes a discussion of the topic in the penultimate chapter of the book ("Universality and the Traversal of Differences"). In it, Badiou defensively reminds the reader that he certainly recognizes ethnic differences in the world: "*The fact is* that there are Greeks and Jews" (98). But, following Paul's paradoxical description of the "things that are not" in 1 Corinthians 1:28–29, he flips the facticity of ethnic identity on its head: "The ontology underlying Paul's preaching valorizes nonbeings against beings, or rather, it establishes that, for the subject of a truth, what exists is generally held by established discourses to be nonexistent, while the beings validated by these discourses are, for the subject, nonexistent. Nevertheless, these fictitious beings, these opinions, customs, differences, are that to which universality is addressed; that toward which love is directed; finally, that which must be traversed in order for universality itself to be constructed" (98). Badiou equates ethnic identities with things that exist according to "established discourses," which is why they have a facticity in experience; however, they are really fictions with respect to the real. This perceptual shift reminds us of Jacques Ellul's claim that the state is always already disempowered, even if it actually isn't. Though they are really nothing, identities are that which provide the space within which universality emerges. This is why, according to Badiou, Paul can say that he has "become all things to all people" in 1 Corinthians 9:19–23: Paul accommodates people's (ethnic/cultural) differences "so that the process of their subjective disqualification might pass through them, within them" (99). We consume our differences, but unlike Valentinus's Jesus, we shit them out. The Christian subject becomes that which embodies an "indifference that tolerates differences" (99). Badiou's Paul recognizes difference in the world but sees it with such indifference that it might as well be shit.

Badiou worries that such a reading will leave him (and his Paul) open to the charge of anti-Semitism. As a result he deflects. He lays the blame for anti-Semitism on the canonical Gospels, particularly John's, for blaming the death of Jesus on the Jews (101–2). He finds none of this blame leveled against Jews in Paul (though he might have included 1 Thess. 2:14–16 or 2 Cor. 3:12–16 alongside the mention of Judean resistance in Rom. 15:31). He argues that Paul recognizes Jewishness as the origin point for the event of Christ's resurrection, as the point giving this event historical particularity; however, the event transcends its Jewish origin, requiring those who are Jewish to be "resubjectivated" (103). Consequently, Paul rejects Moses, embodiment of the subjectivizing Law, for Abraham: "A Jew among Jews, and proud of it, Paul only wishes to remind us that it is absurd to believe oneself a proprietor of God, and that an event wherein what is at issue is life's triumph over death, regardless of the communitarian forms assumed by one or the other, activates the 'for all' through which the One of genuine monotheism sustains itself" (103). For Badiou's Paul, it is fine if someone wants to remain Jewish or Greek or a Black homosexual or a disabled Serb while in fidelity with the event of the Resurrection; but that person should not be fooled into thinking that those identities mean anything or have anything to do with the event itself, with what really matters. Truth is indifferent to them. They are not worth collecting at the garbage dump for recycling and reuse.

Badiou's choice of Paul as a theoretician for his notion of the event creates serious problems. First, his framing of Paul as an ideal militant/poet-thinker shifts Paul's canonical function from the religious to the secular, but it also leaves Badiou in the same position as the Christian theologian: Paul cannot be critiqued but must always be right. Badiou must find ways to exonerate Paul from his problematic statements that have contributed to the history of anti-Semitism and misogyny. Second, by grounding his reading of Paul in a premise of universal legibility, Badiou is forced to route his theory of the event through Paul's terminology. One of Badiou's persistent concerns is that philosophy needs to engage and emulate the precision of mathematical logic and presentation.[33] By limiting himself to Paul's language to articulate the theory of the universal, he traps himself within the discourse that has shaped the interpretation of the Pauline archive for two millennia. As Neil Elliott rightly notes, Badiou's reuse of Paul's ethnic binaries within his own theory of the event unintentionally mimics Protestant Pauline theology and "wrongly places a supposed opposition to Judaism, Jewish identity, and the 'exceptionalism' of Jewish law as such at the center of Paul's thought."[34] Badiou's Paul thus sounds like an anti-Semitic misogynist, and his invocation of the new Christian discourse that transcends and traverses the Jewish one cannot be read as anything but a secularized form of Christian supersessionism. This is one unredeemable remainder deposited in the cesspool left by Paul's transformation into a radical militant.

Another equally fetid remainder of Paul's redemption is what happens to slaves in the declaration of the event. Badiou's Paul does not address slavery as an institution, though he states that slaves are not inhibited from joining Pauline communities, insofar as all are addressed in the declaration of the Resurrection event (*Saint Paul*, 13–14, 73–74, 92). Slavery is for Badiou's Paul a state of mind, much like Ellul's realized eschatology: it shows that one is trapped within the cosmic order (the Jewish and Greek discourses) (49, 59, 63). Badiou's indifference to the difference that makes the slave is perhaps best heard as he brings his study to a close: "With regard to the world in which truth proceeds, universality must expose itself to all differences and show, through the ordeal of their division, that they are capable of welcoming the truth that traverses them. What matters, man or woman, Jew or Greek, slave or free man, is that differences carry the universal that happens to them like a grace.... Differences, like instrumental tones, provide us with the recognizable univocity that makes up the melody of the True" (106). I would venture to say that the melody of the True would be cold comfort to actual slaves in their enslaved particularity, just as would Ellul's notion that oppressive governments are always already disempowered by the cross. By constructing a Paul, a reader, and a philosophy that disregard the historically situated bodies of real humans, Badiou shows a problematic indifference to anti-Semitism, misogyny, and slavery. His reading of Paul also never wrestles with what Paul's archive says about slavery as an institution, a problem we have returned to repeatedly. One would think that if Paul were truly the radical militant that Badiou paints him as, he would have addressed himself to the most exploitative systems in his historical context!

In an excellent engagement with Badiou's work on Paul, L. L. Welborn has shown that resources within the Pauline archive could have rendered Badiou's theorizing able to address itself to the material and embodied suffering of the oppressed.[35] Welborn shows that Badiou neglects the potential of rendering the Pauline event as the Crucifixion, not the Resurrection, of Christ. If the Crucifixion becomes the Pauline event, then "the purpose of God's intervention in history was not the liberation of a universal subject from the path of death, but rather the redemption of the many oppressed, whose identities are submerged in shame, and whose lives are in danger of disappearing, on account of the annihilating power of the cross."[36] The problem, of course, is that Badiou eschews the Crucifixion because it was real and particular. Within his framework, it cannot be universalized. Welborn rightly shows how the particularity of the cross could, in fact, be universalized, not by the erasure of its specificity but by submerging within it.

Badiou's militant Paul leaves behind him a massive, unredeemed remainder on his way to the realm of the Platonic forms: the embodied masses of the oppressed.[37]

Those subjected to the horrific violence of crucifixion by the Roman state were considered criminal scum. Jesus's body, abject, bloodsoaked, broken, and shameful, might have been worth considering as an eventual site. But Badiou is too concerned with keeping out of the muck of history. He would rather rescue his Paul from the dump, polish him up, and put him high up on the mantel.

THE PAULINE MURDER MYSTERY

In *Moses and Monotheism*, Sigmund Freud famously renarrated the history of Israel as a cover-up for a collective act of repression of a violent act: the murder of Moses.[38] Like a trauma that returns through subterranean psychic channels, the murder of Moses, himself a devoted follower of the monotheist pharaoh Akhenaton, is repressed by the Israelites, only to return, according to the great psychoanalyst, in the form of monotheism. Monotheism as return of the repressed. In other words, the shit we do always comes back to us. Freud's *Moses* is a fascinating and utterly spellbinding psychoanalysis of a people.[39] For Ward Blanton, it offers a key to redeeming Paul.

Blanton is a strikingly interesting thinker among modern biblical scholars. His works have charted the many subterranean entanglements between biblical studies and Western philosophy. His first book renarrated the work of some of the founding figures of New Testament studies, showing that they were much more actively engaged in philosophical discussions beyond the boundaries within which the modern academy has sequestered various humanistic disciplines.[40] Instead of Badiou, Agamben, and Žižek, the major nineteenth-century figures in New Testament studies were reading the likes of Hegel and Kant. Blanton's more recent work has focused on Paul, seeing in the apostle an opportunity to envision a "materialism for the masses."[41]

Taking inspiration from Freud's murdered Moses, Blanton recasts the history of the Pauline archive as a repressed murder mystery: the real, Historical Paul was murdered by later Christians—particularly the fourth-century church historian Eusebius of Caesarea but also the author of the canonical Luke-Acts—and substituted with a Paul who has offered, in Nietzsche's famous phrase, a Platonism for the masses. This "weaponized"

narration of Christian origins involved more than just the proverbial Marxist opiate for the masses. The Platonist Paul offered not only a theology
of future, otherworldly salvation but tools for anti-Semitism and imperial
violence. For Blanton, the Historical Paul presided over an experiment in
radical community that was killed quite early on in the history of Christianity and swapped out for the Platonist Paul of the church. And ever since
there has been a cover-up in which the polymorphic Pauline experiment has
been left as a rotting corpse, hidden behind the figure of Paul the founder
and guarantor of Christian orthodoxy. But the nose never lies, and you can
hide the smell of a dead body for only so long.

For Blanton, the Paul of Christian orthodoxy has been the culprit behind
all the evils done in Paul's name that I have pointed to in the preceding pages.
He has also been the reason the Historical Paul got such a bad rap in recent
centuries. Even the contemporary radical philosophers who have engaged
with the Pauline archive, according to Blanton, "remain starstruck to one
degree or another by a narrativized spectacle, an instauration of a particular
biblical and early Christian tradition . . . [that is] the ghastly or sublimated
afterimage of a brutal act of repression. This repression . . . operates around
the narrations of Paul as the first Christian and foundation of an emergent
Christianity" (4). Affirming the judgments against the Orthodox Paul by the
likes of Nietzsche, Marx, Freud, Derrida, and others, Blanton wonders why
they didn't turn their critical faculties, their deconstructive optics, to asking
whether the Paul they encountered in their day was the real Paul. If Derrida
could rehabilitate Plato in the machinery of deconstruction, why didn't he
do the same for Paul? The answer, he suggests, is that the critics of orthodox
Christianity and the Western tradition were just as invested in the Orthodox
Paul as his defenders were (186). They needed someone to rebel against, and
the Orthodox Paul fit the bill.

The formation of the Orthodox Paul begins early, on Blanton's retelling.
Paul was useful to early Christians as "a hero invested with a foundational
greatness to the same degree as key threads of his legacy needed to be forgotten" (6). What was forgotten, principally for Blanton, was Paul's identity
as a Jewish partisan for Jesus. The reason for this was that early Gentile
Christians quickly became concerned about their ties to a Jewish movement
in the wake of the various Jewish rebellions against the Roman Empire.[42]
Blanton traces the early layers of this "distancing" to the canonical Acts of
the Apostles (*Materialism for the Masses*, 19–25). Over time, this project built
layer on layer of material on top of the now dead body of the Historical Paul,
such that by the time of the fourth-century church historian Eusebius, Paul's

story had become "a retrospective *historical narration* of Paul as founding figure of a new religion, as someone who named a profound break (and therefore a new start) in relation to Judaism" (13; emphasis in the original). Via the renarration of Paul's story, early Christianity effaced the traces of its own emergence (14). From there a Paul serviceable to empire and anti-Judaism entered the Western cultural imaginary, only lately to be overturned. The cover-up was successful, and the real Paul was fodder for worms.

And here Blanton makes a move that is surprising for its traditionalism: he quietly elevates biblical historical criticism as one of the keys to unraveling the conspiracy around the church's apostolicide and its cover-up. Paul's corpse was discovered through a "surprising turn of events" that was "made possible by a series of technical developments within apparently disconnected forensic and archaeological spheres, above all recent work in continental philosophy and biblical studies" (187). The rotting Paul that Blanton discovers under the concrete of orthodoxy is, first of all, a Jewish Paul (24, 35–38). As part of breaking with Judaism, the Orthodox Paul had to become a "Christian" (23). In this, Blanton's Paul follows in the wake of biblical scholars who have constructed what is commonly called the New Perspective on Paul (69).[43] Starting in the mid-twentieth century, this scholarly movement "rediscovered" the fact that the Historical Paul was Jewish, not (a proto-)Christian, and reconceptualized Paul's theology away from traditional Christian theological concerns. For most Pauline scholars, Paul has been Jewish for a while now. Only recently have the philosophers gotten the memo.

The second discovery that Blanton unveils is also rooted in historical-critical work on Paul: the Pauline archive's similarities to ancient philosophical traditions beyond Plato's dualistic thinking. Blanton's Paul is not, at the core, a Platonist (like Badiou's Paul) but a Stoic, and in that sense he can be read within a "materialist" history of the West (*Materialism for the Masses*, xvi, 34, 107–11, 117–24, 148–54). This aspect of the real Paul has been excavated by biblical scholars, though the idea that Paul was a fellow traveler with the Stoics has not met with the same widespread acceptance in the guild of Pauline scholars as the New Perspective has, as Blanton shows.[44]

From these two cardinal points, Blanton reveals the real Paul ("as solid and real as can be"), no longer the "founding apostle" or "inventor of Christianity" but "a sacred corpse all fitted up with concrete slippers" (*Materialism for the Masses*, 187). It is from here that the exhumed Jewish partisan of Stoic immanence takes two divergent directions in Blanton's thinking: backwards to a reinscribed myth of Christian origins and forward through

the dense and shifting negotiations of Paul's archive through the subterranean currents of Western philosophies of immanence. The latter offers an
exciting model for thinking about how Paul might be grafted into new configurations and spark new movements, while the former ties Paul back into
the Christo-capitalist cycle of redemption, with a remainder. Blanton's Paul
may be a reaction to the Orthodox/Eusebian Paul of Western tradition, but
he also wants his Paul to anchor a new myth of origins for radical, immanent
philosophies of resistance that really don't need one.

To be fair to Blanton, he makes clear to his readers that *A Materialism
for the Masses* is much more about Paul's "afterlives" in the recent history
of materialist philosophy than about the Historical Paul (5). He promises a
future companion volume comprising readings of his Historical Paul alongside ancient philosophers (5–6). Regardless, it is clear that the Paul that
Blanton has discovered under the concrete is tasked with rewriting history:
"What if a consistently creative—but ultimately marginal and shortlived—
praxis of Paul the partisan Jew had not been co-opted and buried beneath
what can only be called a weaponized form of Platonic-historical narration . . . ?" (xii)

Blanton's revivified Paul is cast in ways similar to Alain Badiou's militant
Paul. His Paul engaged in "peculiarly risky social experimentations" and
was an "exemplar of unexpectedly and riskily creative openings imminent
to tradition, identity, and the panoply of techniques which constitute these"
(xii–xiii). Paul's movement "maintained itself in blissful vibrancy and exposure to risk and weakness before passing away" (xiii). "Characteristic of the
Pauline movement" were "immanently borne pressures, fissures, and risky
forcing into newness or a new vibrancy of inherited identities, tropes, and
ideas" (19). Blanton's Paul reemerges as a countermyth of origins for Christianity that anchors an as-yet-untold renarration of its history: "I have argued
that we can subtract the lynchpin, the origin, the founding father from a
story of Western religion as Christianity by pointing out that Paulinism was
ultimately shortlived, ephemeral, an explosion of impossible rhetoric about
the transformation of embodied and engendered habituations for the creation of the new" (192). It is this Paul that we must "put on" or "become" if
we are to become faithful to the real Paul behind the conspiracy: "A new
materialism cannot simply criticize or exclude Paul; it must rather *become*
him. . . . My own framing of concerns will never be more or less than this,
to search for those ready to be the least and greatest of Paulinists" (12–13).
The concerning aspect of Blanton's project is not so much his invocation of
a Paulinism that is creative and risky, but that his Paul is presumed to be

so and, by extension, presumed to be a necessary component of thinking through liberative futures. Why do we need to become Paul?

In place of the Orthodox Paul, Blanton sets up the Paul of Immanence as a touchstone for a new materialism; however, like Badiou, he does not show a willingness to grapple with Paul's darker side, except insofar as that darker side is merely projected on the Orthodox Paul: "The future of the discussion about subversive Paulinisms, reworked philosophemes, and a differently constituted 'West' depend on our creativity in thinking around the early apologetic self-presentations and their co-optation of Paulinism to these ends" (25). It is the conspiracy of the Orthodox Paul that must be wrestled with and overcome, not Paul himself. After all, "it is not Paul's fault" (11). The goal is to imagine "what would have emerged were Paul to be for us resurrected thus outside the theologico-political frame of the old 'Platonism for the masses'" (xiii).

To put the matter bluntly, "there are—and continue to be—occlusions, elisions, repressions, and murders in the co-optation of Paul" into a Platonism for the masses (185), but does the Pauline archive really bear no responsibility? In the prelude to his book, Blanton thinks back on protests in which he participated in the lead-up to the Iraq War. What might have happened, he wonders, had those protests taken a different form, found a way to unleash greater countervailing forces to the drive to war, conquest, and death? In the aftermath of this failed resistance, Paul became "a beloved touchstone" to Blanton: "I wonder with and against him about how to snatch an undying life from imperial apparatuses which have, somehow and much to our horror, become more living than the living" (xvi). I wish that Blanton could dwell longer on that "against," for the history of Christianity has been one in which Paul more often than not would have been found standing on the other side of those protests as a support for state violence. It is not enough to just say that all the bad that has come from Paul's archive is the result of a theological-political conspiracy. We must see that there is something in a revivified Paul that is worth it, beyond whether Paul might be made to say some things similar to contemporary philosophers.

Blanton's Paul is, in many ways, a resacralization: strip away Paul the priest, the representative of the oppressive "church," and you'll find Paul the saint, who also happens to be the embodiment of a vibrant, radical potentiality. Paul's exhumed body can sit alongside the eerily embalmed saints that populate saints' shrines. One can hear echoes here of Pier Paolo Pasolini's Paul (to be discussed in the next chapter). For Pasolini, Paul embodies both the saint and the priest but always at the same time, an unresolvable contradiction. Blanton's Paul is split vertically: below is the saint rotting in his crypt; above, blocking our view, is the garishly dressed priest. Take away the priest and Paul the saint is set free. Blanton offers a new figure of Paul, wrapped up in the philosophical garb of immanent philosophy. One wonders whether this is just a fancier version of the Paul of biblical historicism, replicating the distinction often used in historical Jesus studies but with a twist: the Paul of history versus the Paul of faith. Regardless, Blanton's Paul has been sanitized. He may be a corpse, recently exhumed from his unmarked grave, but he bears the sweet aroma of the saintly relic.

Paulus non olet.

Ward Blanton's revivified Paul is problematic as a replacement hero for the Orthodox Paul, but his turn to reading Paul within a longer history of immanent philosophical projects gestures toward alternatives to a Pauline return of the repressed. The bulk of Blanton's book explores the deep, complex, and often unseen connections between Pauline motifs and what he calls "an underground current" of materialist philosophical thinking in Western philosophy (185). Blanton is attuned to this larger conversation and can see the work that the Pauline archive does for philosophers like Agamben, Badiou, and others. For the philosophers that have begun to use Paul for their own radical projects, "the name Paul in these encounters functions as a site on which to analyze more rigorously some high modern and contemporary paradoxes of power that are in this respect indistinguishable from an ontology of contemporary social life" (6). Pauline texts, in some of these projects, "afford an intriguing comparative touchstone to think about a kind of excess of life (a 'surplus of immanence'), an irreducible excess *in* life itself, an openness or freedom within things" (5). As a detective hunting for Pauline traces within this strain of philosophical thought (including thinkers like Lacan, Foucault, Freud, Nietzsche, Althusser, and many, many others), Blanton is unparalleled among scholars today. To follow him as he narrates the circulation of Pauline tropes as uses and negotiations between, say, Lacan and Pasolini is to feel some of the optimism about what the recent turn to Paul among modern philosophers might produce (163–81). Further, Blanton can see surprising possibilities for disciplinary critique, as when he shows the subterranean alliances between Michel Foucault and the conservative New Testament scholar Theodore Zahn (97–128). His forays into the underground current show that Paul's archive has shaped and been reshaped by the subterranean currents in Continental philosophy.

For Blanton, such openness to transformation is a call to counter the "weaponization" of the Pauline archive with a counterinterpretive violence (xvii, 25).

> We must rework the cultural function of the apostle, as if to allow another gospel to ring out from him, as if to witness to another type of collectivity or other solidarities confronting other political catastrophes, all these forming alongside a repetition of this name now *within* the path of an "underground current" of a new materialism. . . . What we need is a rethought political or social canon of Western "origins," one in which we find in Paul a "materialism for the masses," an origin itself split into a multiplicity, constituted by difference, and therefore the farthest thing from a foundational idealism. (187)

This important passage from the conclusion to Blanton's opus shows the promise and peril of this fight over Paul's corpse. On the one hand, his valorization of a Saint Paul returned from the dead is on full display here. We must rework Paul's cultural function but keep him at the center. A new Gospel, yes, but it must be *from him*. Paul must remain canonical, though in a materialist rather than a Platonist canon. And we must keep Paul as part of a new myth of origins. Paul is dead. Long live Paul!

What doesn't seem to occur to Blanton is that we might make space for new collectivities or coalitions if we refuse Paul's canonicity or the need for a myth of origins.[45] What if we diffused or dispersed Paul, following out the resonances that his myth generated in the history of the West, without trying to anchor a new materialism in Paul? In other words, chart indebtedness rather than become disciples.

═══════════════════════════════════

In this chapter we looked at how three Pauline interlocutors ("a sociologist, a philosopher, and a biblical scholar walk into a bar . . .") have sought to redeem Paul from his inscription into the canon of Western Christian tradition. For each, Paul must be redeemed, from oppressor to militant, Platonist to Stoic, shit to fertilizer. But these recycling projects leave a remainder. All interpretations of sacred or secular texts are imperfect and provisional, and all leave a remainder that will spark reinterpretation. The thing to attend to is what that remainder is, or on whom that remainder falls.

In these three scholars' work, a remainder is produced by the work done to redeem Paul and keep him at the center. What might it look like if Paul wasn't the center of the search for inspiration for anarchist, Marxist, or Stoic-Immanent political figuration? We can hear echoes in Blanton's poetic musings in his book's prelude of what might happen if we gave up on Paul's ghost.

> What if that name, Paul, or that figure Paulinism, were not naturally linked to metaphysical dualisms, to brutally supersessionist anti-Judaisms, or to the economies of salvation with which both of these are tied? What if, in a word, we were to trace a Paul who, as a force of thought, did not play the guarantor in relation to all those tropes and tricks that Nietzsche diagnosed so beautifully with the gloss: "Platonism for the masses"? . . . What if the only way latter day Paulinists were to imagine that this kind of originary Paulinism could be repeated, therefore, was at tangents or in fits and starts, in the oddly singular or vibrant comparison as coding networks shift and swerve, opening and closing, folding and unfolding ecological spaces for a time of life immeasurable because without original version, authorized copy, or prefabricated purpose? What new Paulinists would arise! (*Materialism for the Masses*, xii–xiii)

This is exactly the point: the new Paulinists that would arise would be Paulinists without Paul, Paulinists who may play with Paul as a force of thought but who do not rely on either the repetition of the Platonism for the masses that the "Paul" of tradition is composed of or even the "Paul" who was really the true revolutionary of thought buried under orthodox tradition. For those who hope for a mass movement to emerge that might counter the forces that have been so able and willing to deploy Paul against the living, would it not be better to unleash Paulinists without origin, without saints, without limits?

SPLITTING PAUL

WHILE THE READERS OF PAUL that we explored in the last chapter returned to the Pauline dump to find something valuable for use in their political and theological projects, in this chapter I look at two readers—the filmmaker Pier Paolo Pasolini and the biblical scholar Brian Blount—who go back to that dump in hopes of finding answers for how Paul has affected them and their communities. These catadores figure Paul's legacy by splitting him in two: militant and monster, liberator and oppressor. Pasolini and Blount try to redeem Paul, fissured between two countervailing forces and legacies, for the former against the latter in these binaries. Paul becomes the garbage I produce at home: some of it is just waste, while some goes in the recycling bin. These projects have moved me in how they construct and then wrestle with a split, bipolar Paul, at once shit and gold but never simply one or the other. The recognition that Paul's archive is traversed by irreconcilable fissures disrupts the Christo-capitalist discourse of shit, within which Paul's archive is always already redeemed and points toward a possible way out.

SAN PAULO: MILITANT AND/OR MONSTER?

In 1966 the controversial Italian director Pier Paolo Pasolini began circulating a draft screenplay for a film about Saint Paul. The film was never made for various reasons, but the screenplay Pasolini drafted was published in 1977 and translated into English in 2014 by Elizabeth Castelli.[1] When he drafted his script, Pasolini had already made a film about Jesus (*Il Vangelo secondo Matteo* [1964]), in which he limited himself to using only the actual words of the Gospel according to Matthew. For his Paul film, he decided to follow the same principle: all the dialogue spoken by Paul would be taken directly from the apostle's letters. However, while his Jesus film was set in the first century, Pasolini's story of Paul's life would be set in the director's contemporary moment: Europe and America in the postwar period. The goal of this transposition was to emphasize Paul's contemporaneity: "Why would I want to transpose his life on earth to our time? It is very simple: to present, cinematographically in the most direct and violent fashion, the impression and the conviction of his reality/present. To say then explicitly to the spectator, without compelling him to think, that 'Saint Paul is *here*, *today*, *among us*,' and that he is here almost physically and materially. That it is our society that he addresses; it is our society for which he weeps and that he loves, threatens and forgives, assaults and tenderly embraces."[2] Paul's legibility as a contemporary would be achieved by juxtaposing his words to modern questions from other characters in the film: "The 'questions' which the evangelized will pose to Saint Paul will be questions of modern men— specific, detailed, uncertain, political questions, formulated in a language typical of our time; Saint Paul's 'answers,' by contrast, are what they are, that is exclusively religious, and moreover formulated in a language typical of Saint Paul: universal and eternal, but not current."[3] Modern questions, ancient answers.

Pasolini's Paul starts off as a bourgeois Pharisee living in Nazi-occupied France.[4] After the death of Stephen, he travels to Barcelona to persecute Christians and is struck with his "road to Damascus" moment along the way. In Franco's Spain, he converts to an antifascist Christian movement. Now plagued by an escalating mystical affliction (his "thorn in the flesh"), he travels to Germany (the equivalent of the Historical Paul's Macedonia), Rome (= ancient Athens), Paris (= Jerusalem), and finally to New York (= Rome). Here Paul is martyred on a hotel balcony, though Pasolini hoped to film on the same spot where Martin Luther King Jr. had been assassinated just weeks before Pasolini finished his screenplay.[5]

Pasolini's script was a major influence on Alain Badiou's portrait of Paul.[6] From the filmmaker's introductory statements, we can see where Badiou borrowed his sense that Paul's thought was universally legible, able to speak directly to the present with a militant urgency. Further, Badiou's sense that Paul could be stripped of his historical particularity and engaged directly as an abstract philosophical project took its cues from Pasolini's attempt to place the apostle's words and biography in a contemporary setting. However, I would argue that for Pasolini, Paul's legibility in the contemporary moment results not from his universality but from the possibility of retelling his story via analogy.

> Such temporal violence toward the life of Saint Paul, made to take place
> in the heart of the 1960s, naturally requires a long series of transpositions.
> The first and most important of these transpositions consists in substi-
> tuting for the conformism of Paul's times . . . a contemporary conform-
> ism, which will therefore be the conformism of present-day bourgeois
> civility. . . . Such a large transposition, founded upon analogy, inevitably
> implies many others. In this game of transpositions, which are mutually
> implicated and therefore require a certain coherence, I would like never-
> theless to keep myself free.[7]

Paul's legibility must be constructed; it is not given by the universality of his
prose. Pasolini does not follow the path of Giorgio Agamben in suggesting
that Paul's contemporary legibility results from a unique sync (a *Jetztzeit*)
between ancient Rome and the neoliberal now that arrests the multiplicity
of interpretations of Paul.[8] Pasolini moves Paul from the past to (his) present
by a series of transpositions by analogy (ancient Rome = modern-day New
York because of X, Y, and Z reasons) that are never exact or complete and
could, theoretically, be done in different ways by different artists.

Despite this, Badiou sees in Pasolini's screenplay an argument for the
apostle's universality, from which the philosopher goes on to build a picture
of Paul as the ideal militant/theoretician of universality. What Badiou only
pauses over, however, is how Pasolini constructs a Paul who is fundamentally split between two contradictory poles: the saint and the priest. Badiou
sees Pasolini's Paul as a saint betrayed by a conspiracy between the church,
the institution Paul creates in the service of his militant program, and Luke,
the author of the canonical Acts of the Apostles, who in the screenplay is an
agent of the devil. These forces betray Paul and convert him from saint into
priest, in ways not unlike Ward Blanton's Pauline conspiracy.

However, Badiou's conspiracy theory, much like Blanton's, misses how
Paul's duality is presented in the screenplay as constitutive of a split in Paul
himself. The duality emerges repeatedly. One example, among many in the
screenplay, comes from a scene in the house of Prisca and Aquila. The scene
is set in Geneva, which is constructed as an analogy for ancient Corinth.
Paul is a guest of Prisca and Aquila and works as a laborer in their factory,
underscoring the working-class positionality he has affected in the script. In
their house, stuffed full of the city's cultural and intellectual elite, he gives a
speech that is basically a reading of 1 Corinthians, intercut with comments
made by the audience out of his earshot. Pasolini describes Paul at the start
of his sermon: "Paul speaks with inspiration, healthy, hard, strong, self-

assured, paternal albeit with maternal tendencies, authoritatively."[9] As he loses the attention of the "intellectuals" in the crowd, his delivery changes. Amid Paul's rejection of *porneia* in 1 Corinthians 6, Pasolini describes a different Paul: "Paul's face is not as inspired as it was in the beginning of the speech: something dark, violent, and perhaps disturbed is in him."[10] He recognizes that Paul's actual words carry the force of militancy but also the sexual repressiveness of the church. Paul is saint and priest at the same time.

Pasolini made this duality within Paul clear when he spoke about the screenplay, which Elizabeth Castelli's superb introduction to her English translation makes available through her research into Pasolini's larger archive of extant interviews and writings. In the first draft of the script, Pasolini writes, "Paul too was full of duality! There were two Pauls! There were two natures in Paul! Paul had two faces. And you will see them: a hard and sure face, a weak and lost face; a sane face and a mad face . . . a reactionary face and a revolutionary face. Thus he reproduced the duality of God, and he provoked scandal. Rather, he *provokes* scandal."[11] In an interview in 1974, Pasolini further elaborates on the doubleness of Paul:

> I make a double Saint Paul, I mean schizophrenic, completely dissociated in two: one is the saint (obviously Saint Paul had a mystical experience— that's clear from the letter—that was also authentic), the other instead is the priest, ex-Pharisee, who recuperates his prior cultural situations and who will be the founder of the Church. For this I condemn him: insofar as he is a mystic, that's all right, . . . but rather I violently condemn him as the founder of the Church with all the negative elements of the Church already present: the sexophobia, the anti-feminism, the organization, the collars, the triumphalism, the moralism. In sum, all the things that have created the evil of the Church are all already in him.

In the same interview, speaking of whether his film about Paul is a religious film, Pasolini says,

> Yes, in a certain sense yes. It is called *Blasphemy*: and you know very well that in ancient sacred rites, as in all the peasant religions, every blessing amounts to a curse. Thus every blasphemy is a sacred word. Obviously, this, my violence against the Church is profoundly religious insofar as I accuse Saint Paul of having founded a Church rather than a religion. I do not revive the myth of Saint Paul, I destroy it.[12]

Hence Pasolini's screenplay is not a straightforward valorization of Paul as militant saint, as we might have expected based on Badiou's reading. In fact, he intended his film to be a destruction of Paul's mythology. If we place Pasolini's Paul alongside the Pauls of Badiou and Blanton, we can see their attempts at redeeming Paul in a new light.

First, Badiou's Paul relied on the assumption that a theorist of the universal is legible regardless of sociohistorical difference. This trapped Badiou into valorizing and justifying Paul's ethnic rhetoric in ways mirroring the history of Christian anti-Semitism. Because he affirmed Paul's bona fides as a militant, Badiou could not see other gaps in Paul's optics, particularly around women and slaves. By contrast, Pasolini renders Paul a militant by analogical transposition. He justifies each decision to move a component of Paul's biography into a (for him) modern militant biography. Within these transposed narrative frames, Pasolini highlights the sentences in the Pauline archive most amenable to radical rereadings. He thus creates a militant Paul via creative analogy.

But crucially, he does not ignore the sayings within the Pauline archive that reveal nonliberative tendencies. The scene in Geneva is a useful case in point. The intellectuals in the crowd nod along with the opening chapters of Paul's first letter to the Corinthians, with all its talk of countercultural wisdom and paradoxes of nothings becoming somethings. But they balk when Paul shifts to the topic of sex, taking positions that would remind the audience of Catholic sexual mores, a frequent target of Pasolini's larger oeuvre.[13] Pasolini's Paul is always both things, revolutionary and reactionary, split right down the middle. "In fact here the story of two Pauls is narrated: the saint and the priest . . . I am all for the saint, while I am certainly not very tender toward the priest. . . . [The screenplay leaves] the spectator to choose and to resolve the contradictions and to establish whether this THEOLOGI-CAL FILM be a hymn to Holiness or to the Church."[14]

Contrast this approach with Blanton's apostolic conspiracy. His Paul relies on a horizontal split: the Orthodox Paul must be cut away to reveal Paul's corpse beneath. Pasolini's Paul is split vertically: an unresolvable fissure remains between the priest and the saint. He leaves Paul's split there for the audience to decide. This is the key transgressive move he makes that will be repeated by Brian Blount in the next section. We may want to choose, as does Pasolini, Paul the saint over the Paul the priest. And we are free to make that choice—but we cannot erase, as Blanton's Pauline conspiracy does, the dark side that will always remain in any appropriation of Paul.

In her work on Pasolini's screenplay, Castelli frames the project as a broader meditation on the act of translation: "It is possible to consider Pasolini's *Saint Paul* as a broader theoretical reflection upon translation itself—that delicate process of transferring, transmitting, ferrying-across the expressions and commitments and affect of one textual-political world into another. Yet as its theorists will argue, translation is also an act of violence and an act of betrayal. And so, the ambivalent and contradictory meanings of translation—to carry across and to betray—make Pasolini's *Saint Paul* itself a space of ambivalence and contradiction."[15] Castelli's reading of *Saint Paul* shows what sets this project apart from other modern Pauline redemptions. Pasolini clearly sees something of interest in Paul's words, something that reminds him of leftist political struggle in the postwar world. His transposition, his carrying across, of Paul from the first to the twentieth century gives that image of the apostle a space of possibility, a chance to stretch its legs. But we don't just get to have a leftist Paul without a cost. His saintliness in *Saint Paul* is haunted by Paul the priest. We are left to wonder which is the betrayal in translation and which is the transfer; and though we may decide for ourselves (clearly Badiou and Blanton read Pasolini and chose the saint), there will always remain a nagging doubt. What if we chose poorly . . . ?[16]

LIBERATING PAUL . . . SOMETIMES

In 1833 the Reverend Charles Colcock Jones, a white Methodist minister in Georgia, preached a sermon on Paul's letter to Philemon to a congregation of slaves.[17] As Jones later recounted the experience, half his audience walked out as he was explaining how Paul's letter enjoined slaves to be obedient to their masters and condemned the practice of slaves running away from slavery. The remaining half of the congregation, according to Jones, remained after his sermon had concluded and challenged him: "After dismission, there was no small stir among them; some solemnly declared 'that there was no such an Epistle in the Bible'; others, 'that they did not care if they ever heard me preach again!'"[18] This critical analysis of how Paul's archive was used by pro-slavery whites in the American South forms the background for Brian Blount's important and illuminating reading of Paul's archive.[19] While Blount does not engage with the philosophical reuse of Paul that we have charted so far, his choice of interlocutors shapes a reading of Paul that challenges how he has been reconfigured as a champion of radical, liberative politics. Blount's reading of Paul draws from the experiences and voices of those who found themselves bound, beaten, dehumanized, and killed by Paul's letters. In this way, he comes close to reading Paul in fidelity to a Badiouian event: he listens to and remains in solidarity with the words uttered by those who were not counted, who have been present but invisible in (white) America. He thus reads Paul from within the plantation, the paradigmatic site for thinking about the shit that comes from capitalism, neoliberalism, racism, and colonialism. Blount sits down in the shit with those who have been dehumanized by white supremacist Christianity, and he listens to what these astute theorists of scripture have to say about Paul. By reading Paul with and alongside enslaved Africans, he shows that extricating the apostle from the shit his epistles produced can never really hide the smell that hangs over those letters.

Blount's reading of Paul is based on how enslaved Africans engaged with the Bible more generally. Those enslaved in the New World regularly found themselves the object of missionary preaching and teaching that attempted to convert slaves to Christianity while also asserting that Christianity supported their enslavement.[20] We can hear the utterly dehumanizing effects of slavery and its alliance with Christianity and the Bible in a passage from the 1770 memoir of James Albert Ukawsaw Gronniosaw, a freed slave.

> [My master] used to read prayers in public to the ship's crew every Sabbath day; and when I first saw him read, I was never so surprised in my life, as when I saw the book talk to my master, for I thought it did, as I observed him to look upon it, and move his lips. I wished it would do so with me. As soon as my master was done reading, I followed him to the place where he put the book, being mightily delighted with it, and when nobody saw me, I opened it, and put my ear down close upon it, in great hopes that it would say something to me; but I was very sorry, and greatly disappointed, when I found that it would not speak. This thought immediately presented itself to me, that every body and every thing despised me because I was black.[21]

Enslaved audiences were often preached to by missionaries like Jones, who told them that the Christian god expected them to be obedient to the slavers and honest and hardworking in their labors. This god also expected them to stay slaves and not seek their own liberation. Paul was central to this ideological violence. As Clarice Martin has shown, "Pauline texts functioned as the linguistic, ideological, and religiously sanctioned lynchpins in the stolid and death-dealing institution of American slavery."[22]

In response to this dehumanizing situation, enslaved Africans developed forms of Christianity that resisted the white slaver rhetoric directed against them.[23] They created an oral Bible from the written text they were presented with, composing a Bible that spoke to and against their situation as slaves via a process involving extraction and addition,[24] what Delores Williams has described as a hermeneutics of survival and biblical appropriation.[25] As Jones discovered, slaves cut material from their Bible that was dehumanizing to them while adding to and expanding on biblical materials: "Theirs was a *compositional* process. Fusing biblical material with their own life situations and concerns, their space, they *composed* a biblical witness that was uniquely their own and spoke to their uniquely tragic circumstances."[26] This process was not simply editorial, as it involved an openness to fusing biblical stories with beliefs and practices that the enslaved brought with them from West Africa. In particular, Blount notes that many slaves retained their African belief in a high god who cared about justice and mercy for both the community and the weak.[27]

This creation of an oral Bible led, for example, to the transformation of the biblical Exodus account into a story of slave liberation directed specifically toward the liberation of African slaves.[28] The Exodus of the Israelites from Egypt (Exod. 1–19) is not inherently a call to the liberation of all slaves in every place they are found; it is a story of one enslaved people's liberation through the intervention of their god. Blount argues that the creative work of enslaved Africans transformed the Exodus narrative by combining it with West African traditions of a high god who cares about justice for the weak. This new narrative came to reveal, for enslaved Africans, the true liberative nature of god.[29] In addition, this story of a liberating god of justice came to be a story not of Israel's god but of theirs: "Israel's myth became their myth" (32).

The resignifying of the Exodus narrative had ripple effects that reconfigured other aspects of white Christian biblical interpretation. Moses was reconfigured from the giver of the Jewish Law superseded by the advent of Christ to the precursor of the suffering liberator Jesus. Jesus becomes, then, a second Moses, not as the giver of a new law in the Gospel of Matthew but as one who comes to suffer as and alongside the enslaved in the service of their liberation (32–33). Jesus might still have suffered for sin, but his sufferings also were undertaken in service to the destruction of slavery. Jesus, and by extension god, suffers in the shit in solidarity with his people. Further, this emergent theology changed the very definition of sin itself. For the enslaved, sin came to name the breaking of social solidarity within the community of the oppressed (40). What seemed to white Christians to be immorality was actually an ethics rooted in principled resistance to white oppression: lying and deceiving to protect a fellow slave, stealing from the slaver's property (itself a product of the slave's work), and violent rebellion.[30] These practices came to be markers of virtue, because they cohered with the belief that god had passed judgment on the slave system and those who supported it, justified it, and benefited from it.[31]

In the process of constructing their Bible, slaves like those addressed by Jones could not accept Paul's sacrality or canonicity.[32] Paul was either marginalized or rejected outright, in what Blount calls an "exercise in internal critique of the Bible."[33] In contrast, Paul's archive was the go-to source for sermonizing to slaves and defending slavery as an institution, in response to abolitionists.[34] Clarice Martin notes that virtually every major pro-slavery tract relied heavily on that archive.[35] As she shows, in the sermons, tracts, and writings of pro-slavery church leaders, Paul's archive was mobilized to argue that (1) Paul addressed slaves and slavers without ever challenging slavery as an institution; (2) Paul permitted slavers to be members of his churches; and (3) Paul's archive presumed that social class and status (particularly as it pertained to slaves and slavers) were given by god.[36] As a result, Paul was excised from the Bible of the enslaved because he could not and did not speak to their experience. These enslaved Christians knew that a real Bible existed out there somewhere, but that the Bible preached to them was just the slavers' Bible.[37] Paul was in the slavers' Bible.

Blount, however, is not content to leave Paul in the garbage dump of the slavers' Bible. Following earlier scholarship that attempts to read Paul as having been unfairly used for nefarious ends,[38] he offers several arguments for how Paul might be redeemed. In this he follows a tradition noted by Allen Callahan in which liberatory readings of Paul are produced by using the tools of academic biblical scholarship.[39] First, Blount notes, like Ward Blanton and Eric Smith, that according to academic biblical scholars many of the worst texts in the Pauline archive regarding slavery were written by the Pauline school, not the Historical Paul (notably, Colossians, Ephesians, 1 Timothy, and 1 Peter).[40] Paul is not responsible, then, for things said in his name. This leaves us to make sense of Paul's admonition that slaves stay slaves in 1 Corinthians 7 and the letter to Philemon, which so incensed Rev. Jones's audience in Georgia.

For this task, Blount follows biblical scholars working in the so-called New Perspective trajectory of Pauline scholarship.[41] Without getting lost in the weeds, the New Perspective reads Paul's theology as concerned primarily with how Gentiles might become reconciled to the god of Israel through the death and Resurrection of Jesus. Paul, on this reading, is concerned not with saving humanity from original sin but with negotiating the ethnic complexity of communities dedicated to the veneration of Jesus as the eschatological agent of Israel's god. Blount describes this as Paul's "boundary-breaking theology," in which the apostle attends to breaking down the ethnic boundaries between Jews and Gentiles.[42] Blount suggests that a liberative theology emerges as a secondary effect produced by this ethnic boundary breaking. As he works out this radical strain of theology, his Paul opens up avenues for thinking about further boundary breaking, epitomized by Paul's famous saying in Galatians 3:28 that in Christ there are neither Jew nor Greek, slave nor free, male and female (137).

At this point in his argument, Blount has constructed a Paul that could be placed alongside the Paul of Alain Badiou and Blanton. The apostle theorized a radical theology that breaks down difference (in this case, ethnic difference) in such a way that it creates a template for the universalizing of this radical erasure. His theology is tied tightly to his ethics, much as Badiou's Pauline militant unites thought and life (125–26). Finally, the real Paul was hidden behind a conspiracy theory of deutero-canonical writings that occluded the radicality of his theological project. Blount's Paul sounds as though he would fit right in with Badiou's and Blanton's; however, Blount's slave interlocutors pull him back.

Blount's Paul is liberative . . . sometimes. "Sometimes" is the pivot around which Blount skirts the drive to redeem the apostle, rendering him more like Pier Paolo Pasolini's split Paul.

> Paul's theology has as one of its primary goals the breaking down of religious, social, and political boundaries between Jews and Gentiles in the first-century believing communities. . . . His, then, was a boundary-breaking motivation. Sometimes. For the apostle, it seems to me, does not in the end always maintain the courage of his own somewhat shocking convictions. The liberating ethics his theology enables on the one hand is often disabled on the other by less egalitarian theological and practical considerations. (123)[43]

The reason for this split in Paul, for Blount, is that Paul simultaneously adhered to a "creation theology," in which god established an order of creation in which certain differences are set in advance. Sometimes Paul followed his boundary-breaking theology—though Blount really only shows that he did so with regard to Jews and Gentiles. Most times he followed his creation theology and sided with the forces of order, hierarchy, and inequality: on the relations between church and state, marriage and sexuality, common first-century patriarchal virtues and vices, and, crucially, slavery (Blount, *Then the Whisper*, 150–55). Caught between the radical and the conservative, the charismatic and the institutional, the militant and the reactionary, Blount's Paul bears the irreconcilable fissure, like Pasolini's Paul. Were we to bring Paul to our ethical deliberations in the present, Blount suggests, a lot would depend on which Paul showed up (155).

Blount's hope is that some semblance of that radical theology that he has isolated in Paul will spur the creativity of contemporary African American churches to look at the apostle differently: either to bring him into the fold, if tentatively, or to use his radical side to resist the readings of Paul that support conservative views on politics, sexuality, and gender (157). These are real concerns, as Clarice Martin has shown. Martin points to the fact that while most white and African American Protestants have come to reject pro-slavery statements in Paul's archive, they have not brought a similar hermeneutic of suspicion to bear on Pauline texts condoning the inferiority and subjection of women.[44]

But Blount knows that the redemption of Paul is a hard sell. Even as he argues for a reading of Paul's views on slavery that puts the apostle at odds with the worst of antebellum pro-slavery theology, he admits that this is not enough. Even if we grant that Paul was better than we thought regarding slavery, he was no abolitionist (and neither was Jesus for that matter, but that's another story). Paul was rejected by the enslaved Christians who sparred with the Reverend Charles Colcock Jones as woefully insufficient to their experience and needs.[45]

In light of the creative work that enslaved Africans did to fashion a liberative Bible out of the slavers' text, Blount wonders why they did not put their tremendous creativity into redeeming Paul, retrofitting the radical side of Paul's theology for their own liberation. Some enslaved African readers and their descendants did find ways to reclaim and make use of parts of Paul's archive, as Callahan and others have noted;[46] yet Blount is right to dwell on why Paul has remained such an ambivalent scriptural presence in African American Christianity. Somewhat mournfully he writes, "Why could not the slaves see in and do with Paul what they were able to do successfully with the rest of the biblical tradition? I suspect that it was because they came to believe that the problem lay as much with Paul as it did with the perverted interpretations coming out of slaveholding Christianity."[47]

Back to the Dump

It seems only fair. If I am going to ask these scholars why they keep going back to the Pauline junkyard, I should answer the question too. It seems contradictory (does it not?) that I am writing a book about Paul in which I am arguing that we should throw him out with the trash. I sound like that friend who constantly tells you he is over his ex but still talks about that person all the time. "Sure . . . you're over Paul. I'm glad you can tell yourself that."

This contradictory position (Do I love Paul? Do I hate him?) is hard to dissociate from what it feels like to break up or get divorced. The pain and the trauma are felt as both a chasm and a scar, an absence and a newly intimate presence. That person whom we loved so much is now gone from our lives, but that absence takes on its own presence. Our loved one is here in that absence. That moment where you wake up expecting Paul to be in the bed next to you. That sound that makes you think he is walking through the door. The memories of the harms we suffered or the harms we caused. We feel that absence as an intimate presence.

I broke up with Paul not long after I arrived at graduate school. There wasn't one moment when the relationship broke down. It was a gradual process by which I came to see that my relationship to Paul was something akin to what Lauren Berlant calls "cruel optimism."

> A relation of cruel optimism exists when something you desire is actually an obstacle to your flourishing. It might involve food, or a kind of love; it might be a fantasy of the good life, or a political project. It might rest on something simpler, too, like a new habit that promises to induce in you an improved way of being. These kinds of optimistic relation are not inherently cruel. They become cruel only when the object that draws your attachment actively impedes that aim that brought you to it initially.[1]

My defenses of Paul became increasingly harder to hold together. My friends and teachers kept showing me all the ways he was bad for me. More important, he had a history, a trail of literal broken hearts and broken bodies. It was a slow, simmering intervention for a jilted lover who couldn't see what was right in front of him.

As a college student, I remember reading the gut-wrenching opening of Neil Elliott's *Liberating Paul*, where Elliott chronicles examples of evils committed in Paul's name, from the enslavement of Africans, to the subjugation of women, to the Holocaust, to US imperialism.[2] At the time, I could feel both the horror of what Christians had done with Paul *and* anger at how they had misinterpreted him. How dare they misrepresent Paul's radicality? How dare they not make careful distinctions between the Historical Paul and the deutero-canonical one? I was defensive of my apostle, my lodestar, my intimate.

As with any unhealthy relationship, the realization that what you are attached to is not good for you comes on slowly. Over time the parade of similar stories, stretching miles and miles, made me rethink my relationship to Paul. Contrary to detectives like Ward Blanton, I started to suspect it was more likely that the forces of empire and violence took up Paul and canonized him *because* he was useful to their projects. There was no conspiracy to hide a radical Paul behind a reactionary façade. The reactionaries had always recognized in Paul one of their own.

The Paul I had built as an undergrad and held on to as a graduate student, a Paul who was liberal and maybe a little progressive, was no longer recognizable to me. The Paul I had fallen in love with was a Paul shaped by the white male interests of historical criticism to be an image of those ideals. Maybe I could say that Paul wasn't a slavery apologist, but I needed him to say now that slavery was an abominable moral and ethical and theological evil. But he wouldn't and couldn't do that. At the Presbyterian church where I was first an intern and then an elder, my occasional guest sermons felt increasingly strained. I had to find ever-more ingenious ways to work around and against the liturgical text for the day rather than with it.

I wrote him a breakup letter in the form of a dissertation, then a book, and then this book. As ever, he said the same things to me to win me back. He apologized and tried to explain. "For if I cause you pain, who is there to make me glad but the one whom I have pained? . . . For I wrote you out of much distress and anguish of heart and with many tears, not to cause you pain, but to let you know the abundant love that I have for you." He turned my past against me. "For you put up with it when someone makes [a slave] of you, or preys upon you, or takes advantage of you, or puts on airs, or gives you a slap in the face. To my shame, I must say, we were too weak for that!" He gaslit. "I say nothing about you owing me even your whole self."

He threatened. "What would you prefer? Am I to come to you with a stick, or with love in a spirit of gentleness?"[3]

I have resisted. But I keep writing about Paul. Why is that?

When we talk about love and the hold it can have over us, we often speak of its magic. Love casts a spell on us, bewitches us. We've all read stories of love potions, maybe even been tempted to acquire them. Love's magic is ambivalent. It can name the euphoria of requited love or the power that holds us, suspended between will and coercion, *in* love. The pleasures of this magic are, as Roland Barthes might say, not simple.[4] They are a flux of countervailing desires and repressions, fantasies sublime and perverse.

I'm not sure that I can explain why I keep writing about Paul. It isn't out of love in any traditional sense. The answer, if it exists, certainly lies somewhere in the countervailing pleasures of love and hate offered to the privileged male reader of Paul's archive. I never had to read Paul to survive or read Paul against other readers of Paul to protest my enslavement or my persecution. I did not come to love Paul for the ways in which he allowed my community to resist Pauline violence.

Lacan says that love is giving what you don't have.[5] What he means by this is that when we love someone, we offer that person what we lack, something we can't even name for ourselves but know is missing. The vulnerability of sharing what we lack with someone else is the risk at the heart of love. At the same time, we love the person we love because of something our beloved does have, an excess that is more than this person's specific traits, qualities, or actions. This supplement to the object of our affections (what Lacan calls the *objet a*) is what allows us to love despite the beloved's imperfections.

Maybe I loved Paul because of a lack in myself, something I couldn't articulate fully and probably can't now. For my younger self, Paul as sacred text bled into the god whose Word was said to reside there. Couldn't that god's presence in the text have been the supplement, the *objet a*, that allowed me to love Paul and the Bible for something other than what they are? I came to this god hoping to resolve my own shame, on the promise that my fractures could be mended into a fantasy image of a good life. Was I offering Paul my lack? Did he accept, could he have accepted, what I didn't have?

Was Paul for me a fetish object? Barthes, having pronounced the death of the author, sees the author as a haunting absence within the text, not behind it but lost in its midst. Again it comes down to a lack, an absence, that perhaps causes desire—"*I desire* the author: I need his figure."[6] Paul's archive has no author except the one we create for it. It is an anthology, curated and edited. Despite this reality, desire, Barthes suggests, creates the author.

I'm trying to own my shit by talking about how love, even love for an absent apostle, can make us feel shitty and do shitty things, but perhaps I'm deferring with all this talk of love and desire. That is part of the appeal, part of the desire for an author, for Paul: deferral. The work that it took to make a Paul, to sustain and nurture Paul as the author, for me, of an archive of texts, was a deferral of my own responsibility. I needed someone else. I needed god/Paul to affirm what I needed to believe, what I wanted to do. And not only that. Reading from a position of privilege, I wanted others to do what my Paul said—not because I was trying to survive, but because I had a notion of what was right and just and needed Paul to say it for me.

This is the unspoken blindness and cynicism at the heart of even the most superficially altruistic biblical studies work that sits within or appropriates its frameworks from the white male center: a blindness to naming and interrogating our own enmeshed assumptions and biases but also our desires and pleasures, and a cynicism that there are audiences who will credulously believe and therefore will do what our Pauls demand that they do.

Joan Copjec argues that for Lacan, a different love is possible when "our appeals to the Other have been abandoned, once we accept the fact that there is 'no Other of the Other.' . . . The Other possesses nothing that we want, nothing to validate our existence."[7] Bruce Fink calls this "transference love," the love that an analyst has for her patient, a love that loves without wanting to be loved in return.[8] It is transference love, Fink argues, that disrupts repetition and makes analytic change possible. It also cannot work unless the analyst finds something to love in the patient.

I'm still writing about Paul. It's probably clear now that I don't like Paul very much. But I'm still writing. That could mean that I still love him and want something from him that he can't give me. In other words, I'm straddling the thin line between love and hate, my desires unmet. It could also mean that I have found something to love in Paul's archive that keeps me in the room.

I could also be paranoid. Eve Sedgwick has diagnosed academics like myself as paranoid, always looking for evidence of systemic oppression, always vigilant about what might come, reliant on a naïve belief that exposing oppression will solve it.[9] When I see in Paul all the evils that have been done in his name, am I not living by the paranoid aphorism "You can never be paranoid enough"?[10] Sedgwick lifts up an alternative for critical analysis. Reparative readings remain open to surprise, to building something new out of the old, to finding resources in otherwise barren landscapes to nurture the self and the community.

I suspect there is a reparative impulse in many readers of Paul, a recognition that there is power in Paul's archive that could be mobilized for good. If Paul can become a liberal hero, then maybe Christians will follow suit. Sadly, I think that such readings return us to that cynicism of what it means to interpret a canonical archive and what assumptions we make about readers of sacred texts. I also think they risk following a similar path as my paranoia: they push too quickly for reconciliation without having found justice. When Sedgwick speaks about what reparative readings look like, she emphasizes that they are defensive projects, temporary shelters, and assemblages of parts into a whole different from what came before.[11]

I'm not ready to repair Paul. Frankly, I enjoy hating him too much. In her engagement with the terrifying interpretive history of Genesis 9 and the curse of Canaan, Jennifer Knust resists the call to simply repair the text and its interpretation.[12] For one, there is a pleasure to be found in paranoia, in being what Sara Ahmed calls a "killjoy."[13] It can be fun to hate on Paul. But there is also joy in seeing a student give up the ghost, realize that she doesn't have to keep working hard to find her life, actions, or love justified in Paul's words. Knust suggests that paranoia can and must be retained so long as we "stop confusing paranoia with *the way things really are* and *always have to be*."[14] Paranoia and repair go hand in hand: the former is a strategy for survival, while the latter risks in the hope of finding shelter . . . for a time.

The catadores who make their way back to Rio's dump each day straddle this position between paranoia and repair. As they collect, sort, and reassemble that which has been deemed waste, unusable, garbage, they do so fully aware of the dehumanizing effects of capitalism. This work is a result of capitalist consumption and despoliation, the neoliberal decimation of safety nets and workers' rights, the utter lack of imagining a future that doesn't just replicate the way things are. But the catadores make lives there in the waste, lives where they have flexibility and a measure of freedom and community, if only for a time. Whether such communities spark a new politics or new models of collectivity is an open question.[15]

If most reparative readings of Paul might be characterized as extractive returns to mine gold and shape it anew, I would argue that feminist readers of Paul have been catadores. Feminist biblical scholars have scoured his archive to write histories of those with whom he worked and debated.[16] As

Sheila Briggs argues, feminists rightly gave up on asking *whether* Paul could envisage social egalitarianism and instead focused on *how* he resisted it. This created the ethical drive to "search for the silent residues of that which [Paul] refused."[17] In this they have pressed on Barthes's "figure" of the author who is "lost in the midst of a text (not *behind* it, like a *deus ex machina*)."[18] In other words, they go back to Paul's garbage dump to find something other than Paul, something valuable and recoverable in the midst of the text. It might be stained by Paul's toxicity, but, perhaps, it could be repaired.

Digging through this garbage involves seeing the possibilities for what might be made from the refuse. In this sense these reconstructions resemble "found object" art, artistic projects built out of found materials. Practitioners of found object art or trash art find and assemble discarded materials so that they speak anew.[19] Feminist reconstructionists scavenge through the garbage heap of the Pauline archive, reconstructing new voices that are simultaneously art and refuse. They point us to possibilities of ancient futures that were silenced, marginalized, and discarded.

Why do I keep returning to Paul's dump? It may be this that I love about Paul's archive that keeps me coming back: I enjoy hating Paul. I enjoy reading around him and finding something that might be repaired for a time into something else. And I find joy in the community that gathers around this archive, doing the same work. But I think the image of the catadores heading to and from the Pauline garbage heap helps explain the contradiction that sits at the heart of this book. While there is an ethical exigency to go back to the dump to find possibilities for what capitalism or historicism or orthodox Christianity has thrown out, the production of those possibilities comes at the cost of returning over and over again to a toxic site. If there is any optimism in such a pursuit, Lauren Berlant captures it: "The urgency is to reinvent, from the scene of survival, new idioms of the political, and of belonging itself."[20] What better place to do that than among scavengers on a dung heap?

PROFANING PAUL

WHEN EUROPEAN MISSIONARIES ARRIVED in Africa in the early colonial period, they brought their Bibles with them. It must have seemed strange to the Africans these missionaries encountered that the sacred could be located in a book. As Vincent Wimbush has argued, "Only someone thoroughly socialized in a culture of the (sacred) book . . . could think of the textualization of divine communication as anything other than odd."[1] Bruno Latour has imagined a similarly tense (mis)communication around icons and idols in the initial colonial encounter.[2] The idea that the sacred could be limited to a book was strange because local traditions regarded the sacred as potentially omnipresent, able to be anywhere.[3] The disconnect between notions of sacrality might have remained mere curiosity, but the intensification of European interference and the forced theft of Black bodies changed the dynamics of power. Those caught up in the asymmetries of European colonial power no longer had the luxury of viewing the Europeans and their sacred book as strange. To survive they had to figure out how to understand and then navigate a dominant culture centered on a set of written scriptures.[4] The centrality of the Bible, and by extension Paul, to a textualized notion of the sacred has shaped Paul's canonical function, his continual redemption as saint.[5] Control over his canonical function has been governed by an evolving and diffuse set of rules that have informed both ecclesiastical and academic study of his archive. In previous chapters we've seen some of the mechanisms by which (largely) white male readers have kept Paul at the center of their interpretations, redeemed him for new, leftist uses. The history of biblical studies and Brian Blount's intervention in Paul's redemption show that these mechanisms are rooted in a longer history that privileges (and obscures) whiteness.

By bringing to the fore the voices of those who, like the first Africans

encountered by European missionaries, find this not only strange but violent, Blount gestured toward a way of approaching the Pauline archive from
the perspective of those who have had to survive it rather than merely interpret it. In this chapter I theorize this distinction in a different key, drawing
from, but also critiquing, the work of Giorgio Agamben. Most reuses of the
Pauline archive, whether by academic biblical scholars or Continental philosophers, effect a "secularization" of the archive, which merely transports
Paul's canonical function from the realm of the church to another locale.
Profanation, by contrast, divests a text of its sacrality, making possible a
mode of reading that embraces betrayal, impropriety, and transgression.[6]
While I show that Agamben's reading of Paul is problematic and reinscribes
a white male reading of the apostle's archive, I dwell here on his category
of profanation because I think it can be allied with other analytic frames
that recur throughout this book to read Paul as shit: Wimbush's scripturalization, Sedgwick's paranoid/reparative readings, and (later) Jasbir Puar's
homonationalism.

PROFANATION

Profanation is the act of returning something to common use. In his "In
Praise of Profanation,"[7] Agamben rethinks the genealogy of consecration
and profanation.

> And if "to consecrate" (*sacrare*) was the term that indicated the removal
> of things from the sphere of human law, "to profane" meant, conversely,
> to return them to the free use of men. The great jurist Trebatius thus
> wrote, "In the strict sense, profane is the term for something that was
> once sacred or religious and is returned to the use and property of men."
> And "pure" was the place that was no longer allotted to the gods of the
> dead and was now "neither sacred, nor holy nor religious, freed from all
> names of this sort."[8]

Agamben's archaeology of the profane flips common assumptions about the
nature of the religious and the secular. Scholars of religion have long specu-
lated, following Durkheim, on how the sacred is produced and what consti-
tutes it.[9] This focus on the sacred as the quality that instills a new value or
charisma in people and things has left the profane undertheorized. Typically

the profane is defined by the quality of not-being-sacred. Thus Durkheim can write, "Sacred things are things protected and isolated by prohibitions; profane things are those things to which the prohibitions are applied and that must keep at a distance from what is sacred."[10] Freud centered his definition of the sacred on the arbitrary prohibition of the primordial father, which is why, for him, the Latin *sacer* means both "sacred" and "worthy of disgust."[11] Both the sacred and shit are defined by their inability to be touched. Agamben's definition follows Durkheim in seeing the sacred as a space of prohibition, of abstraction from a set of relations by an arbitrary choice, but fundamentally Durkheim sees the profane as merely that which is not sacred after this sovereign decision.

While the sacred captures our attention by the specialness it bestows on an object, Agamben is correct that sacralization simultaneously removes something from common use. Sacred objects have a use, of course, but by being coded as sacred they participate in a different assemblage of forces. A sacred vessel still might transport wine from bottle to lips, but it does so as part of a different economy of relations from that of a wineglass at a dinner party.

Trebatius's description of the profane generates for Agamben a challenge to the assumption that the profane is simply the not-sacred. Something that has been profaned has been returned to use and is now free in a way it was not when bound to the gods. As Agamben puts it, "To profane means to open the possibility of a special form of negligence, which ignores separation or, rather, puts it to a particular use."[12] Ignoring or transgressing the sovereign act of separating the sacred from the profane, what Agamben here calls "negligence," offers the possibility of putting the no-longer-sacred to use. What might it look like for Paul to be profaned in this sense?

SECULARIZING PAUL

The dominant mode within the academy of rendering Paul "historical" has been the deployment of the historical-critical method to read Paul's letters. Historians of early Christianity convert his letters into historical documents that they analyze in a reconstructed ancient context. As a result, Paul is treated not explicitly as a mythical saint but as a person whose words and deeds are meaningful in his particular time and place. The context of meaning-making is produced by the historian who sets the limits on what Paul's statements can mean within the time and place in which he lived. In this way, Paul is treated as a human among other humans and not as a saint writing inspired or sacred texts. He shat like everyone else.

Yet historical criticism cannot truly profane Paul in the way that Agamben suggests, because historicizing Paul is not profanation but what Agamben calls secularization. According to him, the colloquial definition of *secularization* follows a trajectory identified by Max Weber, in which secularization "was an aspect of the growing process of disenchantment and detheologization of the modern world."[13] The advance of secularization is, by Weber's definition, the increasing absence of the religious or the theological from the public sphere. Agamben follows an alternative definition of *secularization* advanced by the Nazi legal theorist Carl Schmitt, who argued that secularization is really just Protestant theology that has gone underground: "All significant concepts of the modern theory of the state are secularized theological concepts."[14] For Schmitt and Agamben, theology is still present at the core of our conceptions of the state. To explain how this works, Agamben calls secularization a "signature": "Signatures move and displace concepts and signs from one field to another . . . without redefining them semantically."[15]

As a method of making knowledge, historical criticism "secularizes" Paul but does not profane him.

> In this sense, we must distinguish between secularization and profanation. Secularization is a form of repression. It leaves intact the forces it deals with by simply moving them from one place to another. Thus the political secularization of theological concepts (the transcendence of God as a paradigm of sovereign power) does nothing but displace the heavenly monarchy onto an earthly monarchy, leaving its power intact. Profanation, however, neutralizes what it profanes. Once profaned, that which was unavailable and separate loses its aura and is returned to use. Both are political operations: the first guarantees the exercise of power by carrying it back to a sacred model; the second deactivates the apparatuses of power and returns to common use the spaces that power had seized.[16]

My "transgressive" suggestion that would-be tourists sit on a public toilet in an ancient Roman city doesn't go far enough. In fact, it likely renders the toilet sacred. Reading Paul's letters as "historical documents" merely displaces them: Paul may no longer be simply a set of divinely inspired texts, but he remains a "great Man" of history, a religious "genius," or, more commonly, a historicized author of authoritative religious texts. While historicism may challenge Paul's authority in certain ways, it does not necessarily render him profane. Historical criticism alone neither challenges Paul's authority within Christian history and tradition nor offers an ethical critique of Paul's writings.

PAUL'S SECULAR LEGIBILITY

For Agamben, there is only one way to profane something: "The creation of a new use is possible only by deactivating an old use, rendering it inoperative."[17] If we are to deactivate the Pauline archive, we must attend to the compulsion to read Paul in the first place. In previous chapters we have seen how Alain Badiou turned to Paul and rendered him a secularized saint, a poetic thinker of Badiou's event. But we might ask Badiou: Why does he read Paul at all? Would Alain Badiou feel compelled to read Paul if Paul were not already accorded a status within the Christian canonical archive? Why doesn't Badiou feel the same compulsion to engage with Melito of Sardis or Epiphanius of Salamis, themselves perfectly interesting early Christian authors? From whence does Paul's legibility and power derive if not the deep well of Christian scripturalization that has rendered him authoritative and legible by force through two millennia? The profanation of the Pauline archive must begin with deconstructing this impulse not only to read Paul but to assume that reading him and reconstructing him will grant us insight into some kind of universal sacred/secular truth. It thus might be a name for the resistance to what Wimbush has called the white men's magic of biblical sacrality and interpretation.

Lacking a critical analysis of why Paul was fashioned into the scriptural center of Western culture, Agamben draws from Walter Benjamin's theorization of materialist historiography and the "now" (*Jetzt*) of messianic time to describe Paul's universality. In his commentary on the first ten words of Paul's letter to the Romans, Agamben seeks to "restore Paul's Letters to the status of the fundamental messianic text for the Western tradition."[18] He attempts to wrestle Paul's letters away from the "anti-messianic tendencies" operating within the church and the synagogue.[19] In a move that (inadvertently) mirrors his own description of "secularization," he seeks to skirt the concerns of Christian theology (namely, Christology) to ask "more modestly and more philosophically, . . . What does it mean to live in the Messiah, and what is the messianic life? What is the structure of messianic time? These questions, meaning Paul's questions, must also be ours."[20] With this pivot,

Agamben secularizes Paul, moving from Christian theology to the secular descriptor of the "messianic," while presuming Paul's legibility must be marshaled to resolve political questions that have lost their temporality ("Paul's questions must also be ours"). Paul is moved from the realm of the church to the "more modest" domain of philosophy while the authority structure around his letters is maintained. They must be transferred from the domain of the church and restored to their proper status as *the* "fundamental messianic text" of the West. Notice in the first quotation that Agamben shifts from the singular to the plural: from Paul's *Letters* to *the* text. Whatever pluriform uses Paul's letters have had, Agamben's project is to render them singularly as messianic, though embodying a messianism that has not found a place within church or synagogue, Christianity or Judaism. It is through this process of secularization, not profanation, that Paul's questions become (ambiguously) "our" questions.

At the conclusion of his commentary, Agamben shows his cards regarding how Paul can be singularly secularized under the heading of the messianic. He sees Paul's messianism as the secret source of Benjamin's secular messianism, an unacknowledged conversation partner underlying Benjamin's enigmatic *Theses on the Philosophy of History*.[21] Paul's letters become singularly legible via this secret connection.

> Whatever the case may be, there is no reason to doubt that these two fundamental messianic texts of our tradition, separated by almost two thousand years, both written in a situation of radical crisis, form a constellation whose time of legibility has finally come today, for reasons that invite further reflection. *Das Jetzt der Lesbarkeit*, "the now of legibility" (or of "knowability," *Erkennbarkeit*) defines a genuinely Benjaminian hermeneutic principle, the absolute opposite of the current principle according to which each work may become the object of infinite interpretation at any given moment. . . . Benjamin's principle instead proposes that every work, every text, contains a historical index which indicates both its belonging to a determinate epoch, as well as its only coming forth to full legibility at a determinate historical moment.[22]

For Agamben, Paul becomes legible through a historical sync, a recapitulation of historical moments, in "our" tradition. Paul's "situation of radical crisis" syncs up with Benjamin's (and therefore our own?) in such a way that he becomes fully legible.

Agamben secularizes Paul within Benjamin's materialist messianism, which merely shifts the authority of Paul within the church to the realm of political theology, and in so doing he makes himself the hermeneute of Paul's secularized yet covertly sacred text. He finds the key to Pauline legibility via this secularization. But Agamben misses the chance to profane Paul in his very own terms. He dismisses out of hand the idea that Paul might be subject to "infinite interpretation at any given moment." We might read this as a resistance to the universalism of Paul's canonical status: Paul cannot be made to speak in any context save our time. But how are we to judge Paul's "full legibility"? I would suggest that Agamben's dismissal of infinite interpretation hides what is really the problem: Paul has always been legible in the Western tradition precisely because he has been canonical, which means he has always been reinterpreted to remain relevant. Agamben's dismissal of other readings of Paul is his attempt to capture Paul's sacrality for his own secular messianism. It is an assertion of hermeneutical authority over a still-canonical text.[23]

This move to capture Paul via a "Benjaminian hermeneutic" is mirrored in work by scholars trained in biblical studies.[24] They have tried to render something like Agamben's messianic *Jetztzeit* (the now time) as a sync between the Roman Empire and postcolonial modernity. Paul's world, dominated by Rome, is said to parallel in enough ways the world of the present, dominated by Western neoliberalism and colonialism, that his letters become readable again.

This merely extends the problem of legibility and interpretation introduced by Agamben: how does one know when a text has become fully legible, particularly a text that, by virtue of its canonical status, has been made universally legible for almost two millennia? Paul is the dominant theological voice in the West. His concepts have haunted Western philosophy, political theory, and economics, as well as other domains of human knowledge. What I suspect is that Paul's newfound "legibility" is the result of a new demographic synergy. On the one hand, Marxists like Badiou have been in search of resources in texts that have ceased to carry practical authority in an increasingly secular Europe. They have taken to scouring the garbage bins for new ways to revive their political projects in the wake of neoliberal dominance of the globe. On the other hand, white American, mainline Protestant Christians have become progressively liberal and have sought for ways to read their sacred texts to support those views. In short, Paul's legibility as a leftist is the result of an alliance of interest that secularizes/historicizes his archive, without ultimately questioning whether that archive is worth using in the first place.

While these modern readers of Paul align themselves with one aspect of Benjamin's messianism, they ignore his caution around precisely the kind of historical artifacts that make up the Pauline archive: those that have been used, circulated, and preserved by history's victors. According to Benjamin, we ought to always ask, With whom do the adherents of historicism sympathize?

> The answer is inevitable: with the victor. And all the rulers are the heirs of those who conquered before them. Hence, empathy with the victor invariably benefits the rulers. . . . Whoever has emerged victorious participates to this day in the triumphal procession in which the present rulers step over those who are lying prostrate. According to traditional practice, the spoils are carried along in the procession. They are called cultural treasures, and a historical materialist views them with cautious detachment. For without exception the cultural treasures he surveys have an origin which he cannot contemplate without horror. . . . There is no document of civilization which is not at the same time a document of barbarism.[25]

Benjamin's caution gets at the core of the problem with which this book is concerned: Paul has been and continues to be used to authorize oppression and violence; at the same time, many proponents of liberal, socialist, or communist forms of politics invest a great deal of effort in expunging Paul's record. His archive is simultaneously civilized and barbaric, gold and shit.

I sympathize with the goals of philosophical readers of Paul like Giorgio Agamben and Alain Badiou. Confronted by the dominance of neoliberal economic governance; the rise of new, potent forms of political barbarism, nationalism, and xenophobia; and impending ecological catastrophe, they have turned to Paul to find something, anything, they can use to help think otherwise. I sympathize as well with biblical scholars who, whether they see Paul as scripture or just (unwittingly) treat him as such, are concerned with grounding their theology and politics in something that feels solid, in a "correct" historical reading of what Paul really thought, even if I sense a note of cynicism in this project. But Paul's legibility for these purposes comes with an unacknowledged cost, which is itself a serious risk. Viewed from the vantage point of two millennia, his archive has been implicated in, to use Benjamin's terms, more barbarism than civilization.

PAUL IS SHIT(TY)

That messy line between barbarism and civilization is, as we have seen, traversed by the history of shit. Shit sits at the intersection of public and private, clean and unclean, death and life, healthy and sick, barbarism and civilization. Profaning Paul and his archive means seeing them as shit, not as simple feces that we flush away and never remember but as excrement that is both feces and fertilizer at the same time. And, as with shit, there is no Away for Paul's archive. All our excrement, waste, and garbage stay in our global ecosystem . . . somewhere. At some point, none of us will be able to get away from it, but in the meantime the brunt of the fantasy that we can easily dispose of our shit and stay clean is borne by the most precarious among us. Paul's archive is not going to be taken out of the Christian canon anytime soon, which means that it will continue to straddle the line between barbarism and civility. And as it does so, it will offer fertilizer to some and waste to others.

Profanation offers a way of surviving Paul's archive. If the sacred is that which cannot be touched, which is set apart, profanation brings that which was sacred back to the rest of us. As Benjamin warns, such an object must be handled carefully, for it has a history of barbarity. Many will need to find ways to recycle Paul's archive to survive, as those who have been made to carry Paul's shit have always had to do to protect their people. Those of us who do not need to wrestle with Paul to survive should celebrate and learn from these recycled readings, not because they reveal something liberating about Paul, but because they reveal their virtuosity, creativity, and power as readers. It is their genius that gives Paul's words a liberative force that lands where it is most needed. To return us to Eve Sedgwick's terms, these are reparative readings that offer a chance at survival, for a time.

In addition, I think there is another way to return to Paul's archive that I will explore in the next chapters by sitting longer with the enslaved Africans in Brian Blount's account of Paul. I suggest that some of these voices offer a different form of profanation that intertwines Sedgwick's paranoid and reparative readings. These reading strategies sometimes reject Paul and sometimes play with his archive so as to render his violent logic inoperative. In this they offer a way of reconceptualizing a profaned Paul, of seeing Paul as shit.

A SOMETIMES PAUL

WHAT IF WE GIVE UP ON Paul's redemption? Throughout this book I have played with a number of different frames for thinking about Paul's canonical function and how it might be interrogated and subverted: scripturalization, secularization, profanation, reparative and paranoid readings. I have conscripted each frame into thinking with and about shit: excrement, waste, garbage, recycling, redemption. I have done so to stage an intervention in the circuit of perpetual recycling, redemption, and restoration of Paul. Far too many readers of Paul come to his archive primed to repair him. Some do this because they have always been able to make Paul say what they want, say what will maintain their privileged place in society. Others try to repair Paul in the hopes of reading themselves into that power structure. In this chapter I argue for a halt to Paul's always-already redemption, for a state of suspension between the elucidation of Paul's harms and his reuse. I do so by following the lead of Nancy Ambrose, whose body was stolen from her by white Christians evoking Paul's authority. By stopping this cycle of Pauline redemption, we make space to sit in the shit, refusing redemption (for now), and, we hope, create new forms of communal life by listening and risking with one another. "Sitting is sitting," Lauren Berlant writes, "and preparation for moving."[1]

PAUL AND THE DISINHERITED

Howard Thurman was a prominent African American theologian and civil rights leader in the mid-twentieth century, ultimately serving as dean of Marsh Chapel at Boston University. In one of his most famous books, Thurman deals with Paul, setting him alongside Jesus's radical solidarity with the oppressed.[2] His Jesus sits squarely within the tradition of Jesus as a second Moses, a liberator of the oppressed.[3] For Thurman, Christianity has betrayed the "religion of Jesus" and become largely a religion of domination that posits another world to justify and sustain oppression in this one (29–30). For Thurman, Christianity has been an opiate for the masses. And by Christianity, he means Paul.

On Thurman's reading, Paul is a Jew who was not of the same class as Jesus and his apostles. He was educated and (following the biography of Paul in Acts) a Roman citizen. He was thus "of a minority, but with majority privileges" (32). That his privilege was guaranteed by the state meant he was not troubled by the idea that slaves should stay in their place. He possessed "that quiet sense of security which comes from knowing that you belong and the general climate of confidence which it inspires" (33). It is Jesus, not Paul, who Thurman thinks lived in conditions most approximating those of twentieth-century African Americans and who could and did speak to those very conditions (34). Predating Pier Paolo Pasolini's insight into Paul as doubled, Thurman sees Paul's privileged minority, what Homi Bhabha might call his "postcolonial hybridity,"[4] as bearing an inherent ambiguity.

> It would be grossly misleading and inaccurate to say that there are not to be found in the Pauline letters utterances of a deeply different quality— utterances which reveal how his conception transcended all barriers of race and class and condition. But this other side is there, always available to those who wish to use the weight of the Christian message to oppress and humiliate their fellows. The point is that this aspect of Paul's teaching is understandable against the background of his Roman citizenship. It influenced his philosophy of history and resulted in a major frustration that has borne bitter fruit in the history of the movement which he, Paul, did so much to project on the conscience of the human race.[5]

Thurman's Paul foreshadows Pasolini's and informs Brian Blount's. There is a boundary-breaking quality to some of Paul's thought, but that other side is always there, always ready to be used "to oppress and humiliate." The womanist scholar Renita Weems takes a similar view of Paul's relative privilege and its effects on his ethics: "These credentials, in view of his teachings on women and slaves, appear to have restricted his vision of the kingdom of God to that of a vindicated community of religiously oppressed men; it appears, then, that he did not envision the kingdom as a totally reconstructed and reconciled humanity."[6] Unlike Blount, Thurman sees no real need to redeem Paul. He can be explained, but he can't be saved. He's just too dangerous.

Thurman's critique of Paul and unwillingness to save him is echoed in writings by a number of twentieth-century Black thinkers. James Baldwin called Paul "mercilessly fanatical and self-righteous."[7] Albert Cleage rejected Paul as one who offered a different religion from that of Jesus, the Black Messiah.[8] James Cone, a pivotal figure in Black Theology, rarely drew from Paul's writings, but he did register a similar ambivalence about Paul as Thurman's. He was also keenly aware that a critique of Paul was inseparable from a critique of the whiteness suffusing the interpretation of Paul's archive.

> We cannot forget that whites used Paul to justify slavery, and biblical scholars have done little to heal racial wounds deep in black history. In their scholarship, they ignore black people, and do not talk about the influence of Pauline scholarship on white supremacy in America. . . . I do not have a problem with Paul, since he affirmed that "we are all one in Christ Jesus" (Gal 3:28), and when saying that slavery didn't matter (1 Cor 7:20–21) he had in mind the coming end of time. But whatever Paul may have said, does not make much difference to me or to blacks who were enslaved and lynched in Paul's name. What matters is that white theologians have done almost nothing to liberate him or themselves from white supremacy.[9]

"AT LONG INTERVALS"

Thurman's reticence to save Paul, he suggests, comes from his grandmother, Nancy Ambrose, whose response to Paul offers perhaps the clearest example of how Paul can be profaned.

> During much of my boyhood I was cared for by my grandmother, who was born a slave and lived until the Civil War on a plantation near Madison, Florida. My regular chore was to do all of the reading for my grandmother—she could neither read nor write. Two or three times a week I read the Bible aloud to her. I was deeply impressed by the fact that she was most particular about the choice of Scripture. For instance, I might read many of the more devotional Psalms, some of Isaiah, the Gospels again and again. But the Pauline epistles, never—except, at long

intervals, the thirteenth chapter of First Corinthians. My curiosity knew no bounds, but we did not question her about anything.

When I was older and was half through college, I chanced to be spending a few days at home near the end of summer vacation. With a feeling of great temerity I asked her one day why it was that she would not let me read any of the Pauline letters. What she told me I shall never forget. "During the days of slavery," she said, "the master's minister would occasionally hold services for the slaves. Old McGhee was so mean that he would not let a Negro minister preach to his slaves. Always the white minister used as his text something from Paul. At least three or four times a year he used as a text: 'Slaves, be obedient to them that are your masters . . . as unto Christ.' Then he would go on to show how it was God's will that we were slaves and how, if we were good and happy slaves, God would bless us. I promised my Maker that if I ever learned to read and if freedom ever came, I would not read that part of the Bible."[10]

Thurman's story of his grandmother's biblical hermeneutics has spurred many responses among African American biblical scholars and theologians. Weems frames Ambrose's devotional practices within the realm of the aural. The "aural hermeneutic" of African American women "enables them to measure what they have been told about God, reality, and themselves against what they have experienced of God and reality and what they think of themselves as it has been mediated to them by the primary community with which they identify."[11] In a later interview, Thurman recounts how his grandmother told another story about her time as a slave. Occasionally she was allowed to attend church services in which the preacher was a fellow slave.

Always, no matter what his subject was, [the slave preacher] ended his sermon in the same way. She said he would stand and look at them. Then he would say, "You are not slaves, you are not niggers—you are God's children." When my grandmother would tell us about this, we would all wait for that moment because a faraway look would come into her eyes, with a slight stiffening of her spine, and for me, there was a contagion that came to me as a little child in knowing that the Creator of Existence also created me.[12]

This second anecdote shows the embodied affect of the aural experience to which Weems points. The Bible preached to enslaved Africans wasn't just a text read and studied but one that landed. And how it landed mattered. For Ambrose, hearing that she was not a slave or of an inferior race but a child of god spoke not to an abstract sense of religious belonging but to the contradiction at the heart of her embodied existence. The thrill of it still affected her body so many years later ("a faraway look would come into her eyes, with a slight stiffening of her spine"). As Vincent Wimbush writes, the Bible was often a site around which Blacks, navigating a white slaver world, attempted to find security and inclusion.[13] So, too, did Paul's letters land in Ambrose's experience, but with the opposite effect. They expressed the contradiction not of her embodied existence but within the slavers' Bible itself: the Bible could not at the same time endorse her servitude and her status as a child of god. Paul had to go.

Earlier, we saw the aural discernment of enslaved audiences in the rejection of Rev. Charles Colcock Jones's sermon in Georgia. A similar story is related by former slave Lunsford Lane: "There was one very kind hearted Episcopal minister whom I often used to hear; he was very popular with the colored people. But after he had preached a sermon to us in which he argued from the Bible that it was the will of heaven from all eternity we should be slaves, and our masters be our owners, most of us left him; for like some of the faint hearted disciples in early times we said,—'This is a hard saying, who can bear it?'"[14] Lane's fellow slaves rejected biblical interpretation that endorsed their servitude, but like Ambrose they also juxtaposed biblical texts as part of their critique. Lane's quotation of John 6:60 is itself an ironic play. In context, the disciples are unable to accept Jesus's admonition to eat his flesh and drink his blood (6:52–59). Lane ironically appropriates the judgment of John against the disciples, as if to say, "Clearly we were 'faint hearted disciples' for not endorsing our own enslavement. OK boomer." To hear Paul's admonitions that god had willed them to be slaves was something these slaves could not bear.

The embodied experience of Pauline endorsements of slavery created a new hermeneutic of hearing and a curation of an aural Bible. As Wimbush has argued, enslaved African readings of the Bible, in the many forms and spaces in which such readings took place,

> reflect a hermeneutic characterized by a looseness, even playfulness, vis-à-vis the biblical texts themselves. The interpretation was not controlled by the literal words of the texts, but by social experience. The texts were heard more than read; they were engaged as stories that seized and freed the imagination. Interpretation was therefore controlled by the freeing

of the collective consciousness and imagination of the African slaves as they heard the biblical stories and retold them to reflect their actual social situation, as well as their visions for something different.[15]

Wimbush's invocation of the playfulness of slave interpretation, ranging from Ambrose's discernment of what counted as the Bible for her to the creativity of biblical citation and allusion in spirituals, recalls Giorgio Agamben's reflections on profanation.

THE BIBLE AT PLAY

For Agamben, profanation is the act by which something sacred has been removed from the realm of the gods and returned to common use.[16] He suggests one way to profane the sacred: "The passage from the sacred to the profane can, in fact, also come about by means of an entirely inappropriate use (or, rather, reuse) of the sacred: namely, play."[17]

Can the playfulness that Wimbush names be read as Agamben's profanation through play? Citing, as he so often does, the philologist Émile Benveniste, Agamben argues that play represents an overturning of the sacred: "The power of the sacred act, he writes, lies in the conjunction of the myth that tells the story and the rite that reproduces and stages it. Play breaks up this unity."[18] When enslaved listeners creatively reconfigured the Bible read to them, they broke up the unity of the Bible's sacred white power, which lies not in the book itself but in the book as read in church to an audience that knows its place.[19] The resistance faced by white preachers was a refusal to accept the unity of Bible—Slave—Ideology—Audience on which the proslavery Bible's authority was based.

Agamben's thinking on play and profanation extends to how the Bible was not simply rejected by enslaved Africans but refashioned. Citing the example of children who can turn anything, regardless of worth, use, or sacrality, into a toy, Agamben writes, "What is common to these cases and the profanation of the sacred is the passage from a *religio* that is now felt to be false or oppressive to negligence as *vera religio*. This, however, does not mean neglect (no kind of attention can compare to that of a child at play) but a new dimension of use."[20] Slavers and white preachers often found themselves baffled by the resistance of slaves to their preaching and found their morality, which reconfigured the codes of virtue and vice common to white society, antinomian.[21] The blinders of slave ideology, which saw Africans as inferior to whites, made them see these practices as infantile. But for slaves, their play was not infantile but deadly serious political and theological resistance: by reconfiguring the Bible and Christian theology through neglect of slaver ideology, they gave the Bible a new use, no longer simply religion but *true* religion (*vera religio*) for them in their embodied particularity.

This wasn't, as modern Bible readers might expect, a return to the "true" nature of the Bible as a text that was against slavery: "Profanation does not simply restore something like a natural use that existed before being separated into the religious, economic, or juridical sphere. . . . This operation is more cunning and complex than that and is not limited to abolishing the form of separation in order to regain an uncontaminated use that lies either beyond or before it."[22] The resistance to slavery that characterized how slaves interpreted and reused biblical stories was not based in a "real" anti-slavery Bible that preexisted this activity. The Bible was not restored to its proper role as champion of human liberation. It was the work of enslaved Africans that created a new anti-slavery Bible in performance and directed toward the future. Wimbush shows, in his study of the life of the eighteenth-century ex-slave Olaudah Equiano, how this work occurs via mimicry: "Equiano seemed not only to have figured out what games the dominant culture had been playing with scriptures . . . he seemed aware of what game he might play in the engagement of scriptures in order to free himself from the negative effects of the binding, in which black skin color had been made to signify strangeness, the margins, absence."[23] Enslaved African uses of biblical materials took similar forms to those used by white Christians (sermons, devotional practices, singing), but these behaviors had been stripped of their sense and their ends: the staging of the hierarchies of the "Southern way of life."

One example, among many, of such serious play with the Pauline archive comes from a 1774 petition penned by enslaved Africans to the government of Massachusetts. Amid their petition, which sought an end to their enslavement, the writers use Paul to argue against Paul.

> Our lives are embittered to us. . . . By our deplorable situation we are rendered incapable of shewing our obedience to Almighty God How can a slave perform the duties of husband to a wife or a parent to his child? How can a husband leave master to work and cleave to his wife How can the wife submit themselves to their husbands in all things How can the child obey their parents in all things? There is a great number of us sencear . . .

members of the Church of Christ how can the master and the slave be said to fulfil the command Live in love let brotherly Love contuner [continue] and abound Beare ye one anothers Bordens How can the master be said to Bear my Borden when he Bears me down with the Have [heavy] chains of slavery and operson against my will and how can we fulfill our parte of duty to him whilst in this condition as we cannot searve our God as we ought in this situation.[24]

The writers skillfully juxtapose Paul's command in Galatians 6:2 to "bear ye one another's burdens" to references to Pauline texts outlining the relationships in a patriarchal household (Eph. 5:22, 24; 6:1–4; Col. 3:18–20). They argue that slavery precludes the commandments laid down by Paul for Christians. The asymmetries of slavery make it impossible to bear one another's burdens, which presumes a certain social equality. And the violence of the slave system makes it impossible for patriarchal family relationships to function. Yet the writers leave out of their citations the nearby verses in Ephesians and Colossians that enjoin similar requirements of obedience to slaves (Eph. 6:5–8; Col. 3:22–25). This is not just selective editing. The fact that the authors do not cite chapter or verse suggests that they expected their readers to know they were interpreting scripture. By leaving out the verses that everyone knew were also there, the writers deconstruct Paul's authority itself. If slavery makes it impossible to do one's Christian duty, then why did Paul support and condone slavery? This astute subversion of Paul's authority comes without any citation of Paul by name as an authority figure. The writers were not claiming that Paul was on their side but brilliantly pointing out the aporias and contradictions in Paul's archive itself.

By constructing a Bible from their experience through such playful interpretation and reuse, enslaved Christians profaned the white Bible, arresting its old use as a tool in their own oppression and putting it to new use. This profanation opened up the space for something called Bible to take up a position opposed to the institution of slavery. This is not to discount the work done by white and Black abolitionists in the North in building arguments that resisted pro-slavery ideology, nor is it to overlook the violence that brought the institution of slavery to an end in the South. To survive the horrific contradictions of their lives, slaves profaned the slavers' Bible to tell a new story of their suffering, humanity, and hopes for liberation.

A SOMEWHERE BIBLE

In their autobiography, former slaves Lewis and Milton Clarke reflect on their answers to common questions they were asked in their travels around the North, speaking on the evils of slavery: "What do slaves know about the Bible?—They generally believe there is somewhere a real Bible, that came from God; but they frequently say the Bible now used is master's Bible; most that they hear from it being, 'Servants, obey your masters.'"[25] The idea that there is a real Bible out there, somewhere, leaves open the space for repeating the profanation of the Bible by enslaved Africans. What would it mean to have a Bible that is always somewhere but not here?

Nancy Ambrose's discerning aural palette suggests a model for thinking about such a Bible. A Somewhere Bible is what speaks to us now in our thrownness in embodied existence. That which would comprise such a Somewhere Bible would be that which is useful, that which is available to play with freely. In other words, a Somewhere Bible can only include the profaned. Ambrose's choice of texts ("Psalms, some of Isaiah, the Gospels again and again") comprise those biblical materials that had been profaned by enslaved Christians, removed from their use as sacred justifications for slavery and racism and fashioned into narratives and figures of liberation. They were texts that spoke to Ambrose's embodied experience as a slave, an African American, and a woman. Her rejection of Paul's letters, she clearly explains to her grandson, was because these texts could not be redeemed. They had been wielded with such violence against her and those like her. They were not in god's Bible, nor were they useful.

But . . . "at long intervals" she could listen to 1 Corinthians 13. What I find so interesting about Ambrose's admission of this chapter back into her aural canon is that it comes after she has thoroughly rejected Paul's very canonicity over the course of a lifetime.[26] She tells her grandson that as a slave, she had vowed to god that she would not read Paul ("I promised my Maker that if I ever learned to read and if freedom ever came, I would not read that part of the Bible"). And she held to that commitment, except for this one chapter from Paul's archive.

We've all heard 1 Corinthians 13 at some point. It is frequently intoned at Christian weddings ("Love is patient; love is kind; love is not envious or boastful or arrogant . . ."). Something of a digression from Paul's larger conversation around spiritual gifts among his Corinthian audience members, this short chapter reads like a hymn to love, making it fodder for all manner of sappy Hallmark cards. It is not hard to see why someone like Ambrose might want to hear the aurally pleasing lines in praise of love intoned to her periodically by her grandson. But how is it that she can be so clear in her opposition to Paul, and yet invite his occasional presence?

I would suggest that it is because Ambrose listens to Paul scatologically. She has profaned Paul, rendered him and his writings as garbage and refuse. Paul is no longer canon by default for her. He is not required to be there alongside Moses, Isaiah, and Jesus. He is not an authority endowed by god to which the reader must submit. He is not a saint to be emulated or obeyed. His words do not carry the force of law. And because he is not required to be there, he can occasionally come over, for just a bit, when the mood strikes. A profaned Paul can become part of a Somewhere Bible, but only if he says something worth listening to. If Paul is sacred, if he is not fully profaned, we must make him work for everything and every time. We must take all the bad, and there is a lot of it, with a little good. But if he isn't sacred, if he is no longer the family patriarch but the weird uncle we occasionally invite to Thanksgiving, we can ignore him until he becomes useful, until he offers something necessary. Maybe then he can become part of god's Bible, somewhere.

PAUL'S SHIT

IN HIS LETTER TO THE PHILIPPIANS, Paul speaks about shit. He says that he considers his previous life, the life he led before his calling by Christ, to be *skubala*, excrement. He drops a dirty word here not merely for emphasis. The letter is replete with rhetoric that draws from the discourse of shit. Paul writes of out-of-control bellies, mutilated flesh, shame and exaltation, purity and impurity, precarious and glorified bodies. Attention to his shit and its uses exposes his attempts to draw boundaries between civilized and barbarous, insider and outsider, us and them, the living and the dead. Read as part of a discourse of the body, Paul's reference to his shit helps us see new patterns in the rhetoric of the letter. Critical attention to Paul's shit also creates new possibilities and perspectives. Feces can be fertilizer for new life. Enslaved Africans created a Bible for themselves, their Somewhere Bible, through creative invention.

In this chapter the collectivity I look to for inventive readings of Paul comprises feminist and queer biblical scholars. These are the scholars who have shown how Paul's rhetoric, in all his letters, is shaped by concerns with unity, hierarchy, and control. Because they reject readings that unquestioningly identify the interpreter with Paul, feminist and queer approaches can read Paul while simultaneously staking out a position from which to critique what Paul says.[1] From such a horizon, feminist and queer readers of Paul's letters study them for echoes of diversity, disagreement, and debate, making space for voices other than the apostle's to emerge from his writings. Such modes of reading are similar in many ways to that of Nancy Ambrose: Paul is unredeemable, but reading his letters might yet introduce us to new ideas that are not his. Moreover, these modes offer ways of reading Paul by attending to his shit rather than carting it off or pretending it's not there.

PHILIPPIAN BODIES

The only reference to excrement in Paul's archive comes in his letter to the Philippians (3:8). Writing from prison to the collective of Jesus followers in a Roman colony in Macedonia, Paul struggles rhetorically over his body. The body is, as he begrudgingly admits, a necessity if one wants to do things in this world, but it is also a site of shame, always ready to become a problem. The body is for Paul a body of humiliation (3:21). It would be better to flee and put on the new body of the resurrected (1:23). We could read Alain Badiou's anxieties easily into the Paul of Philippians: both see the limitations of the body's particularities and long for escape to a resurrected body stripped of all that. Paul calls the particularities that have attached to his body shit (*skubala* [3:8]). In what follows, I read this reference to shit in the broader context of Paul's letter, paying attention to how the body that produces excrement is sidelined and problematized in Paul's rhetoric. My reading draws from the work of Joseph Marchal and Sheila Briggs.[2] What emerge from paying attention to Paul's shit are two insights: (1) Paul worries over his body and prefers to denigrate it in favor of a hoped-for resurrected body of glory; (2) his fears of an abject body offer jumping-off places for thinking otherwise about the body.

Paul writes to the Philippians from prison (1:7, 12–14).[3] This confinement of his body shapes his letter, as he attempts to reframe this potential shame as something beneficial. Recognizing that some of his opponents have rejoiced in his incarceration, Paul claims to be indifferent (1:15–18) and expresses confidence that his imprisonment is benefiting the spread of the gospel (1:12–14). But his bluster only barely conceals his fears of being shamed.

> I know that this will end in my salvation, through your prayers and the provision of the spirit of Jesus Christ, according to my expectation and hope, that I will not be shamed in any way but that Christ will be exalted in my body, as always as now, by completely frank speech, whether by life or by death. For to me living is Christ and dying is profit. If it is life in the flesh, this is profitable work, and what I should choose, I do not know. I am held together between the two, having a desire to be set loose and to be with Christ, for that is much better. But remaining in the flesh is more necessary for you. And having been persuaded by this, I know that I will remain and stand beside you all for your progress and joy of faith, so that

your boast may overflow in Christ Jesus in me through my arrival again
to you. (1:19–26)

Paul notes that his imprisonment could be read as shameful. He thus presents
himself as confident that Christ will be exalted in his (potentially shameful)
body. The key to reading his body rightly, according to Paul, is to see it as
a necessity suffered for the Philippians. The expectation is that Paul's body
will be profitable as a commodity, so long as the Philippians follow his teachings and accept his authority. Throughout the letter, Paul equates the proper
Philippian response to his teaching with the performance of unity (1:27–28;
2:2; 4:2) through imitating him (3:17).[4] He expresses a preference to be set
free from the body, but, passive-aggressively, he makes a concession that no
one asked for: "I'd rather pass into glory and hang with Jesus, but you need
me, so I will stay around." Later, Paul will call himself a libation being poured
out over the sacrifice of the Philippians' faith (2:17). His shameful body is
converted through metaphors of profit and food into a vehicle for glory.[5]

Paul makes clear that he is ready to be with Christ, but that for the time
being he will remain in a fleshly body. To distinguish himself from his opponents, who might seek to shame him for his imprisonment, Paul contrasts his
preference for the body of glory with the terrestrial bodies of his opponents.

> Many live, as I have told you many times and about whom I am now
> speaking while lamenting, as enemies of the cross of Christ. Their end is
> destruction and their god is their digestive system and their glory is in
> shame, being those who think about terrestrial things. For our citizenship
> is in the heavens, from which we eagerly expect a savior, the lord Jesus
> Christ, who will transform our body of humiliation to be of the same
> form as his body of glory according to the active force by which he is able
> to subject all things to himself. (3:18–21)

Paul casts his opponents as fleshly, in contrast with the bodies of glory
that he and his followers will receive. He describes these enemies as being
focused on the terrestrial, the things that are on the earth (*epigeia*), and he
claims that their god is their digestive system. The term used here is *koilia*,
which can mean "belly," "intestines," or "excrement." Paul evokes the whole
cycle of consumption and excretion involved in nourishing the body. To care
about the body is to set oneself up for destruction (*apōleia*).[6]

Paul's followers, by contrast, are promised a body of glory (*doxa*) if they continue to imitate him (3:17). This body will transform their fleshly one, marked here as a humiliation or abased (*tapeinōsis*). Such a transformation results from their citizenship (*politeia*) in the heavens as believers along with the work of Christ. It further sharpens the contrast between the humiliated fleshly bodies destined for destruction that walk on the earth and the glorious bodies that result from the believers' translation into their true place in the heavens. Accordingly, Paul is concerned about the purity of the Philippians. He frequently enjoins them to be pure, innocent, blameless, and without blemish (1:10; 2:14–15; 4:8–9), qualities he ties to unity in obedience to his own teaching (2:12–13; 3:17; 4:2). Paul not only hopes for transformation, but he ties it to a fascination with power. Jesus can transform debased bodies into glory because he is able to subject all things to himself (3:21). Mayra Rivera rightly sums up Paul's dueling bodies in Philippians: "The dream of glorious bodies freed from the weight of earthly substances is alluring. But their brilliance is fueled by the exhaustion of flesh."[7]

FROM GLORY TO SLAVERY AND BACK

This fascination with power and domination in the face of humiliation and shame recurs frequently in the letter. Feminist scholars have long pointed out that the flesh, humiliation, and shame are frequently gendered as feminine, both in antiquity and in the present.[8] As Paul reflects on his own incarceration and on Jesus's crucifixion, he treats both events as potentially shameful. The crux of this contrast between feminine humiliation and masculine authority is the famous Christ hymn.

> Have this mind in you that was also in Christ Jesus, who being in the form of god did not consider equality with god as something to be exploited, but he evacuated himself and, taking the form of a slave, was born in the image of humans. And being found in form as a human, he abased himself, becoming obedient unto death, even a death on a cross. Therefore also god has hyper-exalted him and favored him with the name that is beyond every name, so that in the name of Jesus every knee should bend of those from the heavens, from the terrestrial, and from under the earth and every tongue should confess that Jesus Christ is lord to the glory of god the father. (2:6–11)

There have been lively debates as to whether Paul is the author of the Christ hymn or merely quoting from a hymn sung in collectives of Jesus followers.[9] Regardless, his use of this hymn anchors the bodily juxtaposition throughout the letter between an abject fleshly body and a glorious and powerful heavenly one. In the myth presented here, Christ descends into an abject physical form likened to a slave, in which he suffers a slave's death, death on the cross. But because of Christ's obedience (*hypēkoos*), he is transformed back into a hyperbody (the Greek prefix *hyper-* is used twice) so powerful that it makes the whole universe submit. What is dramatized here for Paul is that a body undergoing humiliation or shame from obedience will be transformed into a powerful, conquering body. He buys into a fantasy of ultimate revenge.

In her work on the Christ hymn, Sheila Briggs challenges the extent to which we can read this hymn as liberative for the oppressed,[10] a position often taken by biblical scholars.[11] Drawing from the work of Orlando Patterson,[12] Briggs shows how the Christ hymn reinforces the social reality of ancient slavery rather than critiques it. As she reads the hymn, the narrative pivots on the surprising reversal: Christ was in the form of god and then entered into slavery as a human before then being exalted again as universal lord (*kurios*) through his obedience. As Briggs rightly points out, what is considered virtuous about Christ in the hymn is his obedience to empty himself and become a slave-human, not his death on the cross. In this sense, "God is . . . described as having the same expectations of Christ in the form of a slave as a human master had of the slave in the world of the New Testament."[13] Further, while the enslavement of Christ into an inferior human form might have been a site for thinking about the violence of ancient slavery, where just about anyone was in danger of being captured and enslaved, Christ's obedience neutralizes the scandal: by going willingly Christ does not suffer the violence of enslavement, nor does he come to bear the moral inferiority that attached to enslaved persons (148).

While god plays the role of slaver in the hymn, the human condition is figured as universal slavery ("taking the form of a slave, was born in the image of humans"). Although Christ's *kenosis* (self-emptying) has been read as an act of solidarity with humanity, the figuring of the human condition as "universal human slavery reinforces the social reality of a particular institution of slavery by encouraging endurance of the human condition rather than transformation of it" (146). Ultimately, Briggs concludes, the Christ hymn is a kyriocentric text that "does not challenge the interests or beliefs of slavemasters" (149).[14] One might go further and ask what sort of Christ is represented here. Christ's *kenosis* is something that can only be done by free and privileged agents. Is Christ just slumming it here with us slaves, knowing full well he will return to his privileged place in heaven?

ALL THIS IS SHIT

It is in this context that we can read Paul's own description of the particularities of his biography as "shit" (*skubala*), what Badiou might call a Paul with the "details abolished."[15] Scholars have long read Paul's self-description in 3:1–11 as a parallel to the Christ hymn; however, that consensus has recently been challenged persuasively by Dorothea Bertschmann.[16] While Paul's account of his background as shit is not the counterpart to Christ's self-enslavement, it does trade on the same anxieties about the body and its precarity that return throughout the letter. While Jesus received (back) an exalted body for his kenotic obedience, Paul hopes to earn resurrection from the dead, a new, glorious body to replace his current one.

Paul's line of argument focuses on a comparison between himself and his opponents. He describes his opponents as "dogs" (*kynes*), "evil workers," and "the mutilation" for advocating circumcision for followers of Jesus, which he frames as having "trust in the flesh" (3:2–3). To flip the tables on his opponents, Paul claims to have more qualities that should give him confidence in the flesh but then radically reverses, calling these qualities "shit."

> If some other person seems to have confidence in the flesh, I have more: circumcised on the eighth day, from the *genos* of Israel, of the tribe of Benjamin, a Hebrew from Hebrews, a Pharisee according to the law, a pursuer of the collective according to zeal, perfect according to justice in the law. But whatever profits were mine, I have accounted them losses because of Christ. And further I deem everything to be a loss because of the excessive value of the knowledge of Christ Jesus my lord, because of whom I have lost everything, and I deem it all shit so that I might gain Christ and be found in him, not having my own justice from the law but through the faithfulness of Christ, the justice from God according to faithfulness, which knows him and the power of his resurrection and the solidarity of his sufferings, taking a similar form to his death, if somehow I might arrive at the resurrection from the dead. (3:4b–11)

Here Paul rehearses aspects of his own biography, from birth through his turn to following Christ. He renders this in language of accounting, treating aspects of his identity as values in a ledger he compares with the value of knowing Christ.[17] This value is determined by what it offers: achieving resurrection from the dead (3:11), which is acquired through solidarity with Christ in his sufferings and through the power behind his own resurrection.

Paul revises the value of his biography and his achievements in light of the value of the Resurrection: it's all shit. Here he sounds something like Alain Badiou's Paul: a subject straining to only know Christ and the Resurrection, in the process stripping off all the particularities of his previous identity in fidelity to this event. Unlike Badiou's Paul, however, the apostle makes a calculated accounting in a ledger to describe his fidelity to the Resurrection of Christ, an action Badiou would call subjecting the event to a count, something that does not fall under the sign of the true universal.[18] As Bertschmann rightly shows, Paul does not reject his past outright, in some kind of Christian supersessionist rejection of Judaism and the Law, but rather has radically reevaluated a list of valuable objects compared with one (Christ) immeasurably more valuable.[19] Following Jennifer Quigley's work on Philippians, we can see that Paul regards the Resurrection of Christ as a commodity that has value within a wider theo-economy.[20] This points to a key problem in Badiou's reading of Paul: the Resurrection is countable as a value (even if it is uniquely massive) within the situation, as Paul understands it. He does not proclaim a rupturing event of the Resurrection but sells the Philippians on a commodity they should buy, as opposed to that sold by his opponents (the "dogs" [3:2]).

Reading Paul's reversal with the discourse of shit helps us see how Christ and his resurrection function like commodities in the apostle's logic. In his work on waste, Brian Thill has argued that the things we throw away are effects of an economy of desire.

> The things we call our waste exist in an interzone between two states of mind and two structures of feeling about the glittering, shattered object-worlds we have built around ourselves. These relics float between the poles of desire and discard. More than mere trash or hazard, a better way to think about waste is to think of it as the unsatisfactory and temporary name we give to the affective relationships we have with our unwanted objects. Waste is the expression of expended, transmuted, or suspended desire.[21]

In light of the new commodity he has his heart set on acquiring, Paul has come to see his past and the identities and qualities associated with it as feces. He dramatizes his reevaluation of value akin to how Thill describes litter: "Mere litter is a special category of waste because its existence depends more than anything else on individualized indifference. The indifference engine that drives litter is the flip side of desire. It's the waste we could not bring ourselves to care even a little bit about, when we had, just moments before, cared about some part of the thing we're throwing out very much: the potato chips in the unwanted bag or the gum inside the tossed wrapper."[22] The language of indifference that Thill uses for litter resonates with Badiou's claim that for Paul, the event has rendered him indifferent to his Jewishness and to particular identities in general.[23] But this is not an indifference borne of the radical newness of the universalizing event. Paul is repulsed by his old life because the affective connection with it has been severed as his desire has been redirected to the new commodity of Christ, like a child desperately wanting that new toy. Quigley has shown how this passage (and all of Philippians) is saturated in language of "theo-economics," in which Paul is constantly tallying up the costs, losses, profits, and ventures that come with his work with and for Christ and the Philippians.[24] He is indifferent, not because of his fidelity to a universalizing event, but because his desire has turned to a new, more valuable commodity.

Central to this cycle of desire-consumption-waste-desire is Paul's anxiety about the body. The ultimate commodity for Paul is a body that cannot be shamed because it has been made glorious. In his ritual of taking out the garbage each morning, Italo Calvino saw a chance to be free of the "detritus of myself." As Thill narrates Calvino's ritual, we can hear echoes of Paul's transformation.

> Through this ritual, [Calvino] confirms the need to separate himself from a part of what was once his, so that tomorrow, he says, "I can identify completely (without residues) with what I am and have." Waste thus signifies something more than just a certain stage of an object's life cycle; it is our specific affective relationship to an object that makes it "waste" in the first place. Once desire has been squeezed out of it, we're left with the waste products of those desires. The thing loses its thingness, and becomes something to eliminate. It is as if the real dread we feel about our own waste is not its undesirable and ignoble putrescence, but the creeping fear that its unwanted proximity to us somehow threatens to erase or disturb our very sense of ourselves as discrete bodies.[25]

Like Calvino, Paul separates himself from his waste so that he can identify with a new, clean self. That self is tied to a new desire for Christ and the Resurrection. These commodities and the body that comes with them offer further distance from his own shit: the promise of a glorified body that no longer suffers humiliation and shame.

Paul's excremental reevaluation of his past, his radical redefinition of value, is jarring; however, by following imagery of the body, digestion, and excrement through Philippians, we can see a recurring set of thematics that help clarify his logic. He persistently devalues the fleshly body: his own, those of his opponents, and human bodies more generally. This devaluation draws from imagery of digestion and excrement to separate the fleshly, earthy body from Paul's idealized visions of Christ's glorified and powerful body and the pure resurrected body Christ offers. The latter is made available to those who obey Paul in unity and is backed by divine power that has subjected all things and all people to its will. Christ suffered by willfully taking on a servile human form. Paul also suffers, leaving behind the things he previously valued in the mad rush for even greater profit. This profit is the promise of resurrected life and a kind of cosmic vengeance, in which those who persist in the flesh will find destruction.

We can see, perhaps, why this passage, which presents a Paul so like Badiou's, is only briefly discussed by him.[26] This is the dark triumphalism of the proclamation of the Resurrection, in which Paul shows his fascination with a power that both brings others into submission and transforms his body from flesh to glory, from shit to gold. His shit traces an economy of desire that abandons the past and the body in favor of power and vengeance. Paul may envision, sometimes, a humanity in which divisions separating us from one another can be overcome; but that drive to unity, homogeneity, and transcendence, which so drives Badiou's reading of Paul as well, is bound up with fantasies of violence and control. It is not hard to feel in Paul's hopes for resurrection a fascistic universalism.

SITTING IN THE SHIT

Paul's shit is tied to a troubling economy. It is not a sign of the militant herald of the universalizing event. It is tied to a disparagement of the body that drives violence and vengeance. Paul's bodily preoccupations are directed toward a new commodity of desire: a resurrected body free from the vaga-

ries of embodied existence. What do we do with this theo-economy, to bor-
row Quigley's term, of excrement and desire?

As we saw above, in her work on the Christ hymn Sheila Briggs shows
that taken on its own terms, the narrative of the hymn does not challenge
but rather reinforces the slave system of the ancient world. She rightly points
out that what the hymn *also* does is introduce the idea that Christ, and by
extension god, could be enslaved.[27] For ancient and modern slaves, the idea
of a god in solidarity is meaningful, particularly one who sits in the shit
with the enslaved and oppressed. The text may be kyriocentric (and we must
admit that), but "the imagination of the slaves in confronting the Philippians
hymn was not circumscribed by the logical associations of the text within
the dominant symbolic universe."[28] If read from the perspective of enslaved
readers who don't care about what Paul thinks—in other words, if Paul is
read as a profaned text—the hymn can become a pivot on which to imagine
other pasts and invent other associations. Liberative readings do not come
from following Paul's intentions, thought, or theology; rather, they come
from imagining readers of his letters who would use their own creativity,
ingenuity, and intelligence to address their context.

So what would it look like to imagine a god who sat in the shit with the
most marginalized? What would it look like if modern readers saw our lives
as shit, disposable, precarious, exploited by capitalism, all to varying degrees,
not as prelude to taking up a glorious resurrected body but as something to
sit and wrestle with, alongside those whose precarity and disposability are
greater than our own? Joseph Marchal's work on Philippians presents one
compelling option for how to read against Paul in this way.

Marchal suggests that rather than following Paul down the path of desire
for transcending the fleshly body, we might instead take the occasion of
Paul's invocation of his shit to think about what he wants to run from.[29] He
seeks to flee from the precarious body to the glorious one promised by and
through Christ's resurrection. He deploys triumphalist rhetoric, from shit
and death to exaltation and glory. This triumphalist fantasy might best be
summed up in Paul's claim that Christ's strength allows him to do anything
(4:13). Of Paul's rhetoric, Marchal rightly asks,

> How different would such demonstrations look, however, if Paul then
> or people now did not rush to such (likely overinflated) claims about
> comprehensive strengths and sufficiencies? Instead of a set of practices
> that demarcate differences, could we bear in mind our mutual condition,
> what makes us human together? . . . Rhetorically, historically, and even

theologically, it seems important to attend to the moments before a narration of victory or strength, to tarry over the process of humanization
rather than deification. . . . This, indeed, is what connects community
and Christ: a shared permeability and, yes, possibility as humans, even a
shared mortality so starkly stressed in the "hymn." If we stop stressing the
"him" (Paul's masculine construction of himself as a model) and abide a
bit more in the beginning of the "hymn," that moment of tension becomes
a resource for a different kind of repetition.[30]

Marchal's interruption of Paul's drive to exaltation creates an important
space within the text to press, as did Briggs's enslaved readers, for a different
reading that does not follow Paul's own logic. It also gestures toward a mode
of reading that can elicit a universalism borne not by Badiou's genericity but
by a precarity that is generally specific and specifically general for subjects
within the regime of global, financialized capitalism.

Skirting Paul's naming of his own past as shit, Marchal draws out the
gastrointestinal metaphor within the Christ hymn. He notes that *kenoō*, the
Greek word used to describe Christ's emptying of himself, can also refer to
emptying one's bowels. Christ's transition from equal to god to slave-human
is effected by shitting. Jesus's body, beaten, bloodied, and shamed on the
cross, is divine shit. This first movement of the Christ hymn is what calls for
a pause in the interpretive machinery. Pausing over this imagery allows us
to read the discourse of shit in Paul's letter differently.

First, it forces us to dwell on the porousness of the body and its entanglements: "The shame and stigma attached to practices like defecation
does remind us of the permeability of our bodies. Since the boundaries of
our bodies are not nearly as hard and firm as dominant discourses so often
declare, any activity that moves across these boundaries has the potential
to highlight what also defines us as humans: our vulnerability and fragility.
In short, our mortality."[31] Marchal sees shit as an uncomfortable reminder,
for Paul and us, of the lack of clear boundaries around the body. A wide
array of scholarship in the sciences and the humanities, often referred to
as posthumanism, has pushed for a rethinking of the body, its plasticity,
and its porousness. Posthumanist scholarship particularly challenges the
unified notion of the human subject, paying attention to the ways in which
our selves are entangled rather than autonomous.[32] Much posthumanist
work has focused on modern technology and science: genetic modification,
artificial intelligence, the virtual landscape of cyberspace.[33] Some work has
focused on interspecies coevolution,[34] while others have focused on sys-

tems analyses that flatten the distinctions between humans and the environment.[35] Pausing to reflect, as Paul refuses to do, opens up space to think in new ways about the body.

A posthumanist framing of shit allows us to imagine alternative politics of precarity. "Dwelling upon Christ's kenotic evacuation," Marchal writes, "underscores how forces cross and act upon bodies, as well as how the body exceeds itself and its ostensible boundaries."[36] The body extends past our skin and invites other entities to pass through it. Thus the self is constituted not by individual agency but by both its vulnerability and the forces affecting it. A politics of a posthuman body could figure itself around a messy assemblage of human and nonhuman, of agencies of various kinds, that make for a good life. Rather than rooting political imaginaries in a monolithic notion of the human or notions of class, nation, or rights, our bodies' relative precarity and interdependability become frames for thinking universally from the particular: "While this is often seen as one of the basest things we humans do, it is one that we must do with some regularity: to survive as embodied entities, we must manage and expel waste. If all humans must do such base and shameful things, then, in becoming human Christ too would have to do similarly. In short, and as the children's book states, *every*one poops!"[37]

Marchal's reading of Philippians approaches what I might call a shit theology of universalism. Decentering Paul from the conversation, a shit theology reorients how we read. It dwells on moments of abjection and resists exaltation, the drive to turn shit to gold. It doesn't sell pie in the sky but sits on the refuse pile with our embodied precarity, shared mortality, and the suffering that both entail.

In this way, shit offers a way of thinking a universalism that does not rely on Badiou's Platonic genericity, the hunt for that which is (potentially) common to all yet unattached to materiality and particularity. Judith Butler, whose work informs Marchal's reading of Philippians, has argued that the precarity and vulnerability of the body offer a frame for the kind of coalitional politics of difference that so bothered Badiou. As she writes, "Precisely because bodies are formed and sustained in relation to infrastructural supports (or their absence) and social and technological networks or webs of relation, we cannot extract the body from its constituting relations—and those relations are always economically and historically specific."[38] In other words, there is no way to abstract ourselves from the webs of relations that constitute us as subjects: "Perhaps it helps to put it this way: the body is exposed, to history, to precarity, and to force, but also to what is unbidden and felicitous."[39] This shared capacity to affect and to be affected, to use Spinoza's oft-repeated phrase, in the very particularity of our interdependencies may be a way to think a universal from within and not as an abstraction from the particular.[40]

Zygmunt Bauman has similarly argued that what defines subjectivity under global capitalism is a shared "redundancy."[41] As he suggests, "To be declared redundant means to have been disposed of *because of being disposable*—just like the empty and non-refundable plastic bottle or once-used syringe, an unattractive commodity with no buyers, or a substandard or stained product without use thrown off the assembly line by the quality inspectors. 'Redundancy' shares its semantic space with 'rejects,' 'wastrels,' 'garbage,' 'refuse'—with *waste*."[42] Might a universal subjectivity come from recognizing that we are all, to varying degrees, disposable and vulnerable? We all live precarious lives, some more than others; and the systems we have created to govern our nations, economies, and ecologies are indifferent to whether any of us suffers. We are disposable. We are not special. We are vulnerable.

But that very vulnerability, Butler reminds us, is also a vulnerability to be affected by and to affect others. To sit in the shit with those whose precarity is markedly more severe than one's own offers a way through embodied life into, perhaps, some different way of organizing collectivities. We have no glorious bodies to which to escape. All we have are these decaying bits of matter. But perhaps something can emerge when bodies come together "to enact the world we wish to see, or to refuse the one that is doing us in."[43]

Paul would have us escape all this. To hope for something away from here. But the simple truth is we'll all be garbage at some point. We might as well embrace it.

REFUSING PAUL

THE GARBAGE WORKERS' UNION is one of the most organized and respected unions in Dakar, the Senegalese capital. It is also a key site of resistance to the neoliberal transformations that have been pushed on African nations by global institutions in the name of modernization and development. Rosalind Fredericks documents how it achieved this in her study of urban infrastructure in Dakar.[1] Beginning in the late 1980s, garbage, its collection, and its geography became highly contested sites for figuring citizenship, inequality, and the failures of the neoliberal state in Senegal. At the turn of the twenty-first century, public protest of inequalities in waste infrastructure led to "trash revolts" throughout the city, involving both garbage worker strikes and the strategic, voluntary movement by citizens of household garbage to public spaces. As Fredericks notes, these protests "deploy[ed] the power of dirt to creatively subvert ordering paradigms and contest the stigma and abjection implied by living and working in filth" (13). The garbage workers themselves have framed their work as acts of Islamic piety. As the union leader, Madany Sy, told Fredericks, "To be a true believer, a true Muslim, one must be clean. One must not be sullied; cleanliness is essential. Thus those who collect the trash of the markets, hospitals, the households, they have a surplus with regard to God. . . . I sacrifice myself today so that people don't have to be contaminated by illnesses" (141–42). The union has been so successful because it has assembled itself with the precarious urban poor, Islamic piety, and the vitality of the city's garbage.

Garbage and waste are vital agents—"vibrant matter," to use Jane Bennett's phrase—at work in our social, economic, and political orders, large and small.[2] As Fredericks observes, "The high organic content, stench, and propensity for quick putrefaction in the Senegalese heat makes household trash in Dakar visceral, lively matter" (*Garbage Citizenship*, 18). As those who manage the "toxic vitality" of trash, the garbage workers have found a potent leverage point through which to mobilize the force of garbage's agency and organize the energy of Dakar's urban poor (18). I have likened biblical scholarship in the pages of this book to a sanitation service for the Bible, dutifully collecting and disposing of Paul's shit. If that is true, what would it look like for readers of Paul to become like the Dakarois garbage workers, harnessing and mobilizing Paul's shit, not to dispose of it but to fight back?

Paul, too, sees toxic vitality in garbage and refuse, though he casts himself not as their manager but as toxic waste itself. In his correspondence with the Corinthians, he often speaks of the hardships he has experienced because of his work on behalf of the cult of Christ (2 Cor. 4:7–12; 6:3–10; 11:21–33). In these lists of afflictions, Paul speaks of physical punishments and hardships, as well as threats and experiences of violence. These torments are meant to indicate to his Corinthian audiences that he is steadfast and brave, that he is willing to suffer for the sake of his message of a crucified Judean messiah.[3] As a result, he expects the Corinthians to follow his lead.[4] A similar list of hardships occurs in 1 Corinthians 4:8–13. In addition to the usual elements of his hardships, Paul describes himself and his fellow apostles as garbage.

> Already you are adorned! Already you have become rich! Quite apart from us you are ruling! Indeed, I wish that you were ruling, so that we might rule with you! For I think God has displayed us apostles last of all as sentenced to death, so that we have become a spectacle to the cosmos, both to angels and to humans. We are fools because of Christ, but you are wise in Christ. We are weak, but you are strong. You are honored, but we are dishonored. Until now we are hungry and thirsty, we are naked and beaten and homeless, and we are tired from working with our own hands. When verbally abused, we bless; when pursued, we stand firm; when spoken ill of, we speak kindly. We have become like the *perikatharma* of the cosmos, the *peripsima* of all things, and we still are.

The Greek words that I have left transliterated here only occur once each in Paul's letters and are themselves rarely used in ancient Greek literature. Both terms evoke what we would call garbage or waste. *Perikatharma* can refer to the leftovers from a sacrificial offering or the slag that remains after smelting. It names refuse, but it also came to refer to those who themselves are outcasts and scapegoats.[5] *Peripsima* can refer to that which is scoured off the plate when a meal is finished, the unwanted leftovers headed for the garbage dump. Like *perikatharma*, it can also be extended to refer to vile people and, by extension, to a slave, a person who, for the ancients, was not a person at all.[6] In this list of hardships, Paul names himself and his fellow apostles as garbage and waste, the refuse of the world and the offscouring of all.

I want to conclude this book by resisting the urge to valorize Paul's (seeming) self-abasement and dwell with the refuse with which he identi-fies himself. Paul names himself as refuse in what Margaret Mitchell calls a "paradoxical encomium," a surprising act of self-praise meant to reinforce the apostle's own contested authority in Corinth.[7] Instead of following Paul's incitement of praise, I want to follow Joseph Marchal's injunction to stop and sit with the disposability Paul disavows. Refuse, like shit, is an ambivalent substance. It is that which can, nay must, be separated out and discarded, but it is also that which can be recycled and put to new use. We are refuse and, as Bruno Latour suggests, compost at the same time.[8] I want to think too with the garbage workers in Dakar, who have not run from waste but embraced it as a site for contesting what justice, community, and citizenship look like. Can we refuse Paul? And if so, what would an alternative look like?

TAKING OUT THE TRASH

Paul's claim that he and his fellow apostles are trash in 1 Corinthians 4 serves two interrelated functions in the letter's argument. First, it functions as a cat-alogue of Paul's hardships, meant to underscore the sacrifices he has made for the gospel of Christ. These paradoxical accomplishments comprise an argument for Paul's authority within the Corinthian collective of Christ fol-lowers. Second, Paul's self-abasement is paired with his hope and desire for a resurrected body, which he invokes throughout his correspondence with the Corinthians. In this he is consistent with his framing of physical bodies that we explored in Philippians. I will chart each of these functions briefly.

Paul's hardships in 4:8–13 are framed by a concern with judgment (4:1–5) and a claim to authority (4:14–21). He opens the chapter with a claim that, as a slave of Christ and slave manager (*oikonomos*) of the mysteries of god (4:1), he cannot be judged by anyone but god (4:4). As a result, the Corinthians ought not pronounce a judgment on him (4:5). It is unclear what precisely Paul might be concerned about here, but what is clear is that he rebuts a potential judgment against him by the Corinthians by emphasizing how much he has suffered for their sake. He has become weak and foolish, he has suffered and gone hungry, he has become refuse, all so that the Corinthians might benefit (4:8–13; cf. 9:19–27).

Paul writes this, he says, as an admonishment from a father to his children (4:14–15). His sufferings show his paternal love for his Corinthian children (*techna*), but they also indicate that he is the paterfamilias, the head of the household. As the patriarchal father, Paul claims he is willing and able to use corporal punishment to enforce discipline within the household, should the Corinthians remain arrogant and ignore his teachings (4:18–21). Moreover, as a role model, he expects the Corinthians to imitate him (4:16).[9] Paul's claims to be refuse, then, are embedded within an argument that turns his (temporary) marginalized position into a claim to authority over others. In contrast with Jacques Ellul's anarchist Paul, the Paul of 1 Corinthians 4 does not attack the masters; he wants to be one.

Just as in Philippians, so too in his letters to the Corinthians Paul contrasts the present state of his humiliated body with his hope and desire for a resurrected one. To take but a few examples, he speaks of the body as that which is wasting away in anticipation of a new body of glory: "So we do not lose heart. Even though our outer nature is wasting away, our inner nature is being renewed day by day. For this slight momentary affliction is preparing us for an eternal weight of glory beyond all measure, because we look not at what can be seen but at what cannot be seen; for what can be seen is temporary, but what cannot be seen is eternal" (2 Cor. 4:16–18, NRSV). Alternatively, Paul can speak of his body as that which is to be swallowed up by life: "For while we are still in this tent, we groan under our burden, because we wish not to be unclothed but to be further clothed, so that what is mortal may be swallowed up by life" (2 Cor 5:4, NRSV). Paul may invoke his status as refuse, but he is at pains to remind us that it is only temporary. A new body and a new life are just around the corner.

Paul is not the only garbage getting thrown out in his letters, though he is the only waste that will be recycled into gold. In 1 Corinthians 5, he urges the Corinthians to expel an unnamed member of the community for sleeping with his father's wife. As Midori Hartman has perceptively argued, Paul dehumanizes the unnamed man by likening him to yeast that must be expelled, lest he leaven the Corinthians (5:6–8).[10] As old yeast, the offender is to be cast out as refuse, handed over to Satan for destruction (5:5), so that the community can remain ritually pure. Later in the same letter, Paul threatens women who pray and prophesy with their heads uncovered: "For if a woman will not cover herself, then let her be shorn like a sheep [*keirasthō*]" (11:6).

Failure to properly veil means that the women, and therefore the whole community, are not protected from sexual assault by angels (4:10).[11] Finally, in his letter to the Galatians, Paul wishes that those who encourage his Gentile audiences to get circumcised would castrate themselves (*apokopsontai*; Gal. 5:12). Paul may be garbage waiting to be recycled, but he actively seeks to expel those who disagree with him (and even parts of their bodies) as waste that cannot be redeemed.

Paul's self-identification with waste that will be recycled and his identification of his opponents as unredeemable waste can be framed by what Jasbir Puar has called homonationalism.[12] Homonationalism names the "*convivial* relations between queernesses and militarism, securitization, war, terrorism, surveillance technologies, empire, torture, nationalism, globalization, fundamentalism, secularism, incarceration, detention, deportation, and neoliberalism."[13] An example of such convivial relationships is the expansion of marriage equality to gay and lesbian couples at the same historical moment that the persecution of LGBTQ+ populations in Middle Eastern countries is cited as a justification for imperial violence. The inclusion of queer couples in the American neoliberal order fuels an American exceptionalism that transfers queerness so as to target "queerly raced bodies for dying."[14] Paul's claims to a kind of queer subjectivity, to being a substance cast out of the social order, shares a convivial relationship with his expectation that the divine will recycle his own body into spiritual glory and trash his opponents'.

To valorize Paul's self-presentation as refuse as a kind of solidarity with the least among us without paying attention to his larger discursive claims of redemption and violence is to participate in scholarship that, as Maia Kotrosits has noted, reinscribes Christian supremacy.[15] While figurations of Paul as one who gives divine sanction to solidarity with the poor and outcast *might* loosen some of the identifications Christians have made with the state, this loosening comes at a cost: "This idealised resistance, this introduction of a space (however small) of ethical supremacy, of a solely negative or superseded relationship to worldly co-optations and sinister social complexities, runs startlingly close to American claims to and desires for innocence and moral purity."[16] Redeeming Paul, on Puar's terms, participates in a kind of "visibility politics" that obscures the tradeoffs, measured in human lives, that come from inclusion in the social order.

COMPOSTING THE REVOLUTION

This brief foray into the refuse in Paul's letters is a reminder that his interesting turns of phrase do not stand in isolation from his larger arguments and assumptions. While his waste enriches the community (so he claims), he actively expels other wastes to keep it pure. Taken as a whole, Paul's archive is replete with material that is not, shall we say, progressive. A good exegete may cut or ignore or work around ethically problematic passages or lines of thought in Paul's archive, all to manufacture a Paul that is salutary for someone's particular political commitments. However, that which is cast aside as garbage gets dumped on others. Because Paul's archive is never literally torn apart or cut up, as were the Gospels in Jefferson's Bible, the passages treated as garbage become what Graham Harman has called "dormant objects."[17] Problematic passages lie dormant in the archive before registering new effects, which are really just aftershocks of their existence.[18] So long as Paul retains his canonical function, what we ignore will be put on others and can always return in force. A path forward is set by those like Nancy Ambrose who have refused to let Paul off the hook for what he said and did (and for what people felt entitled to do in his name) while also doing the inventive and creative work of envisioning other modes of life over which Paul's figure does not hover.

One of the metaphors that I have drawn from in this book is of sitting, like Job on the rubbish heap or the dunghill (2:8) amid his despair and grief and with his three friends. Sitting with and among shit is a metaphor I offer as a space of possibility that is also fraught with risk. For those with privilege, like myself, sitting in the shit is an act of kenosis that can easily slip into the white savior complex, the kind of solidarity that asserts rather than supports, offers answers rather than listens. It may be too much for those of us who don't now have to live in the dump to risk what Karen Bray has called "becoming feces."[19] Further, there is the risk that a valorization of this particular dunghill will conscript it into convivial relations with neoliberal violence, that whatever form of sociality might come from this sitting could lead to harm for others. Attending to the potential harm of a political or theological figuration is the analytical work afforded by Puar's homonationalism or Eve Sedgwick's paranoid reading: be vigilant, historicize everything. Such vigilance is vital and necessary. Protection and survival depend on it.

Yet the price of that vigilance cannot be the loss of surprise, risk, and even hope. Sitting in the garbage carries with it possibilities as well as pitfalls. Sitting itself can be a way to survive, to nurture the self, while also being inefficient. To sit on the toilet is a waste of commodified time, what Elizabeth Freeman calls chrononormativity,[20] in which we do something necessary for survival while also giving ourselves a few moments of peace or reprieve from the pressures of getting by, of sustaining a life in a neoliberal economy intent on using us up. Lauren Berlant calls this a lateral agency, neither resistant nor acquiescent but a momentary stepping to the side to recover a sense of well-being necessary to survive.[21] Cultivating this recuperative relationship to time might provide potentialities not found in the temporal eruptions of Giorgio Agamben's reading of Paul's messianic time.[22]

A garbage heap is not made up of Pauline flesh, awaiting its spiritual body and vengeance on its enemies, but waste that has ceased to be useful to the demand to consume, to buy, to acquire more and more, and in the process be reborn again and again through our consumption. It sits adjacent to capitalism, not fully divorced from its cycles of desire and consumption, but perhaps at enough distance for new forms of life to emerge. Those of us who sit here in the garbage could become catadores making new forms of social life by sifting and sorting and laboring together. We might be like the pickers of matsutake mushrooms who build new economic and collective lives in landscapes of despoliation, where capitalist economies no longer function at scale. We might even become Dakarois garbage workers, who build alliances with not just those who live under the reality and threat of precarity but also the organic vitality of garbage itself.

Might we even risk a universalism of the garbage heap? Waste is not a singular, organic whole: not the Pauline body of believers, where all our diversities are kept together in and made subordinate to a bounded whole (1 Cor. 12). Nor is waste a transcendence of particularity, where there is neither Jew nor Greek, slave nor free, empty Doritos bag nor crushed soda can. Rather, each piece of trash is unique, with its own story of desire used up, of passing from its time of use to its time of waste. Neither a body nor a site of erasure, somehow a dump nonetheless has its own putrid, oozing vitality, a power to sustain fragile communities and economies, an ecosystem hazardous to life yet somehow still alive. Might a trash assemblage offer an alternative to the stable components and positions of intersectional models of identity?[23]

There is no hierarchy in the dung heap or the dump. Garbage neither produces nor desires masters. "To become feces," writes Bray, "is to refuse to identify with those who seek out mastery: mastery over one's own body, mastery over the social body, and mastery over the body politic."[24] As such, partisans of an anarchism that resists capitalism and the state as Jacques Ellul envisions might name their resistance under the figure of refuse. Garbage has a toxic vitality that might stand as a potent image for revolutionary ferment, the "rebel scum" so often invoked by the empire. Refuse is that which must be separated, what cannot be assimilated to the state or to civilization. Control of waste by the state has always been a "fantasy of power," in which humans and their societies perform their domination of nature.[25] To preserve the fiction of state power, refuse must be cast out, sent to the fictional Away; however, that casting out renders it outside surveillance. As Judith Butler has argued, the dung heap is where new resources might be found. In the places where no one wants to go, new vitalities might emerge, like the matsutake mushrooms at Hiroshima. Those who identify as refuse refuse inscription in the state and refuse hierarchy. These refusals thereby make a new space for radical experiments wherein to engage in new points of attack on things as they are. *We are the offscourings of the global order* (kosmos).

A mass of garbage might also reanimate Ward Blanton's desire for a Paulinism for the masses, though this time without Paul. This dream of Blanton's assembles a mess, but a vibrant mess: "peculiarly risky social experimentations"; "unexpectedly and riskily creative openings"; networks that "shift and swerve, opening and closing, folding and unfolding ecological spaces for a time of life immeasurable"; "ephemeral happenings, events, processes as instances of an undying *life*."[26] Blanton hopes for a vibrant collective of humming actants that will animate something bringing the dead to life and standing against the deadening effects of global capitalism. Litter in the street might be a metaphor for conjuring such a politics of fluidity and vibrancy: "Waste is also an orphan object. It can often be found existing somewhere outside of both the free-floating state and entombment, at least for a time . . . Wastes much larger and more dangerous . . . respect no boundaries; they create their own lines of flight and vectors; they spread their fetor far from home, because in truth they have no home, in the same way that all undesired things lack a home."[27] *We are garbage, set free to trouble the lines between here and there; as such, we exert new pressures, new lines of force.*

An *ekklēsia* of refuse might gain force from what Jane Bennett has called "thing-power": "that strange ability of ordinary, man-made items to exceed their status as objects and to manifest traces of independence or aliveness."[28] In her exquisite study of the vibrancy of things, Bennett reflects on her encounter with a glove, some pollen, a dead rat, a bottle cap, and a stick lodged in a grate over a storm drain in Baltimore. This assemblage of trash resonates with a vibrancy for Bennett: "at one moment disclosing themselves as dead stuff and at the next as live presence: junk, then claimant; inert matter, then live wire."[29] This vibrancy calls to her mind the "undying life," to use Blanton's phrase, of garbage dumps, where the mixing of elements produces noxious gases, oozes toxic streams, and feeds parasitic insects, rodents, and bacteria. That which is thrown away and gathered in its diversity can produce new and surprising forms of life. Ultimately, there is a fine line between rotten garbage and life-giving compost, but one vital to traverse. As Achille Mbembe has written, "The durability of the world depends on our capacity to reanimate beings and things that seem lifeless—the dead man, turned to dust by the desiccated economy, an order poor in worldliness that traffics in bodies and life."[30] New collectivities without Paul might traverse that line, strategically repellant and resilient, in the quest for new forms of life and new collectivities. *We are the toxic vitality of the all.*

Finally, Alain Badiou's own theorizing of the event might benefit from sitting in the garbage. Badiou's events appear at sites that are not counted by the powers that be, that are unimaginable within the constellation of things as they seem. Underneath a veneer of permanence and stability, there is always multiplicity, always a chaos ready to throw the existing order out of whack. Badiou's theory of the event presumes that the sites where something new erupts into the now must be generic, emptied of their historical particularity. Difference is fine, so long as it becomes indifferent in the face of the truth of the event.

Might not garbage be that site from which an event might emerge? As Harman has noted, Badiou's theory of the event is anthropocentric. It requires a human subject.[31] But the actants that structure the situation we find ourselves in are not humans alone. As masses of vibrant matter accumulate in dumps, in the atmosphere, and in the oceans, they remain that which we cannot talk about, that which must be ignored for things to keep working as they have been. Capitalism functions so long as we can believe in the fantasy that our waste can go somewhere from which it will not return. These repressed facts are thus potential evental sites, apart from those we have accounted for. The garbage workers of Dakar have figured this out.

And not only that, but these vibrant masses of carbon dioxide, plastics, and toxic sludge, among others, have already transformed the earth itself, such that not even our societies or our politics understand the ground on which we stand. As Catherine Keller has noted, the ecological crisis that we are already in has created a new earth that we will not recognize.[32] Bruno Latour has argued that climate change has already rendered the earth no longer recognizable to our politics of the local or the global.[33] It is our very waste which has made a new heaven and a new earth, just not the one envisioned by Paul in Romans 8 that groans toward the salvation of the cosmos. Might identifying with the refuse that has transfigured the earth reassemble a politics that can land? There is, as Mbembe reminds us, "only one world, at least for now, and that is all there is."[34] In that sense, then, to ally with our garbage, to sit in the refuse, to become shit, might be a way to be faithful to the event. As garbage workers, might we proclaim not the Resurrection of the Christ but the precarity induced by our shit?

Has this crawl through the muck from the first-century toilet we started on been worth it? The old way of reading was so much easier. I could marshal some Greek lexicons and some ancient literary parallels, consult a few commentaries by eminent European men, trudge through a few articles in German and French, maybe even do some quick searches on the library database. Then I'd make Paul say what I needed him to say, what made me feel good. This way is harder. It demands more listening and historicizing, not just of Paul but of everything, even myself, especially myself. Its risks are great. Is it even possible to do this work without reinscribing some evil, causing some harm? Its rewards also seem smaller: mitigation of harm, tentative, risky hope. Whatever might happen, if it even stands a chance, will be a mess of complicities and convivialities, resistances and setbacks, lateral breaks, advances, and retreats. But maybe something new.

ACKNOWLEDGMENTS

This book has come together in fits and starts over many years. It has lived in the interstices of my other writing. It was written and finished in a dark time for many, full of fears, suffering, tragedy, rage. It was inspired by those lights whose brightness could not be hidden by the darkness. Its faults, and they are many, are my own.

The lights along the way were bright indeed. Jennifer Knust and Katherine Shaner, as they so often have, pressed me to think harder and dig deeper. Many of my colleagues at USC have shared their brilliance and expertise along the way, including Sheila Briggs, whom I have been so fortunate to have as a mentor, and Kelsey Moss, Jessica Marglin, Fred Clark, David Albertson, and Mark Letteney, friends (and occasional coconspirators). I have been fortunate to have supportive colleagues in and outside the School of Religion, including Geoff Von Oeyen, Diane Winston, Lisa Bitel, Jim Heft, Duncan Williams, James McHugh, Lynn Swartz Dodd, Arjun Nair, Sherman Jackson, Peter Mancall, and Victoria Perez. Beyond USC, Taylor Foss, Kasper Teichman, Carly Crouch, Christopher Hays, Maia Kotrosits, Ward Blanton, Larry Welborn, Geoff Smith, Taylor Petrey, and Robyn Walsh have been friends, sounding boards, and supports through all that these last few years have thrown at me.

The revisions of this book were aided by a manuscript review sponsored by Dornsife College and organized by Lori Meeks. I am thankful for Lori's tireless organizing efforts and for her friendship. I am thankful as well for the excellent comments, critiques, and advice from the reviewers.

I also want to thank Kathryn Lofton and John Lardas Modern, the editors of the Class 200 series, for their support of this project, as well as Kyle Wagner and Sandra Hazel at the University of Chicago Press. I am deeply indebted to the three external reviewers of my manuscript; their critiques and insights made the book so much better than it would have been otherwise.

Finally, I am deeply grateful to Jill Hicks-Keeton for reading the manuscript (more than once), for attacking my misplaced modifiers, for celebrating with me the highs and lows, for pushing me to be better, and for providing an example of how to be so.

This book is dedicated to my daughters, Éowyn and Scout. If I have any reason to hope in this world, it is because of them. If you ever read this book, girls, I apologize for all the swearing.

NOTES

Except where indicated, all quotations of Bible verses are my own translation.

SEARCHING FOR PAUL IN THE BATHROOM

1. In his important study of the Bible in early modernity, Vincent Wimbush points to how it is not just naïve to believe that the Bible transcends the vagaries of politics: "In point of fact, such an assumption, which aims to make us believe 'religion' is above and beyond the usual dynamics of power relations, is itself the most profound effect of the power dynamics." Wimbush, *White Men's Magic: Scripturalization as Slavery* (Oxford: Oxford University Press, 2012), 111.

2. It is not the case that slavery was universally accepted in Paul's world. Philo of Alexandria tells us that the Jewish sect he knows as the Therapeutae rejected the ownership of slaves as contrary to nature (*De vita contemplativa*, §70).

3. Taubes's seminar was published as Jacob Taubes, *The Political Theology of Paul*, trans. Dana Hollander (Palo Alto, CA: Stanford University Press, 2004); originally published as *Die Politische Theologie des Paulus* (Munich: Wilhelm Fink Verlag, 1993). Stanislas Breton, *A Radical Philosophy of Saint Paul*, trans. Joseph N. Ballan (New York: Columbia University Press, 2011); originally published in French as *Saint Paul* (Paris: Presses universitaires de France, 1988).

4. Ward Blanton has shown that the philosophical engagement with Paul has a much longer history, even if Taubes and Breton can be credited with starting up the conversation anew in particular ways. See his *Displacing Christian Origins: Philosophy, Secularity, and the New Testament* (Chicago: University of Chicago Press, 2007) and *A Materialism for the Masses: Saint Paul and the Philosophy of Undying Life* (New York: Columbia University Press, 2014).

5. Alain Badiou, *Greece and the Reinvention of Politics*, trans. David Broder (London: Verso, 2018), 2–4.

6. See also on this point Jacques Rancière, *Moments Politiques: Interventions 1977–2009* (New York: Seven Stories Press, 2014), 189–202.

7. One of the earliest and best formulations of this project is Neil Elliott's *Liberating Paul: The Justice of God and the Politics of the Apostle* (Maryknoll, NY: Orbis, 1994). For a critical summary and methodological reevaluation of these studies, which are too many to list, see Christoph Heilig, *Hidden Criticism? The Methodology and Plausibility of the Search for a Counter-Imperial Subtext in Paul* (WUNT, 392. Tübingen: Mohr Siebeck, 2015; reprint, Minneapolis: Fortress Press, 2017).

8. I am reflecting here on the work of Elisabeth Schüssler Fiorenza, *Rhetoric and Ethic: The Politics of Biblical Studies* (Minneapolis: Fortress Press, 1999); and Elizabeth A. Castelli, *Imitating Paul: A Discourse of Power* (Louisville, KY: Westminster/John Knox Press, 1991).

9. Clarice J. Martin, "The *Haustafeln* (Household Codes) in African American Biblical Interpretation: 'Free Slaves' and 'Subordinate Women,'" in *Stony the Road We Trod: African American Biblical Interpretation*, ed. Cain Hope Felder (Minneapolis: Fortress Press, 1991), 218–27.

10. Bernadette J. Brooten, "Paul's Views on the Nature of Women and Female Homoeroticism," in *Immaculate and Powerful: The Female in Sacred Image and Social Reality*, ed. Clarissa W. Atkinson, Constance H. Buchanan, and Margaret R. Miles (Boston: Beacon, 1985), 61–87. See also Dale B. Martin, "Heterosexism and the Interpretation of Romans 1:18–32," *Biblical Interpretation* 3 (1995): 332–55; and "*Arsenokoites* and *Malakos*: Meanings and Consequences," in *Biblical Ethics and Homosexuality: Listening to Scripture*, ed. Robert L. Brawley (Louisville, KY: Westminster/John Knox Press, 1996), 115–36.

11. Michel Foucault, "What Is an Author?," in *Language, Counter-Memory, Practice: Selected Essays and Interviews by Michel Foucault*, ed. Donald Bouchard (Ithaca, NY: Cornell University Press, 1977), 113–38.

12. Elizabeth A. Castelli, "The Philosophers' Paul in the Frame of the Global: Some Reflections," *South Atlantic Quarterly* 109, no. 4 (2010): 653–76.

13. Brian Thill, *Waste* (New York: Bloomsbury Academic, 2015), 8. For a similar project linking waste to temporality, see William Varney, *Waste: A Philosophy of Things* (New York: Bloomsbury, 2014).

14. Melanie Johnson-DeBaufre and Laura S. Nasrallah, "Beyond the Heroic Paul: Toward a Feminist and Decolonizing Approach to the Letters of Paul," in *The Colonized Apostle: Paul through Postcolonial Eyes*, ed. Christopher D. Stanley (Minneapolis: Fortress, 2007), 161–74.

15. Timothy Morton, *Hyperobjects: Philosophy and Ecology after the End of the World* (Minneapolis: University of Minnesota Press, 2013), 112.

16. Thill, *Waste*, 28.

17. Zygmunt Bauman, *Wasted Lives: Modernity and Its Outcasts* (Cambridge: Polity, 2004).

18. I do not claim to speak for or to have done justice to all minoritized and marginalized readers and readings of the Pauline archive. My specific focus on garbage and excrement in the Pauline archive has limited the range of scholarly exegetical work to those who have worked particularly on the passages in Philippians and 1 Corinthians where these images occur. For many marginalized communities, Pauline texts have not always been central to their theological and exegetical work. As such, my curation of voices is limited to authors who have directly engaged Paul and his archive.

19. Though they are not the only texts that purport to speak for and about Paul to survive

from antiquity, they are the only ones, along with the canonical Acts of the Apostles, that are treated as canon by contemporary Christians. In addition, they are the only texts used by academic biblical scholars to reconstruct the historical Paul.

20. Kwok Pui-lan, "Discovering the Bible in the Non-biblical World," *Semeia* 47 (1989): 34–35.

21. I describe this process in the present tense because scriptures are not fixed entities but relational constructions that are continually reaffirmed as scriptures. As W. C. Smith has noted, "People—a given community—make a text into scripture, or keep it scripture: by treating it in a certain way. I suggest: *scripture is a human activity.*" Smith, *What Is Scripture? A Comparative Approach* (Minneapolis: Fortress Press, 1993), 18.

22. Most of my academic work on Paul has operated within and adjacent to the processes of producing a Historical Paul.

23. Kwok, "Discovering the Bible," 35–36. A similar point is made by Stanley Fish regarding literary interpretation. Fish shows that there are no limits on what a text can be made to mean, provided the appropriate external conditions are met: *Is There a Text in This Class? The Authority of Interpretive Communities* (Cambridge, MA: Harvard University Press, 1980), 338–55.

24. Wimbush, *White Men's Magic*, 87. He also offers an alternative definition earlier in the book: "Scripturalization should be conceived as a semiosphere, within which a structure of reality is created that produces and legitimates and maintains media of knowing and discourse and the corresponding power relations" (46).

25. Vincent Wimbush, *Scripturalectics: The Management of Meaning* (Oxford: Oxford University Press, 2017), 154.

26. Wimbush, *White Men's Magic*, 231. In this he shows how biblical interpretation is enmeshed within a broader colonial discourse that attempts to render it impossible, as Spivak has so insightfully noted, for the subaltern to speak. Gayatri Chakravorty Spivak, "Can the Subaltern Speak?," in *Colonial Discourse and Postcolonial Theory*, ed. P. Williams and L. Chrisman (New York: Harvester Wheatsheaf, 1993), 66–111.

27. Wimbush, *White Men's Magic*, 231.

28. Kwok, "Discovering the Bible," 35.

29. Elisabeth Schüssler Fiorenza, *Changing Horizons: Explorations in Feminist Interpretations* (Minneapolis: Fortress Press, 2013), 89–100.

30. Schüssler Fiorenza, 99. Schüssler Fiorenza has continuously and vociferously challenged the field to give up on its commitment to "objective" biblical interpretation and orient itself around an ethics of interpretation. See, in particular, *Rhetoric and Ethic* (Minneapolis: Fortress Press, 1999); *Wisdom Ways: Introducing Feminist Biblical Interpretation* (Maryknoll, NY: Orbis, 2001); *The Power of the Word: Scripture and the Rhetoric of Empire* (Minneapolis: Fortress Press, 2007); *Democratizing Biblical Studies: Toward an Emancipatory Educational Space* (Louisville, KY: Westminster John Knox Press, 2009).

31. Denise Kimber Buell, "Canons Unbound," in *Feminist Biblical Studies in the Twentieth Century: Scholarship and Movement*, ed. Elisabeth Schüssler Fiorenza (Atlanta: SBL Press, 2014), 293–306.

32. Wimbush, *White Men's Magic*, 229.

33. Gilles Deleuze, *The Logic of Sense* (New York: Columbia University Press, 1990), 264–65.

34. Wimbush, *White Men's Magic*, 233.

35. Wimbush, 229. Wimbush and Mitzi Smith both analyze Black readers whose mimetic readings of white scriptural logics mirror and reinforce white fundamentalist ideology or the politics of respectability. See Vincent Wimbush, *The Bible and African Americans: A Brief History* (Minneapolis: Fortress Press, 2003), 63–75; Mitzi J. Smith, "Paul, Timothy, and the Respectability Politics of Race: A Womanist Inter(con)textual Reading of Acts 16:1–5," *Religions* 10, no. 3 (2019); open access at https://www.mdpi.com/2077-1444/10/3/190.

36. On this see Andrea Smith, *Unreconciled: From Racial Reconciliation to Racial Justice in Christian Evangelicalism* (Durham, NC: Duke University Press, 2019).

37. Eve Kosofsky Sedgwick, *Touching Feeling: Affect, Pedagogy, Performativity* (Durham, NC: Duke University Press, 2003), 123–51.

38. "Paranoia for all its vaunted suspicion acts as though its work would be accomplished if only it could finally, this time, somehow get its story truly known . . . as though to make something visible as a problem were, if not a mere hop, skip, and jump away from getting it solved, at least self-evidently a step in that direction" (Sedgwick, 138–39).

39. Sedgwick, 128.

40. Jennifer Knust, "Who's Afraid of Canaan's Curse? Genesis 9:18–29 and the Challenge of Reparative Reading," *Biblical Interpretation* 22 (2014): 388–413.

STAYING WITH THE SHIT

1. Giorgio Agamben, *Profanations*, trans. Jeff Fort (New York: Zone Books, 2015), 86.

2. Agamben, 86.

3. Dominique Laporte, *History of Shit*, trans. Nadia Benabid and Rodolphe el-Khoury (Cambridge, MA: MIT Press, 1993).

4. In his essay on waste, Italo Calvino notes that it was in 1884 that Parisians were ordered to use trash cans to dispose of their waste, earning the containers the name *poubelle*, after Monsieur Poubelle, prefect of the Seine who issued the order. Calvino, "La poubelle agréée," in *The Road to San Giovanni*, trans. Tim Parks (Boston: Mariner Books, 2014), 91–126.

5. Laporte, *History of Shit*, 11.

6. Brian Thill, *Waste* (New York: Bloomsbury Academic, 2015), 28–29.

7. Calvino, "La poubelle agréée," 103–4.

8. Thill, *Waste*, 37–51.

9. Laporte, *History of Shit*, 15–16.

10. Suetonius, *Divus Vespasianus* 23 (the story is discussed by Laporte in *History of Shit*, 77–78). Translation slightly amended from J. C. Rolfe, ed., *Suetonius*, Loeb Classical Library (New York: MacMillan, 1914).

11. Laporte, *History of Shit*, 77.

12. Peter Dauvergne, *The Shadows of Consumption: Consequences for the Global Environment* (Cambridge, MA: MIT Press, 2008).

13. Laporte, *History of Shit*, 28, 30–31.

14. Calvino suggests that there remains a public to which his trash is directed once it leaves his private, suburban domicile; that public is symbolized by the trash can, the *poubelle agréée*. The trash's public is defined by the regulations on the shape, color, and size of the can, as well as the schedule of trash pickup. Calvino, "La poubelle agréée," 98.

15. On the Away, see Timothy Morton, *Hyperobjects: Philosophy and Ecology after the End of the World* (Minneapolis: University of Minnesota Press, 2013), 112.

16. Thill, *Waste*, 50.

17. Laporte, *History of Shit*, 32. Subsequent references will be made in the text.

18. Kate O'Neill, *Waste* (Cambridge: Polity, 2019).

19. On the narrative power of ruins, see William Viney, *Waste: A Philosophy of Things* (London: Bloomsbury, 2014), 127–52.

20. James Buzard, "The Grand Tour and After (1660–1840)," in *The Cambridge Companion to Travel Writing*, ed. Peter Hulme and Tim Youngs (Cambridge: Cambridge University Press, 2002), 40–41.

21. Glen W. Bowersock, *From Gibbon to Auden: Essays in the Classical Tradition* (Oxford: Oxford University Press, 2009), 16.

22. Buzard, "Grand Tour," 38.

23. AnneMarie Luijendijk, "Sacred Scriptures as Trash: Biblical Papyri from Oxyrhynchus," *Vigiliae Christianae* 64 (2010): 217–54.

24. On this see Cavan Concannon, "The Archaeology of the Pauline Mission," in *All Things to All Cultures: Paul among Jews, Greeks and Romans*, ed. Mark Harding and Alanna Nobbs (Grand Rapids, MI: Eerdmans, 2013), 57–83.

25. Paul Clemens, *Punching Out: One Year in a Closing Auto Plant* (New York: Anchor Books, 2012), 253.

26. Thill, *Waste*, 74.

27. Thill, 76.

28. Mary Douglas, *Purity and Danger: An Analysis of the Concepts of Pollution and Taboo* (London: Routledge, 2000).

29. Julia Kristeva, *The Powers of Horror: An Essay on Abjection* (New York: Columbia University Press, 1982), 113. On the complicated history of blood in Christianity and capitalism, see Gil Anidjar, *Blood: A Critique of Christianity* (New York: Columbia University Press, 2014).

30. Kristeva, *Powers of Horror*, 118. Subsequent references will be made in the text.

31. Though even some of these can be monetized, as for the company that owns the landfill or the sewage treatment plant that scrubs dangerous effluent from our water.

32. Achille Mbembe, *Critique of Black Reason* (Durham, NC: Duke University Press, 2017), 13. On the plantation as the model for modern capitalism, see Anna Lowenhaupt Tsing, *The Mushroom at the End of the World: On the Possibility of Life in Capitalist Ruins* (Princeton, NJ: Princeton University Press, 2015), 38–40.

33. Ta-Nehisi Coates, *Between the World and Me* (New York: Spiegel and Grau, 2015), 103–4.

34. Coates, 103.

35. On Paul's Platonist binaries, see Daniel Boyarin, *A Radical Jew: Paul and the Politics of Identity* (Berkeley: University of California Press, 1994).

36. Michel Foucault, *The History of Sexuality*, vol. 1: *An Introduction* (New York: Vintage Books, 1980), 133–60; Michel Foucault, *The Birth of Biopolitics: Lectures at the Collège de France, 1978–1979* (New York: Picador, 2004); Giorgio Agamben, *Homo Sacer: Sovereign Power and Bare Life*, Meridian: Crossing Aesthetics (Palo Alto, CA: Stanford University Press, 1998).

37. Alexander Weheliye, *Habeas Viscus: Racializing Assemblages, Biopolitics, and Black Feminist Theories of the Human* (Durham, NC: Duke University Press, 2014).

38. Kathryn Yusoff, *A Billion Black Anthropocenes or None* (Minneapolis: University of Minnesota Press, 2018), 14–15.

39. Achille Mbembe, *Necropolitics* (Durham, NC: Duke University Press, 2019), 170.

40. Yusoff, *Billion Black Anthropocenes*, 5–6.

41. Orlando Patterson, *Slavery and Social Death: A Comparative Study* (Cambridge, MA: Harvard University Press, 1982).

42. Mbembe, *Critique of Black Reason*, 33–36.

43. Katharine Gerbner, *Christian Slavery: Conversion and Race in the Protestant Atlantic World* (Philadelphia: University of Pennsylvania Press, 2018).

44. Cited in Gerbner, 189.

45. Gerbner, 193–96.

46. Coates, *Between the World and Me*, 71.

47. Mbembe, *Critique of Black Reason*, 36–37.

48. Judith Butler, *Frames of War: When Is Life Grievable?* (New York: Verso, 2010), xiii.

49. Butler, 10. Latour also makes reference to the need to offer a mobile frame: "But as soon as things accelerate, innovations proliferate, and entities are multiplied, one then has an absolutist framework generating data that becomes hopelessly messed up. This is when a relativistic solution has to be devised in order to remain able to move between frames of reference and to regain some sort of commensurability between traces coming from frames traveling at very different speeds and acceleration." Bruno Latour, *Reassembling the Social: An Introduction to Actor-Network Theory* (Oxford: Oxford University Press, 2007), 12.

50. Karen Bray, "Becoming Feces: New Materialism and the Deep Solidarity in Feeling Like Shit," in *Religious Experience and New Materialism: Movement Matters*, ed. Joerg Rieger and Edward Waggoner (New York: Palgrave Macmillan, 2016), 105–33.

51. Bray, 111.

52. Bray, 111–12.

53. Tsing, *Mushroom at the End*, 3.

54. Tsing, 3–4.

55. Tsing, viii.

INTERLUDE: FEELING LIKE SHIT

1. Donovan Schaefer, *Religious Affects: Animality, Evolution, and Power* (Durham, NC: Duke University Press, 2015), 31.

2. Silvan Tomkins, *Affect, Imagery, Consciousness: The Complete Edition* (New York: Springer, 2008), 359.

3. Elspeth Probyn, "Writing Shame," in *The Affect Theory Reader*, ed. Melissa Gregg and Gregory J. Seigworth (Durham, NC: Duke University Press, 2010), 81.

4. Probyn, 82.

5. Ta-Nehisi Coates, *Between the World and Me* (New York: Spiegel and Grau, 2015), 9.

6. Frantz Fanon, *Black Skin, White Masks* (London: Pluto Press, 2008), 2.

7. Fanon, 5.

8. Probyn, "Writing Shame," 84.

9. Alexander Weheliye, *Habeas Viscus: Racializing Assemblages, Biopolitics, and Black Feminist Theories of the Human* (Durham, NC: Duke University Press, 2014), 14.

10. Eve Kosofsky Sedgwick, *Touching Feeling: Affect, Pedagogy, Performativity* (Durham, NC: Duke University Press, 2003), 62–63.

THE BIBLE DOESN'T SMELL

1. Alice Back and Jennifer Glancy, "The Morning After in Corinth: Bread-and-Butter Notes, Part 1," *Biblical Interpretation* 11, no. 3/4 (2003): 449–67; Dale B. Martin, *The Corinthian Body* (New Haven, CT: Yale University Press, 1995), 190–97. The *pharmakon* as poison and cure was central for Derrida's reading of Plato in his essay "Plato's Pharmacy." Jacques Derrida, *Dissemination* (Chicago: University of Chicago Press, 1981), 65–171.

2. See, for example, Albert Schweitzer's classic history of Pauline scholarship, *Paul and His Interpreters: A Critical History* (New York: Schocken, 1964), first published in German in 1911. An excellent exception to this is Robert Paul Seesengood's *Paul: A Brief History* (Malden, MA: Wiley-Blackwell, 2010).

3. On the history of the Bible in European colonialism, see R. S. Sugirtharajah, *The Bible and the Third World: Precolonial, Colonial and Postcolonial Encounters* (Cambridge: Cambridge University Press, 2004).

4. Some colonial missionaries, such as Bartolomé de Las Casas and John Colenso, offered ambivalent dissents from colonial management, using biblical texts to resist the cruelties of colonialism while supporting the idea of a benevolent, Christian missional colonial ideal. See R. S. Sugirtharajah, *Postcolonial Criticism and Biblical Interpretation* (Oxford: Oxford University Press, 2002), 44–52; and Willie James Jennings, *The Christian Imagination: Theology and the Origins of Race* (New Haven, CT: Yale University Press, 2010), 119–68.

5. Tomoko Masuzawa, *The Invention of World Religions, or How European Universalism Was Preserved in the Language of Pluralism* (Chicago: University of Chicago Press, 2005); Brent Nongbri, *Before Religion: A History of a Modern Concept* (New Haven, CT: Yale University Press, 2013).

6. Vincent Wimbush, *White Men's Magic: Scripturalization as Slavery* (Oxford: Oxford University Press, 2012), 91. On the formation of European national identity through

religious and ethnic violence, see Anthony W. Marx, *Faith in Nation: Exclusionary Origins of Nationalism* (Oxford: Oxford University Press, 2003).

7. Robert Allen Warrior, "Canaanites, Cowboys, and Indians: Deliverance, Conquest, and Liberation Theology Today," *Christianity and Crisis* 49, no. 12 (1989): 261–65; Wimbush, *White Men's Magic*, 74–83; R. S. Sugirtharajah, *Exploring Postcolonial Biblical Criticism: History, Method, Practice* (Malden, MA: Wiley-Blackwell, 2012), 39–42; Bruno Latour, *On the Modern Cult of the Factish Gods* (Durham, NC: Duke University Press, 2010), 1–65.

8. Katie Geneva Cannon, "Slave Ideology and Biblical Interpretation," *Semeia* 47 (1989): 9–24.

9. Seesengood, *Paul*, 165–82.

10. On this see Shawn Kelley, *Racializing Jesus: Race, Ideology, and the Formation of Modern Biblical Scholarship* (London: Routledge, 2002).

11. Stephen Moore and Yvonne Sherwood, *The Invention of the Biblical Scholar: A Critical Manifesto* (Minneapolis: Fortress Press, 2011), 46–82.

12. Moore and Sherwood, 49–58.

13. Moore and Sherwood, 58.

14. Jonathan Sheehan, *The Enlightenment Bible: Translation, Scholarship, Culture* (Princeton, NJ: Princeton University Press, 2005).

15. "This reconstitution was first conjured up by a host of scholars and literati who together forged a model of biblical authority that could endure a post-theological era. . . . Enlightenment scholars first made available a version of Biblical authority that could and would compete with the grinding effects of skepticism" (Sheehan, xi).

16. Peter Manseau, *The Jefferson Bible: A Biography* (Princeton, NJ: Princeton University Press, 2020).

17. Robyn Faith Walsh, *The Origins of Early Christian Literature: Contextualizing the New Testament within Greco-Roman Literary Culture* (Cambridge: Cambridge University Press, 2021), 1. My thanks to the author for pointing me to this quotation from Jefferson.

18. Moore and Sherwood, *Biblical Scholar*, 58–59. This is not to say that there were not fierce debates over whether one could question the historical accuracy of the Bible. Biblical scholars like David Friedrich Strauss became pariahs for their use of the new tools of what was called German Higher Criticism, while others, like William Robertson Smith, were charged with heresy for their work.

19. Historicism achieved this bait and switch by changing the subject: "The challenge to theological authority could be blunted by sidelining both the theological and the ethical in favor of the historical. . . . The removal of the theological as the target of critical inquiry ensured that [the biblical scholar] could be both a skeptic and a believer at one and the same time. It became possible to be at once Christian and 'modern,' theologically orthodox yet simultaneously skeptical of the Bible's historicity—though a complex series of markers were set in place to regulate how far one might push one's skepticism" (Moore and Sherwood, 61).

20. Moore and Sherwood, 63.

21. Zygmunt Bauman, *Wasted Lives: Modernity and Its Outcasts* (Cambridge: Polity, 2004), 20–22.

22. Bauman, 21.

23. Kathryn Yusoff, *A Billion Black Anthropocenes or None* (Minneapolis: University of Minnesota Press, 2018).

24. See the important early work on whiteness by Richard Dyer, *White* (London: Routledge, 1997), and Ruth Frankenberg, *Displacing Whiteness: Essays in Social and Cultural Criticism* (Durham, NC: Duke University Press, 1997). On the history of race as a theological project, see J. Kameron Carter, *Race: A Theological Account* (Oxford: Oxford University Press, 2008).

25. Kwok Pui-lan, *Postcolonial Imagination and Feminist Theology* (Louisville, KY: Westminster John Knox Press, 2005), 172. See also Kwok Pui-lan, "Jesus/the Native: Biblical Studies from a Postcolonial Perspective," in *Teaching the Bible: The Discourses and Politics of Biblical Pedagogy*, ed. Fernando Segovia and Mary Ann Talbert (Maryknoll, NY: Orbis, 1998), 69–85. See also Tat-Siong Benny Liew, *What Is Asian-American Biblical Hermeneutics? Reading the New Testament* (Honolulu: University of Hawai'i Press, 2008).

26. Fernando Segovia, *Decolonizing Biblical Studies: A View from the Margins* (Maryknoll, NY: Orbis, 2000), 30–31.

27. As she writes, "The African American female reader of the Bible has, like other women, been taught to suspend her female identity long enough to see the world through the eyes and ears of the male narrator. Failing that, she is expected to agree to become the male reader/audience for whom the text was originally written." Renita Weems, "Reading *Her Way* through the Struggle: African American Women and the Bible," in *Stony the Road We Trod: African American Biblical Interpretation*, ed. Cain Hope Felder (Minneapolis: Fortress Press, 1991), 66.

28. David Horrell, "Paul, Inclusion and Whiteness: Particularizing Interpretation," *JSNT* 40, no. 2 (2017): 130–32.

29. Blossom Stefaniw, drawing from Cheryl Harris's notion of whiteness as property, has argued that maleness is property and commodity within the patriarchal structures governing the study of early Christianity and the Bible. Stefaniw, "Feminist Historiography and Uses of the Past," *Studies in Late Antiquity* 4, no. 3 (2020): 269–71. For Harris's work on whiteness, see her "Whiteness as Property," in *Critical Race Theory: The Key Writings that Formed the Movement*, ed. Kimberlé Crenshaw et al. (New York: New Press, 1995), 276–91.

30. Bauman, *Wasted Lives*, 21.

31. Eric C. Smith, *Paul the Progressive? The Compassionate Christian's Guide to Reclaiming the Apostle as an Ally* (St. Louis: Chalice Press, 2019). Subsequent references will be made in the text.

32. Jennifer Glancy, *Slavery in Early Christianity* (Oxford: Oxford University Press, 2002), 92–96. See also Keith R. Bradley, *Slaves and Masters in the Roman Empire: A Study in Social Control* (Oxford: Oxford University Press, 1987).

33. Joseph A. Marchal, "Pinkwashing Paul, Excepting Jesus: The Politics of Intersectionality, Identification, and Respectability," in *The Bible and Feminism: Remapping the Field*, ed. Yvonne Sherwood (Oxford: Oxford University Press, 2018), 433.

34. Stefaniw, "Feminist Historiography," 262.

35. Moore and Sherwood, *Biblical Scholar*, 101–15.

36. Sugirtharajah, *Postcolonial Criticism*, 114. Sugirtharajah sees this among liberation theologians, whom he also suggests have largely operated within modern Western notions of liberal political frameworks. Moore and Sherwood apply this critique to literary critics like Terry Eagleton and biblical scholars using reader-response methods (*Biblical Scholar*, 116–17).

37. Moore and Sherwood, *Biblical Scholar*, 98.

38. Brittney Cooper has noted that politics of respectability have disproportionately harmed Black women. *Eloquent Rage: A Black Feminist Discovers Her Superpower* (New York: Picador, 2018), 119.

39. Moore and Sherwood, *Biblical Scholar*, 123.

40. Marchal, "Pinkwashing Paul," 438–43; Cynthia Briggs Kittredge, "Feminist Approaches: Rethinking History and Resisting Ideologies," in *Studying Paul's Letters: Contemporary Perspectives and Methods*, ed. Joseph A. Marchal (Minneapolis: Fortress Press, 2012), 117–33.

41. Moore and Sherwood, *Biblical Scholar*, 118.

42. Stefaniw, "Feminist Historiography," 263. Stefaniw draws here from work done by critical race theorists to diagnose the pathologies of the field. On this see Kimberlé Crenshaw, Neil Gotanda, Gary Peller, and Kendall Thomas, eds., *Critical Race Theory: The Key Writings That Formed the Movement* (New York: New Press, 1995).

43. Stefaniw, "Feminist Historiography," 266–68.

44. Nyasha Junior has noted the lack of womanist biblical scholars trained in academic institutions as a hindrance to the advancement of the movement. *An Introduction to Womanist Biblical Interpretation* (Louisville, KY: Westminster John Knox Press, 2015), 95–121. Vincent Wimbush has narrated the complex pathways by which he navigated the largely white domains of graduate school and the professional guild. *White Men's Magic*, 1–11; *Scripturalectics: The Management of Meaning* (Oxford: Oxford University Press, 2017), 4–20.

45. Ellen Muehlberger has catalogued the gender and racial balance of the major journal for the study of early Christianity (the *Journal of Early Christian Studies*) for several years, noting a persistent imbalance toward white male scholars (https://drive.google.com/drive/folders/0By8n-khx7eUOakcyX2VCeEhURms; accessed February 25, 2021).

46. Stefaniw, "Feminist Historiography," 261.

47. Moore and Sherwood, *Biblical Scholar*, 120–22. Subsequent references will be given in the text.

48. Vincent Wimbush's recentering of biblical studies on the history of contact, slavery, and empire in the Black Atlantic shows the value of excavation in transforming the field. See his *White Men's Magic* and *Scripturalectics*. We can also see this program worked out in Wimbush's edited volumes on the category of scripture more broadly. See, for example, *MisReading America: Scriptures and Difference* (Oxford: Oxford University Press, 2013) and *Theorizing Scriptures: New Critical Orientations to a Cultural Phenomenon* (New Brunswick, NJ: Rutgers University Press, 2008).

49. For an important interrogation of the tendency to see philosophical readings of Paul as insufficiently historical, see Paula Fredriksen, "Historical Integrity, Interpretive Free-

dom: The Philosopher's Paul and the Problem of Anachronism," in *St. Paul among the Philosophers*, ed. John D. Caputo and Linda Martin Alcoff (Bloomington: University of Indiana Press, 2009), 61–73.

50. Simon Critchley, *The Faith of the Faithless: Experiments in Political Theology* (New York: Verso, 2012), 155–57.

51. On the necessity of a feminist analysis that both critiques and builds new counternarratives, see Stefaniw, "Feminist Historiography," 280–81.

52. Antoinette Clark Wire, *The Corinthian Women Prophets: A Reconstruction through Paul's Rhetoric* (Minneapolis: Fortress Press, 1990); Elisabeth Schüssler Fiorenza, *In Memory of Her: A Feminist Theological Reconstruction of Christian Origins* (New York: Crossroad, 1994); Elisabeth Schüssler Fiorenza, *Rhetoric and Ethic: The Politics of Biblical Studies* (Minneapolis: Fortress Press, 1999); Elizabeth A. Castelli, *Imitating Paul: A Discourse of Power* (Louisville, KY: Westminster/John Knox Press, 1991).

53. Schüssler Fiorenza, *Rhetoric and Ethic*, ix.

54. Kittredge, "Feminist Approaches"; Sugirtharajah, *Postcolonial Criticism*, 25–30; Joseph A. Marchal, "Queer Studies and Critical Masculinity Studies in Feminist Biblical Studies," in *Feminist Biblical Studies in the Twentieth Century: Scholarship and Movement*, ed. Elisabeth Schüssler Fiorenza (Atlanta: SBL Press, 2014), 261–80; Joseph A. Marchal, *The Politics of Heaven: Women, Gender, and Empire in the Study of Paul* (Minneapolis: Fortress Press, 2008); Wilda C. Gafney, *Womanist Midrash: A Reintroduction to the Women of the Torah and the Throne* (Louisville, KY: Westminster John Knox Press, 2017), 2–9.

55. See, for example, Musa Dube's critique of Elisabeth Schüssler Fiorenza in her *Postcolonial Feminist Interpretation of the Bible* (St. Louis: Chalice Press, 2000), 26–39. Schüssler Fiorenza's later work has expanded to meet this challenge of a more thoroughgoing analysis of what she has called "kyriarchy." See, for example, *The Power of the Word: Scripture and the Rhetoric of Empire* (Minneapolis: Fortress Press, 2007).

56. Schüssler Fiorenza, *Rhetoric and Ethic*, 14. The idea of biblical scholars as public health workers was first suggested by Krister Stendahl, "Ancient Scripture in the Modern World," in *Scripture in the Jewish and Christian Traditions: Authority, Interpretation, Relevance*, ed. Frederick E. Greenspahn (Nashville: Abingdon Press, 1982), 204.

INTERLUDE: OWNING MY SHIT

1. Gustav Adolf Deissmann, *Light from the Ancient East: The New Testament Illustrated by Recently Discovered Texts of the Graeco-Roman World* (London: Hodder and Stoughton, 1910).

2. While many books and articles have been written on this topic since then, I remember reading John Boswell, *Christianity, Social Tolerance, and Homosexuality: Gay People in Western Europe from the Beginning of the Christian Era to the Fourteenth Century* (Chicago: University of Chicago Press, 1980); Robin Scroggs, *The New Testament and*

Homosexuality: Contextual Background for Contemporary Debate (Philadelphia: Fortress Press, 1983); and Jeffrey Siker, ed., *Homosexuality in the Church: Both Sides of the
Debate* (Louisville, KY: Westminster/John Knox Press, 1994).

3. See, for example, Eric C. Smith, *Paul the Progressive? The Compassionate Christian's
    Guide to Reclaiming the Apostle as an Ally* (St. Louis: Chalice Press, 2019), 36–55.

4. Michel Foucault, *The History of Sexuality*, vol. 1: *An Introduction* (New York: Vintage
    Books, 1980), 6.

REDEEMING PAUL

1. Kathleen Millar, *Reclaiming the Discarded: Life and Labor on Rio's Garbage Dump* (Dur-
    ham, NC: Duke University Press, 2018).

2. Millar, 9.

3. Anna Lowenhaupt Tsing, *The Mushroom at the End of the World: On the Possibility of
    Life in Capitalist Ruins* (Princeton, NJ: Princeton University Press, 2015).

4. Jacob Taubes, *The Political Theology of Paul*, trans. Dana Hollander (Palo Alto, CA:
    Stanford University Press, 2004); originally published as *Die Politische Theologie des
    Paulus* (München: Wilhelm Fink Verlag, 1993). On Taubes's reading of Paul, see Eliza-
    beth A. Castelli, "The Philosophers' Paul in the Frame of the Global: Some Reflections,"
    South Atlantic Quarterly 109, no. 4 (2010): 655–60.

5. Carl Schmitt, *Political Theology: Four Chapters on the Concept of Sovereignty*, trans.
    George Schwab (Chicago: University of Chicago Press, 2005). On Benjamin's
    "Theological-Political Fragment," see Taubes, *Political Theology of Paul*, 70–76.

6. Dieter Georgi, *Theocracy in Paul's Praxis and Theology* (Philadelphia: Fortress Press,
    1991); Daniel Boyarin, *A Radical Jew: Paul and the Politics of Identity* (Berkeley: Uni-
    versity of California Press, 1994); L. L. Welborn, *Paul's Summons to Messianic Life:
    Political Theology and the Coming Awakening* (New York: Columbia University Press,
    2015); Giorgio Agamben, *The Time That Remains: A Commentary on the Letter to the
    Romans*, trans. Patricia Dailey (Palo Alto, CA: Stanford University Press, 2005).

7. Quotations follow Jacques Ellul, *Anarchy and Christianity*, trans. Geoffrey Bromiley
    (Grand Rapids, MI: Eerdmans, 1991); originally published as *Anarchie et Christianisme*
    (Lyon: Atelier de creation libertaire, 1988). Subsequent references will be made in the
    text.

8. On the concept of realized eschatology, see C. H. Dodd, *The Apostolic Preaching and Its
    Developments* (New York: Harper and Brothers, 1949), 79–96.

9. Here Ellul comes close to Taubes's reading of Romans 13 (*Political Theology of Paul*, 54).

10. I have similar concerns about the use of Paul's "as if not" by Agamben, *Time That
    Remains*, 41–43.

11. Clarice J. Martin, "The *Haustafeln* (Household Codes) in African American Biblical
    Interpretation: 'Free Slaves' and 'Subordinate Women,'" in *Stony the Road We Trod:
    African American Biblical Interpretation*, ed. Cain Hope Felder (Minneapolis: Fortress
    Press, 1991), 206–31. This tendency has a long history, visible in the narrative of Solo-

mon Bayley, a former slave, who argued that the Bible was against slavery but enjoined female submission to male authority. Emerson Powery and Rodney Sadler Jr., *The Genesis of Liberation: Biblical Interpretation in the Antebellum Narratives of the Enslaved* (Louisville, KY: Westminster John Knox Press, 2016), 135.

12. Martin, *"Haustafeln,"* 228.

13. Alain Badiou, *Saint Paul: The Foundation of Universalism*, trans. Ray Brassier (Palo Alto, CA: Stanford University Press, 2003).

14. Stanislas Breton, *A Radical Philosophy of Saint Paul*, trans. Joseph N. Ballan (New York: Columbia University Press, 2011), originally published in French as *Saint Paul* (Paris: Presses universitaires de France, 1988); Slavoj Žižek, *The Ticklish Subject: The Absent Centre of Political Ontology* (London: Verso, 1999); Slavoj Žižek, *The Fragile Absolute, or Why Is the Christian Legacy Worth Fighting For?* (New York: Verso, 2001); Slavoj Žižek, *The Puppet and the Dwarf: The Perverse Core of Christianity*, Short Circuits (Cambridge, MA: MIT Press, 2003). Other philosophers who have engaged Paul in the wake of these larger engagements include Simon Critchley, *The Faith of the Faithless: Experiments in Political Theology* (London: Verso, 2012), 155–206; Roberto Esposito, *Immunitas: The Protection and Negation of Life*, trans. Zakiya Hanafi (Cambridge: Polity Press, 2011); Roberto Esposito, *Living Thought: The Origins and Actuality of Italian Philosophy*, trans. Zakiya Hanafi (Palo Alto, CA: Stanford University Press, 2012); Clayton Crockett, *Radical Political Theology: Religion and Politics after Liberalism* (New York: Columbia University Press, 2013). See the important edited collection by Ward Blanton and Hent de Vries: *Paul and the Philosophers* (New York: Fordham University Press, 2013).

15. Badiou, *Saint Paul*, 2. This is not all that dissimilar from Blanton's position (see below), except that Badiou is quite clear that this move is thoroughly subjective ("subjective through and through" [2]).

16. Badiou, 2.

17. The fragment is preserved in Clement of Alexandria, *Stromateis* 3.59.3. The translation is from Bentley Layton, *The Gnostic Scriptures* (New York: Doubleday 1987), 239.

18. On the theory of the event, see Alain Badiou, *Being and Event*, trans. Oliver Feltham (New York: Bloomsbury, 2013). Subsequent references will be made in the text. Badiou schematizes the theory in the context of ethics in his *Ethics: An Essay on the Understanding of Evil*, trans. Peter Hallward (New York: Verso, 2001).

19. Ian James, *The New French Philosophy* (Cambridge: Polity Press, 2012), 144.

20. Joerg Rieger and Kwok Pui-lan, *Occupy Religion: Theology of the Multitude* (Lanham, MD: Rowman and Littlefield, 2012).

21. Badiou, *Saint Paul*, 1. While Badiou claims to come at Paul with a sort of secular distance, he is not immune from the effect of Paul's canonicity in the heart of the Western theological and philosophical tradition. As justification for taking up an ancient theologian, Badiou invokes other philosophers who have been forced to grapple with Paul ("found it necessary . . . always in terms of some extreme disposition" [5]): Hegel, Auguste Comte, Nietzsche, Freud, Heidegger, and Lyotard. Badiou's use of Paul is conditioned by his acceptance, not just as canon, but as a timeless classic of the Western canon.

22. Castelli, *"The Philosophers' Paul,"* 661.

23. Badiou, *Saint Paul*, 36. Subsequent references will be made in the text. Badiou credits this sense of Paul's universal legibility to Pier Paolo Pasolini (see below), but it ultimately reflects a philosophical project that locates Truth Platonically in that which can be stripped of all its historical particularity.

24. This procedure involves the articulation of a connection between the subject and the law: "Let us say that, for Paul, it is a matter of investigating which law is capable of structuring a subject devoid of all identity and suspended to an event whose only 'proof' lies precisely in its having been declared by a subject" (Badiou, *Saint Paul*, 5).

25. Badiou surprisingly trades on Paul's biography as conforming to an idealized model of the militant leader. In his chapter "Who Is Paul?," he largely follows the outline of Paul's biography in the canonical Acts, though he draws attention to the legendary aspects of Luke's narrative (*Saint Paul*, 18, 30). Badiou glosses Paul's biography in such a way that it coheres with an unstated model for proper militant behavior. The specifics of Paul's life, it seems, do matter after all. Paul's biography is made to mirror the core theological/philosophical beliefs that his interpreters ascribe to him: his actions, as narrated by the author of Acts, are in sync with what he writes about. The assumption in both cases seems to be that there need be a parity between thought and practice, and that Paul's actions as recorded in his letters or in Acts are consistent with his theological/philosophical commitments. Badiou further reinforces the importance of the form of Paul's life by using it as the basis for his play *The Incident at Antioch: A Tragedy in Three Acts*, trans. Susan Spitzer (New York: Columbia University Press, 2013) and by his valorization of Pasolini's retelling of Paul's life in his unproduced screenplay (*Saint Paul*, 36–39).

26. Badiou is clearly aware of Lyotard's reading of Paul and his valorization of the decipherment of signs, even as he rejects this as a valid position.

27. The event is not a mediation from one form of being to another, nor is it a form of proof that underwrites some set of ideas or beliefs; rather, the event is a rupture that puts language and reason into a deadlock and a radical break that brings nonbeings into being as a "pure beginning" (Badiou, *Saint Paul*, 46–49).

28. Badiou recycles this line of argument by reconfiguring the three discourses as verbs: to demand (Jewish), to question (Greek), and to declare (Christian). Ultimately, it is only through declaration that one avoids the mastery of the other two discourses (*Saint Paul*, 59). For Badiou, the filiation of the discourse of the Son is what allows for the eventful declaration to work universally, in that it makes all into "co-workers of God" (1 Cor. 3:9) and not disciples (*Saint Paul*, 60). The effect that Badiou seeks to create is that of a figure of authority that is not traditionally authoritative; however, what Badiou achieves is mere transposition through secularization.

29. Daniel Boyarin, "Paul among the Antiphilosophers; or, Saul among the Sophists," in *St. Paul among the Philosophers*, ed. John D. Caputo and Linda Martin Alcoff (Bloomington: Indiana University Press, 2009), 132.

30. Beyond the question of ethnic difference, Ben Dunning has offered a brilliant and persuasive reading of how Badiou's marginalization of his own fourth discourse (the mystical) is connected to a larger problem with how sexual difference is treated in the reception of Paul by philosophers like Badiou. Benjamin Dunning, *Christ without*

Adam: Subjectivity and Sexual Difference in the Philosophers' Paul (New York: Columbia University Press, 2014), 39–64.

31. Elizabeth A. Castelli, "Interpretations of Power in 1 Corinthians," *Semeia* 54 (1992): 199–222. See also Castelli's *Imitating Paul: A Discourse of Power* (Louisville, KY: Westminster/John Knox Press, 1991).

32. Castelli also notes how Badiou recycles Christian supersessionism in his reuse of the figures of Jew, Gentile, and Christian ("The Philosophers' Paul," 663).

33. Alain Badiou, *Being and Event*, trans. Oliver Feltham (New York: Continuum, 2005), 1–20.

34. Neil Elliott, "Ideological Closure in the Christ-Event: A Marxist Response to Alain Badiou's Paul," in *Paul, Philosophy, and the Theopolitical Vision: Critical Engagements with Agamben, Badiou, Žižek, and Others*, ed. Douglas Harink (Eugene, OR: Cascade Books, 2010), 149–50.

35. L. L. Welborn, "'Extraction from the Mortal Site': Badiou on the Resurrection in Paul," *New Testament Studies* 55 (2009): 295–314.

36. Welborn, 310.

37. For a similar observation of the absence of attention to the cross and to structural militancy, see Elliott, "Ideological Closure," 150–54.

38. Sigmund Freud, *Moses and Monotheism* (New York: Vintage, 1939).

39. See further Jan Assmann, *Moses the Egyptian: The Memory of Egypt in Western Monotheism* (Cambridge, MA: Harvard University Press, 1998).

40. Ward Blanton, *Displacing Christian Origins: Philosophy, Secularity, and the New Testament* (Chicago: University of Chicago Press, 2007). See also Ward Blanton and Hent De Vries, eds., *Paul and the Philosophers* (New York: Fordham University Press, 2013).

41. Ward Blanton, *A Materialism for the Masses: Saint Paul and the Philosophy of Undying Life* (New York: Columbia University Press, 2014). Subsequent references will be made in the text.

42. "The force of the new, the real (counter?) 'revolution' of Christianity appears in the desire of predominantly Gentile members of a complexly diffuse Jewish collective to distance themselves from the more problematically anti-imperial elements of the movement itself" (Blanton, *Materialism for the Masses*, 33). Elsewhere Blanton argues, "Christian origins stories of the sort we begin to see in Acts always had a great deal more to do with negotiating the ideological aftermath of *this* colonial rebellion and its rapaciously brutal repressions than it ever did with the natural outworking of distinct and distinctly ideal identities, projects, or theologies" (29).

43. For discussions of the New Perspective and its legacies, see John G. Gager, *Reinventing Paul* (New York: Oxford University Press, 2000); Caroline E. Johnson Hodge, *If Sons, Then Heirs: A Study of Kinship and Ethnicity in the Letters of Paul* (New York: Oxford University Press, 2007), 7–9; Magnus Zetterholm, *Approaches to Paul: A Student's Guide to Recent Scholarship* (Minneapolis: Fortress Press, 2009), 95–164.

44. The most thorough Stoicizing of Paul can be found in the work of Troels Engberg-Pedersen, *Cosmology and Self in the Apostle Paul: The Material Spirit* (Oxford: Oxford University Press, 2011), and *Paul and the Stoics* (Louisville, KY: Westminster John Knox Press, 2000).

45. "Still, to think such things by way of a comparative touchstone always transforms our thinking of the present in unexpected ways and with important effects. The Pauline past will not be extricable, finally, from our biopolitical and posthuman futures" (Blanton, *Materialism for the Masses*, 6).

SPLITTING PAUL

1. Pier Paolo Pasolini, *Saint Paul: A Screenplay*, trans. and introduced by Elizabeth A. Castelli (New York: Verso, 2014).
2. Pasolini, 3.
3. Pasolini, 5.
4. The basic plan for the film is sketched in Pasolini, 6-10.
5. Elizabeth A. Castelli, "Introduction: Translating Pasolini Translating Paul," in Pasolini, *Saint Paul*, xli.
6. Alain Badiou, *Saint Paul: The Foundation of Universalism*, trans. Ray Brassier (Palo Alto, CA: Stanford University Press, 2003), 36-39.
7. Pasolini, *Saint Paul*, 3-4.
8. Giorgio Agamben, *The Time That Remains: A Commentary on the Letter to the Romans*, trans. Patricia Dailey (Palo Alto, CA: Stanford University Press, 2005), 145.
9. Pasolini, *Saint Paul*, 62.
10. Pasolini, 65.
11. Pier Paolo Pasolini, *San Paulo*, typescript of various drafts, May–June 1968 (Rome: Biblioteca Nazionale, Dono Eredi Pasolini 1977/80), V.E. 1563 / 1$^{1-11}$-3, p. 14; cited and translated by Castelli, "Introduction," xxxviii.
12. Gideon Bachmann, "La Perdita della realtà e il cinema inintegrabile: Conversazione di Pier Paolo Pasolini con Gideon Bachmann; Chia (Viterbo), 13 settembre 1974," in *Pier Paolo Pasolini: Il cinema in forma di poesia*, ed. Luciano De Giusti (Pordenone: Cinemazero, 1979), 156-57; cited and translated by Castelli, "Introduction," xxxix-xl.
13. In 1963 Pasolini was actually convicted of disrespecting the Catholicism of the Italian state for his short film *La Ricotta*, which narrates the making of a film about the Passion of Jesus by a Marxist director (played by Orson Welles).
14. Pasolini, letter to Don Emilio Cordero, June 9, 1968, cited and translated by Castelli, "Introduction," xvii.
15. Castelli, xx.
16. Recently, George Aichele, Theodore Jennings, and Jay Twomey have analyzed the split character of Pasolini's Paul. See George Aichele, "Pasolini's Pauls," *Biblical Interpretation* 27 (2019): 496-506; Theodore Jennings, "Pasolini's Specters of Paul," *Biblical Interpretation* 27 (2019): 507-17; Jay Twomey, "To an Unknown Apostle: Moments of Pauline Undoing in Pier Paolo Pasolini's *Saint Paul*," *Biblical Interpretation* 27 (2019): 518-32.
17. Jones was part of a missionary association focused on the evangelization of slaves, but there were other missionaries at this time who were hired by plantation owners them-

selves to preach obedience directly to slaves. Allen Callahan, *The Talking Book: African Americans and the Bible* (New Haven, CT: Yale University Press, 2006), 10–11.

18. Jones's account was published in the *Tenth Annual Report of the Association for the Religious Instruction of the Negroes in Liberty County, Georgia* (Savannah, GA: the Association, 1845), 24–25. His narrative was quoted and attacked in Harriet Beecher Stowe's *Uncle Tom's Cabin* (Boston: John P. Jewett, 1854), 483–85. We can see how Jones made use of Philemon and other Pauline texts in his justifications for slavery and the education of slaves in his *The Religious Instruction of the Negroes in the United States* (Savannah, GA: Thomas Purse, 1843).

19. Brian K. Blount, *Then the Whisper Put On Flesh: New Testament Ethics in an African American Context* (Nashville: Abingdon, 2001).

20. On the early history of Christian conversion among enslaved Africans, see Albert J. Raboteau, *Slave Religion: The "Invisible Institution" in the Antebellum South* (Oxford: Oxford University Press, 1978); Callahan, *Talking Book*, 1–18. See also the important comparative work on slavery by Orlando Patterson, *Slavery and Social Death: A Comparative Study* (Cambridge, MA: Harvard University Press, 1982).

21. *A Narrative of the Most Remarkable Particulars in the Life of James Albert Ukawsaw Gronniosaw, an African Prince, as Related by Himself* (Bath: Printed by W. Gye, 1770), quoted in Callahan, *Talking Book*, 13. Vincent Wimbush rightly notes that the "talking book" trope was common in the narratives written by and about early Black authors (*White Men's Magic: Scripturalization as Slavery* [Oxford: Oxford University Press, 2012], 60–67), as do Emerson Powery and Rodney Sadler Jr., *The Genesis of Liberation: Biblical Interpretation in the Antebellum Narratives of the Enslaved* (Louisville, KY: Westminster John Knox Press, 2016), 36–40. See also the earlier treatment of this trope in Henry Louis Gates, *The Signifying Monkey: A Theory of African-American Literary Criticism* (Oxford: Oxford University Press, 1988), 127–69.

22. Clarice J. Martin, "'Somebody Done Hoodoo'd the Hoodoo Man': Language, Power, Resistance, and the Effective History of Pauline Texts in American Slavery," *Semeia* 83/84 (1998): 208.

23. Blount's analysis does not focus on how abolitionist authors developed arguments against slavery with Pauline texts, focusing instead on reconstructing the voices of enslaved Africans. For analysis of the ideological battles in which Pauline texts were conscripted into abolitionist arguments, see Vincent Wimbush, "The Bible and African Americans: An Outline of an Interpretive History," in *Stony the Road We Trod: African American Biblical Interpretation*, ed. Cain Hope Felder (Minneapolis: Fortress Press, 1991), 89–93; Martin, "'Somebody Done Hoodoo'd,'" 213–22; J. Albert Harrill, *Slaves in the New Testament: Literary, Social, and Moral Dimensions* (Minneapolis: Fortress Press, 2006), 165–92. See also the wider discussion of the Bible in Mark Noll, *The Civil War as a Theological Crisis* (Chapel Hill: UNC Press, 2006).

24. Blount, *Then the Whisper*, 23–24; cf. Renita Weems, "Reading *Her Way* through the Struggle: African American Women and the Bible," in *Stony the Road We Trod: African American Biblical Interpretation*, ed. Cain Hope Felder (Minneapolis: Fortress Press, 1991), 61; Powery and Sadler, *Genesis of Liberation*, 1–4. Callahan notes the importance

of the Great Awakening and early evangelicalism's emphasis on the direct experience of God as crucial in inciting and justifying this turn to the aural (*Talking Book*, 3). So also Wimbush, "Bible and African Americans," 86.

25. Delores Williams, *Sisters in the Wilderness: The Challenge of Womanist God-Talk* (Maryknoll, NY: Orbis, 1993), 4–6. See also Wilda C. Gafney, *Womanist Midrash: A Reintroduction to the Women of the Torah and the Throne* (Louisville, KY: Westminster John Knox Press, 2017), 2–9.

26. Blount, *Then the Whisper*, 24. Wimbush calls the Bible a language or a language-world that allowed enslaved Africans to negotiate the doubled strangeness of America and slavery ("Bible and African Americans," 82).

27. Blount, *Then the Whisper*, 30. See also Martin, "'Somebody Done Hoodoo'd,'" 223.

28. Harrill describes this reading as the result of a hermeneutic of typology (*Slaves in the New Testament*, 177–80).

29. Blount, *Then the Whisper*, 31. Subsequent references will be made in the text.

30. Blount, *Then the Whisper*, 40–43; Callahan, *Talking Book*, 6–9, 43–46.

31. The divergent ethics that emerged from slave readings of the Bible caused missionary practice to shift from teaching slaves to read to preaching obedience to their master as a Christian virtue (Callahan, *Talking Book*, 9–10).

32. Wimbush calls the selection and expansion of slave scriptures an emergent "canon" ("Bible and African Americans," 86).

33. Blount, *Then the Whisper*, 33. Martin sees this as a "hermeneutics of critical suspicion" ("'Somebody Done Hoodoo'd,'" 223).

34. Harrill, *Slaves in the New Testament*, 180–91.

35. Martin, "'Somebody Done Hoodoo'd,'" 214.

36. Martin, 214–22.

37. Blount, *Then the Whisper*, 37.

38. Blount mentions as inspiration for his reading Amos Jones, *Paul's Message of Freedom: What Does It Mean to the Black Church?* (Valley Forge, PA: Judson Press, 1984); and Neil Elliott, *Liberating Paul: The Justice of God and the Politics of the Apostle* (Maryknoll, NY: Orbis, 1994). He also follows a similar approach to recontextualizing Paul's thought as that offered by Elsa Tamez, *The Amnesty of Grace: Justification by Faith from a Latin American Perspective* (Nashville: Abingdon, 1993).

39. Allen Callahan, "'Brother Saul': An Ambivalent Witness to Freedom," *Semeia* 83/84 (1998): 248–49.

40. Blount, *Then the Whisper*, 122. Allen Callahan describes attempts by African American readers from the nineteenth to the twentieth century to find emancipatory readings of Paul that are premised on the dissociation of a Historical Paul from the Paul of Acts and the deutero-Pauline literature ("'Brother Saul,'" 235–50).

41. For discussions of the New Perspective and its legacies, see John G. Gager, *Reinventing Paul* (New York: Oxford University Press, 2000); Caroline E. Johnson Hodge, *If Sons, Then Heirs: A Study of Kinship and Ethnicity in the Letters of Paul* (New York: Oxford University Press, 2007), 7–9; Magnus Zetterholm, *Approaches to Paul: A Student's Guide to Recent Scholarship* (Minneapolis: Fortress Press, 2009), 95–126.

42. Blount, *Then the Whisper*, 123–49. Subsequent references will be made in the text.

43. A similar point is made about Paul by James Evans, "Black Theology and Black Feminism," *Journal of Religious Thought* 38 (1981): 47.

44. Martin, "*Haustafeln*," 218–27. Martin thinks that this happened because the Exodus narrative has been the paradigm within African American theology for liberation, but because this narrative is a story of explicit liberation, it is not easily extended to the liberation of wives/women from patriarchal authority (226–27). Martin also suggests that part of the problem is the acceptance by African American Christian communities of the surrounding Eurocentric patriarchal culture (a point also made by Wimbush, "Bible and African Americans," 95–97). James Evans asks a similar question regarding the dissonance created by anti-slavery readings sitting alongside those affirming the submission of women ("Black Theology and Black Feminism," 47).

45. Blount, *Then the Whisper*, 149.

46. On how Paul was reclaimed by early readers, see Callahan, "'Brother Saul,'" 236–40, 242–47; Emerson Powery and Rodney Sadler Jr., *The Genesis of Liberation: Biblical Interpretation in the Antebellum Narratives of the Enslaved* (Louisville, KY: Westminster John Knox Press, 2016), 113–44; Lisa M. Bowens, *African American Readings of Paul: Reception, Resistance, and Transformation* (Grand Rapids, MI: Eerdmans, 2020).

47. Blount, *Then the Whisper*, 157.

INTERLUDE: BACK TO THE DUMP

1. Lauren Berlant, *Cruel Optimism* (Durham, NC: Duke University Press, 2011), 1.

2. Neil Elliott, *Liberating Paul: The Justice of God and the Politics of the Apostle* (Maryknoll, NY: Orbis, 1994).

3. 2 Cor. 2:2, 4; 11:20–21; Philem. 1:19; 1 Cor. 4:21 (NRSV).

4. This is an allusion to Roland Barthes, *The Pleasure of the Text* (New York: Hill and Wang, 1975), 23.

5. Jacques Lacan, *Transference: The Seminar of Jacques Lacan, Book VIII*, trans. Bruce Fink (Cambridge: Polity, 2015), 129. On Lacan's theory of love, see Bruce Fink, *Lacan on Love: An Exploration of Lacan's Seminar VIII, Transference* (Cambridge: Polity, 2016), 33–54; and Joan Copjec, *Read My Desire: Lacan against the Historicists* (New York: Verso, 2015), 143, 148–51.

6. Barthes, *Pleasure of the Text*, 27.

7. Copjec, *Read My Desire*, 151.

8. Fink, *Lacan on Love*, 48–53.

9. Eve Kosofsky Sedgwick, *Touching Feeling: Affect, Pedagogy, Performativity* (Durham, NC: Duke University Press, 2003), 130–43.

10. Sedgwick, 142.

11. Sedgwick, 128.

12. Jennifer Knust, "Who's Afraid of Canaan's Curse? Genesis 9:18–29 and the Challenge of Reparative Reading," *Biblical Interpretation* 22 (2014): 409–13.

13. Sara Ahmed, *The Promise of Happiness* (Durham, NC: Duke University Press, 2010).

14. Knust, "Who's Afraid of Canaan's Curse?," 412.

15. Elizabeth A. Castelli's work on interpretations of Paul in the global South has shown that conservative readings have tended to dominate, even as they intermingle with anticolonialist resistance. "The Philosophers' Paul in the Frame of the Global: Some Reflections," *South Atlantic Quarterly* 109, no. 4 (2010): 666–72.

16. Antoinette Clark Wire, *The Corinthian Women Prophets: A Reconstruction through Paul's Rhetoric* (Minneapolis: Fortress Press, 1990); Elisabeth Schüssler Fiorenza, *In Memory of Her: A Feminist Theological Reconstruction of Christian Origins* (New York: Crossroad, 1994); Elizabeth A. Castelli, *Imitating Paul: A Discourse of Power* (Louisville, KY: Westminster/John Knox Press, 1991); Cavan Concannon, *"When You Were Gentiles": Specters of Ethnicity in Roman Corinth and Paul's Corinthian Correspondence* (New Haven, CT: Yale University Press, 2014); Joseph A. Marchal, ed., *The People beside Paul: The Philippian Assembly and History from Below* (Atlanta: SBL Press, 2015).

17. Sheila Briggs, "Slavery and Gender," in *On the Cutting Edge: The Study of Women in the Biblical World; Essays in Honor of Elisabeth Schüssler Fiorenza*, ed. Jane Schaberg, Alice Bach, and Esther Fuchs (New York: Continuum, 2003), 176.

18. Barthes, *Pleasure of the Text*, 27.

19. See William Viney, *Waste: A Philosophy of Things* (London: Bloomsbury, 2014), 29–75.

20. Berlant, *Cruel Optimism*, 262.

PROFANING PAUL

1. Vincent Wimbush, *The Bible and African Americans: A Brief History* (Minneapolis: Fortress Press, 2003), 16–17.

2. Bruno Latour, *On the Modern Cult of the Factish Gods* (Durham, NC: Duke University Press, 2010), 1–65.

3. Wimbush, *Bible and African Americans*, 17–20.

4. Vincent Wimbush's work on Olaudah Equiano shows the complicated and fraught dynamics of learning how to use the tools of European scripturalization. *White Men's Magic: Scripturalization as Slavery* (Oxford: Oxford University Press, 2012).

5. By "textualized notion of the sacred," I do not mean to limit the Bible to the idea of *sola scriptura*, where the sacrality lies in the words in the text. Rather, I include other ways in which the text as textual object conveys sacrality. On this see W. C. Smith, *What Is Scripture? A Comparative Approach* (Minneapolis: Fortress Press, 1993), 1–20.

6. In this, profaning readings resemble Erin Graff Zivin's anarchaeological reading strategies: *Anarchaeologies: Reading as Misreading* (New York: Fordham University Press, 2020).

7. Giorgio Agamben, *Profanations*, trans. Jeff Fort (New York: Zone Books, 2015), 73–92.

8. Agamben, 73. Quotations from the Roman jurist Trebatius come from Justinian's *Digest* (11.7.2).

9. Émile Durkheim, *The Elementary Forms of Religious Life*, trans. Karen Fields (New York: Free Press, 1995), 33–39.

10. Durkheim, 38.

11. Sigmund Freud, *Moses and Monotheism* (New York: Vintage, 1939), 155–56.

12. Agamben, *Profanations*, 75.

13. Giorgio Agamben, *The Kingdom and the Glory: For a Theological Genealogy of Economy and Government*, trans. Lorenzo Chiesa (Palo Alto, CA: Stanford University Press, 2011), 3–4.

14. Carl Schmitt, *Political Theology: Four Chapters on the Concept of Sovereignty*, trans. George Schwab (Chicago: University of Chicago Press, 2005), 36.

15. Agamben, *Kingdom and the Glory*, 4.

16. Agamben, *Profanations*, 77.

17. Agamben, 86.

18. Giorgio Agamben, *The Time That Remains: A Commentary on the Letter to the Romans*, trans. Patricia Dailey (Palo Alto, CA: Stanford University Press, 2005), 1.

19. Agamben, 1.

20. Agamben, 18.

21. Whether Benjamin would recognize Paul as his source and interlocutor is a different matter. For a critical reading of Agamben's argument for Paul's influence on Benjamin, see Roland Boer, "Paul of the Gaps: Agamben, Benjamin and the Puppet Player," in *Paul in the Grip of the Philosophers: The Apostle and Contemporary Continental Philosophy*, ed. Peter Frick (Minneapolis: Fortress Press, 2013), 57–68.

22. Agamben, *Time That Remains*, 145.

23. Elizabeth A. Castelli observes a similar resistance to "textual ambiguities" throughout Agamben's work on Paul. "The Philosophers' Paul in the Frame of the Global: Some Reflections," *South Atlantic Quarterly* 109, no. 4 (2010): 664.

24. See, for example, John Dominic Crossan and Jonathan Reed, *In Search of Paul: How Jesus' Apostle Opposed Rome's Empire with God's Kingdom* (San Francisco: HarperOne, 2005); Richard A. Horsley, ed., *Paul and Empire: Religion and Power in Roman Imperial Society* (Harrisburg, PA: Trinity Press International, 1997).

25. Walter Benjamin, "Theses on the Philosophy of History," thesis 7, in *Illuminations: Essays and Reflections*, ed. with an introduction by Hannah Arendt and trans. Harry Zohn (New York: Schocken, 1968), 256.

A SOMETIMES PAUL

1. Lauren Berlant, *Cruel Optimism* (Durham, NC: Duke University Press, 2011), 267.

2. Howard Thurman, *Jesus and the Disinherited* (Nashville: Abingdon, 1949); references to this text refer to its 1996 reissue by Beacon Press, Boston.

3. Thurman focuses on Jesus as a member of the dispossessed class of poor Jews under Roman occupation. His historical reconstruction of Jesus follows Vladimir Simkhovitch's *Toward the Understanding of Jesus* (New York: Macmillan, 1921). Thurman sees in Jesus a "Jewish thinker and teacher" who developed "a technique of survival for the oppressed" that is, when isolated from questions of Christian metaphysics, useful for

any oppressed people at any time and place (*Jesus and the Disinherited*, 28–29). Subsequent references will be made in the text.

4. Homi K. Bhabha, *The Location of Culture* (New York: Routledge, 2004). For Bhabha, hybridity helps explain the ambiguous identities forged by people under colonial rule, through mimicry, improvisation, or resistance. For a critical discussion of the term *hybridity* and its legacy in a number of different academic disciplines, see Robert Young, *Colonial Desire: Hybridity in Theory, Culture, and Race* (New York: Routledge, 1995).

5. Thurman, *Jesus and the Disinherited*, 33.

6. Renita Weems, "Reading *Her Way* through the Struggle: African American Women and the Bible," in *Stony the Road We Trod: African American Biblical Interpretation*, ed. Cain Hope Felder (Minneapolis: Fortress Press, 1991)," 74.

7. James Baldwin, *The Fire Next Time* (New York: Vintage, 1962), 44.

8. On Cleage, see Allen Callahan, "'Brother Saul': An Ambivalent Witness to Freedom," *Semeia* 83/84 (1998): 247–48; and Lisa M. Bowens, *African American Readings of Paul: Reception, Resistance, and Transformation* (Grand Rapids, MI: Eerdmans, 2020), 234–38.

9. James Cone, "Wrestling with *The Cross and the Lynching Tree*," *Theology Today* 70, no. 2 (2013): 221.

10. Thurman, *Jesus and the Disinherited*, 30–31.

11. Weems, "Reading *Her Way*," 66.

12. "An Interview with Howard Thurman and Ronald Eyre," *Theology Today* 38, no. 2 (1981): 211–12.

13. Vincent Wimbush, *White Men's Magic: Scripturalization as Slavery* (Oxford: Oxford University Press, 2012), 136–37.

14. Lunsford Lane, *The Narrative of Lunsford Lane, Formerly of Raleigh, N.C. Embracing an Account of His Early Life, the Redemption by Purchase of Himself and Family from Slavery, and His Banishment from the Place of His Birth for the Crime of Wearing a Colored Skin. Published by Himself* (Boston: J. G. Torrey, 1842), 20–21.

15. Vincent Wimbush, "The Bible and African Americans: An Outline of an Interpretive History," in *Stony the Road We Trod: African American Biblical Interpretation*, ed. Cain Hope Felder (Minneapolis: Fortress Press, 1991), 88.

16. Giorgio Agamben, *Profanations*, trans. Jeff Fort (New York: Zone Books, 2015), 73.

17. Agamben, 75.

18. Agamben, 75–76.

19. For how this was done with the Bible as a whole, see Allen Callahan, *The Talking Book: African Americans and the Bible* (New Haven, CT: Yale University Press, 2006).

20. Agamben, *Profanations*, 76.

21. Albert J. Raboteau, *Slave Religion: The "Invisible Institution" in the Antebellum South* (Oxford: Oxford University Press, 1978), 290–318.

22. Agamben, *Profanations*, 85.

23. Wimbush, *White Men's Magic*, 146. This is similar to Agamben's thinking on play: "[Play] consists in freeing a behavior from its genetic inscription within a given sphere. . . . The freed behavior still reproduces and mimics the forms of the activity from which it has been emancipated, but, in emptying them of their sense and of any

obligatory relationship to an end, it opens them and makes them available for a new use" (Agamben, *Profanations*, 85–86).

24. Text taken from Callahan, *Talking Book*, 34. See also the discussion of this petition in Bowens, *African American Readings of Paul*, 21–26.

25. Lewis and Milton Clarke, *Narratives of the Sufferings of Lewis and Milton Clarke, Sons of a Soldier of the Revolution, during a Captivity of More Than Twenty Years among the Slaveholders of Kentucky, One of the So-Called Christian States of North America* (Boston: Bela Marsh, 1846), 105.

26. Here I see Ambrose's rejection of Paul as more forceful than does Callahan: "Her reading of Paul, or, more accurately, her hearing of Paul is not reductive but corrective. She tries to hear Paul's Corinthian voice more often and more intensely than she heard his Ephesian and Colossian counsels to obedience" (Callahan, "'Brother Saul,'" 241). I am not convinced that Ambrose is trying to hear 1 Corinthians 13 "more often and more intensely." Thurman emphasizes that she only rarely asked for this text.

PAUL'S SHIT

1. On the politics of identification, see Elisabeth Schüssler Fiorenza, *The Power of the Word: Scripture and the Rhetoric of Empire* (Minneapolis: Fortress Press, 2007), 87. As Joseph A. Marchal notes, these reading strategies present "a compelling ethical and political horizon for interrogating and negotiating what one finds in biblical argumentation." *Philippians: An Introduction and Study Guide; Historical Problems, Hierarchical Visions, Hysterical Anxieties* (New York: Bloomsbury T&T Clark, 2017), 69.

2. Marchal, *Philippians*, 84–91.

3. For a broader discussion of Paul's imprisonment, see Michael Flexsenhar III, *Christians in Caesar's Household: The Emperors' Slaves in the Makings of Christianity* (University Park: Pennsylvania State University Press, 2019), 27–44.

4. Elizabeth A. Castelli, *Imitating Paul: A Discourse of Power* (Louisville, KY: Westminster/John Knox Press, 1991), 95–98.

5. Paul's anxiety about his potential shame can be seen in 4:11–14. In response to a gift from the Philippians, he is at pains to say that he didn't need their money after all. Yes, he is often hungry and in need, but he knows how to live like that. And anyway, he is still powerful, because he can do all things through god strengthening him (4:13).

6. Paul uses *koilia* in a similar way in Romans 16:18, where he again associates troublemakers with being slaves to their digestive system.

7. Mayra Rivera, *Poetics of the Flesh* (Durham, NC: Duke University Press, 2015), 41.

8. Marchal, *Philippians*, 88–89. See also Meghan Henning, "Weeping and Bad Hair: The Bodily Suffering of Early Christian Hell as a Threat to Masculinity," in *Phallacies: Historical Intersections of Disability and Masculinity*, ed. Kathleen M. Brian and James W. Trent Jr. (Oxford: Oxford University Press, 2017), 282–300.

9. See the important work of Cynthia Briggs Kittredge, *Community and Authority: The Rhetoric of Obedience in the Pauline Tradition* (Harrisburg, PA: Trinity Press, 1998). See

also Gregory Fewster, "The Philippians 'Christ Hymn': Trends in Critical Scholarship," *Currents in Biblical Research* 13, no. 2 (2015): 191–206.

10. Sheila Briggs, "Can an Enslaved God Liberate? Hermeneutical Reflections on Philippians 2:6–11," *Semeia* 47 (1989): 137–53.

11. Several examples of this genre include Michael Wade Martin and Bryan A. Nash, "Philippians 2:6–11 as Subversive Hymnos: A Study in the Light of Ancient Rhetorical Theory," *Journal of Theological Studies* 66, no. 1 (2015): 90–138; E. M. Heen, "Phil 2:6–11 and Resistance to Local Timocratic Rule: *Isa theō* and the Cult of the Emperor in the East," in *Paul and the Roman Imperial Order*, ed. Richard A. Horsley (Harrisburg, PA: Trinity Press International, 2004), 125–54; Peter Oakes, *Philippians: From People to Letter* (Cambridge: Cambridge University Press, 2001), 147–75.

12. Orlando Patterson, *Slavery and Social Death: A Comparative Study* (Cambridge, MA: Harvard University Press, 1982).

13. Briggs, "Can an Enslaved God Liberate?," 145. Subsequent references will be made in the text.

14. See also Katherine Shaner, "Seeing Rape and Robbery: Ἁρπαγμαός and the Philippians Christ Hymn (Phil. 2:5–11)," *Biblical Interpretation* 25, no. 3 (2017): 342–63.

15. Alain Badiou, *Saint Paul: The Foundation of Universalism*, trans. Ray Brassier (Palo Alto, CA: Stanford University Press, 2003), 1.

16. Dorothea Bertschmann, "Is There a Kenosis in This Text? Rereading Philippians 3:2–11 in the Light of the Christ Hymn," *Journal of Biblical Literature* 137, no. 1 (2018): 235–54.

17. On Paul's use of economic language in Philippians, see the important work by Jennifer Quigley, "Divine Accounting: Theo-Economics in the Letter to the Philippians" (ThD diss., Harvard University, 2018).

18. Badiou, *Saint Paul*, 10–11.

19. Bertschmann, "Is There a Kenosis?," 245–47.

20. Quigley, "Divine Accounting."

21. Brian Thill, *Waste* (New York: Bloomsbury Academic, 2015), 8.

22. Thill, 20.

23. Badiou, *Saint Paul*, 23.

24. Quigley, "Divine Accounting."

25. Thill, *Waste*, 29.

26. "For Paul, the Christ-event, which shears and undoes the cosmic totality, is precisely what indicates the vanity of places. The real is attested to rather as the refuse from every place, there where the subject rehearses his weakness: 'We have become, and are now, as the refuse of the world, the offscouring of all things' (Cor. 1.4.13). One must therefore assume the subjectivity of refuse, and it is in the face of this abasement that the object of Christian discourse suddenly appears. One will note the consonance with certain Lacanian themes concerning the ethics of the analyst: at the end of the treatment, the latter must, similarly, consent to occupy the position of refuse so that the analysand may endure some encounter with his or her real. By virtue of which, as Lacan notes, the analyst comes very close to saintliness" (Badiou, *Saint Paul*, 56).

27. Briggs, "Can an Enslaved God Liberate?," 149.

28. Briggs, 149.

29. Marchal, *Philippians*, 91.

30. Marchal, 91.

31. Marchal, 88.

32. Denise Kimber Buell, "Hauntology Meets Posthumanism: Some Payoffs for Biblical Studies," in *The Bible and Posthumanism*, ed. Jennifer L. Koosed, Semeia Studies 74 (Atlanta: Society of Biblical Literature, 2014), 39.

33. See, for example, Rosi Braidotti, *The Posthuman* (Cambridge: Polity, 2013); Catherine Malabou, *What Should We Do with Our Brain?*, Perspectives in Continental Philosophy (New York: Fordham University Press, 2008); and Donna Haraway, *ModestWitness@ Second_Millenium.FemaleMan©_Meets_OncoMouse™: Feminism and Technoscience* (New York: Routledge, 1997).

34. See, for example, Jacques Derrida, *The Animal That Therefore I Am*, trans. David Wills (New York: Fordham University Press, 2008); Gilles Deleuze and Félix Guattari, *A Thousand Plateaus*, trans. Brian Massumi (Minneapolis: University of Minnesota Press, 1987); Giorgio Agamben, *The Open: Man and Animal*, trans. Kevin Atell, Crossing Aesthetics (Palo Alto, CA: Stanford University Press, 2005); and Donna Haraway, *Staying with the Trouble: Making Kin in the Chthulucene* (Durham, NC: Duke University Press, 2016).

35. Manuel DeLanda, *A Thousand Years of Nonlinear History* (New York: Zone Books, 1997); Manuel DeLanda, *A New Philosophy of Society: Assemblage Theory and Social Complexity* (New York: Continuum, 2006); and Clayton Crockett, "Earth: What Can a Planet Do?," in *An Insurrectionist Manifesto: Four New Gospels for a Radical Politics*, ed. Ward Blanton, Clayton Crockett, Jeffrey W. Robbins, and Noëlle Vahanian (New York: Columbia University Press, 2016), 21–60.

36. Marchal, *Philippians*, 89. This might also be fruitfully brought into conversation with Zygmunt Bauman's notion of the universality of redundancy as a category to describe humans in the era of global capitalism. *Wasted Lives: Modernity and Its Outcasts* (Cambridge: Polity, 2004), 9–33.

37. Marchal, *Philippians*, 87. While appreciative of Marchal's point, I want to highlight a comment offered by one of this book's anonymous peer reviewers: "Poop is shit made adorable."

38. Judith Butler, *Notes toward a Performative Theory of Assembly* (Cambridge, MA: Harvard University Press, 2015), 148.

39. Butler, 148.

40. As Butler argues, "The condition of our vulnerability is itself not changeable. This does not mean that we are objectively or subjectively equally vulnerable all the time. But it does mean that it is a more or less implicit or explicit feature of our experience." Butler, 150.

41. Bauman, *Wasted Lives*, 9–33.

42. Bauman, 12.

43. Butler, *Notes*, 153.

REFUSING PAUL

1. Rosalind Fredericks, *Garbage Citizenship: Vital Infrastructures of Labor in Dakar, Senegal* (Durham, NC: Duke University Press, 2018). Subsequent references will be made in the text.

2. Jane Bennett, *Vibrant Matter: A Political Ecology of Things* (Durham, NC: Duke University Press, 2010).

3. See, for example, John T. Fitzgerald, *Cracks in an Earthen Vessel: An Examination of the Catalogues of Hardships in the Corinthian Correspondence*, SBL Dissertation Series (Atlanta: Society of Biblical Literature, 1988).

4. Elizabeth A. Castelli, *Imitating Paul: A Discourse of Power* (Louisville, KY: Westminster/John Knox Press, 1991), 89–118.

5. Margaret M. Mitchell, *Paul and the Rhetoric of Reconciliation: An Exegetical Investigation of the Language and Composition of 1 Corinthians* (Louisville, KY: Westminster/John Knox Press, 1991), 48.

6. Raymond F. Collins, *First Corinthians*, Sacra Pagina 7 (Collegeville, MN: Liturgical Press, 1999), 191; Hans Conzelmann, *1 Corinthians*, Hermeneia (Philadelphia: Fortress Press, 1975), 90; Joseph A. Fitzmyer, *First Corinthians*, Anchor Yale Bible 32 (New Haven, CT: Yale University Press, 2008), 220.

7. Mitchell, *Paul and the Rhetoric*, 221.

8. Bruno Latour, *Down to Earth: Politics in the New Climatic Regime* (Cambridge: Polity, 2018), 86.

9. On the language of imitation, see Castelli, *Imitating Paul*.

10. Midori Hartman, "A Little Porneia Leavens the Whole: Queer(ing) Limits of Community in 1 Corinthians 5," in *Bodies on the Verge: Queering Pauline Epistles*, ed. Joseph A. Marchal, Semeia Studies 93 (Atlanta: SBL Press, 2019), 143–63.

11. Dale B. Martin, *The Corinthian Body* (New Haven, CT: Yale University Press, 1995), 229–49.

12. Jasbir K. Puar, *Terrorist Assemblages: Homonationalism in Queer Times* (Durham, NC: Duke University Press, 2017).

13. Puar, xxii.

14. Puar, xx. Puar's theory is similar to Deleuze and Guattari's juxtaposition of macro- and micropolitics. Gilles Deleuze and Félix Guattari, *A Thousand Plateaus: Capitalism and Schizophrenia*, trans. Brian Massumi (Minneapolis: University of Minnesota Press, 1987), 216.

15. Maia Kotrosits, "The Queer Life of Christian Exceptionalism," *Culture and Religion* 15, no. 2 (2014): 158–65.

16. Kotrosits, 162.

17. Graham Harman, *Immaterialism: Objects and Social Theory* (Cambridge: Polity, 2016), 42.

18. Harman, 63–64.

19. To become refuse and shit, "we will need to experience the discomforts and contingencies inherent in those who have been considered disposable and worthy of expulsion

from the social as well as the religious body." Karen Bray, "Becoming Feces: New Materialism and the Deep Solidarity in Feeling Like Shit," in *Religious Experience and New Materialism: Movement Matters*, ed. Joerg Rieger and Edward Waggoner (New York: Palgrave Macmillan, 2016), 108–9. This will require a radical rethinking of politics itself: "Those in the middle class cannot just make the traditional liberal political move of siding but not identifying with the working class. Rather, we all must try to understand and, I argue, *feel* the growing precarity and disposability to which we *all* are increasingly subjected" (Bray, 113).

20. Elizabeth Freeman, *Time Binds: Queer Temporalities, Queer Histories* (Durham, NC: Duke University Press, 2010). Freeman defines chrononormativity as "the use of time to organize individual human bodies toward maximum productivity" (3). For a use of Freeman's work to destabilize time in the Pauline archive, see James N. Hoke, "Unbinding Imperial Time: Chrononormativity and Paul's Letter to the Romans," in *Sexual Disorientations: Queer Temporalities, Affects, Theologies*, ed. Kent L. Brintnall, Joseph A. Marchal, and Stephen D. Moore (New York: Fordham University Press, 2018), 68–89.

21. Lauren Berlant, *Cruel Optimism* (Durham, NC: Duke University Press, 2011), 115–17.

22. Giorgio Agamben, *The Time That Remains: A Commentary on the Letter to the Romans*, trans. Patricia Dailey (Palo Alto, CA: Stanford University Press, 2005), 59–87.

23. Puar, *Terrorist Assemblages*, 211–16.

24. Bray, "Becoming Feces," 115.

25. Brian Thill, *Waste* (New York: Bloomsbury Academic, 2015), 62.

26. Ward Blanton, *A Materialism for the Masses: Saint Paul and the Philosophy of Undying Life* (New York: Columbia University Press, 2014), xii–xv.

27. Thill, *Waste*, 23. On taking shit to the streets, see also Bray, "Becoming Feces," 115.

28. Bennett, *Vibrant Matter*.

29. Bennett, 5.

30. Achille Mbembe, *Critique of Black Reason* (Durham, NC: Duke University Press, 2017), 181.

31. Harman, *Immaterialism*, 47–48.

32. Catherine Keller, *Cloud of the Impossible: Negative Theology and Planetary Entanglement* (New York: Columbia University Press, 2015), 277.

33. Latour, *Down to Earth*, 2.

34. Mbembe, *Critique of Black Reason*, 182.

INDEX